I0748468

Hundred Years of Indian Cinema

Crisis and Resilience

The Editor

Dr. Bandana Jha

Date of Birth: 02nd july 1973

Village: Basuki Bihari, District: Madubani, Bihar.

Education: B.A.Hons(Economics) from LNMU,Darbhanga. M.A.(Hindi),M.Phil. and Ph.D.from JNU, New Delhi. Diploma in Bahasa Indonesia and Mongolian from JNU,New Delhi.

Book Published : 1.***Women and Political Empowerment*** (translation work) by Institute of Social Sciences,New Delhi.

2. ***Sheel ki Kavita*** published by Ganga Saran and Sons., Varanasi.

3. ***Varuna ka Hona*** published by Antika Prakashan, New Delhi.

4. ***Bhartiya Cinema ka Shatabdi Varsh*** published by Pratishruti Prakashan, Kolkata.

Literary Magzines : Hundreds of poetries, stories, articles, translated works etc. published in magazines like ***Aajkal, Vagarth, Sakkshatkar, Baya, Kadambini, Samved, Antika, Mizan etc.*** and Newspaper like ***Hindustan, Rashtriya Sahara etc.***

Presently : Associate Professor (Department of Hindi and Coordinator, Mass Communication) in Vasanta College for Women (Affiliated to BHU,Varanasi), Krishnamurti Foundation of India, Rajghat, Varanasi-221001.

Contact : Duplex No.-02, Chandra Heritage, Hiramanpur Road, Haweliya, Sarnath, Varanasi-221007.

E-mail : bandana_jnu@yahoo.co.in

Hundred Years of Indian Cinema

Crisis and Resilience

— Editor —

Dr. Bandana Jha

Associate Professor (Department of Hindi),
Vasanta College for Women,
KFI, Rajghat, Varanasi, Uttar Pradesh

2017

Regency Publications

A Division of

Astral International Pvt. Ltd.

New Delhi – 110 002

ISBN 9789387057371 (International Edition)

Published by : **Regency Publications**
A Division of
Astral International Pvt. Ltd.
– ISO 9001:2015 Certified Company –
4736/23, Ansari Road, Darya Ganj
New Delhi-110 002
Ph. 011-43549197, 23278134
E-mail: info@astralint.com
Website: www.astralint.com

Acknowledgement

A book of this nature doesn't just happen within a few short weeks. It involves a host of different people working over many months and I would like to express my gratitude to them.

This book is based on a National Seminar conducted on '*Hundred Years of Indian Cinema: Identity and Resistance*' under the Sponsorship of University Grants Commission, New Delhi at Vasanta College for Women, Rajghat, Varanasi in the month of February 2016.

I am grateful to participants across the country for their Paper Presentation on different dimensions of Indian Cinema which encouraged me to start the work, persevere with it and finally to publish it.

The completion of this book couldn't have been possible without the expertise lectures of well known film Critic Ajay Brahmatmaj, Prof. Jawarimal Parakh of IGNOU, Prof. Kumar Pankaj of BHU, Prof. Mithilesh Kumar Mishra of Univ. of Illinois,USA, Dr. Ravikant of CSDS, Dr.Priyanka Mishra of NFDC and Global Film Critic Dr. Vijay Sharma.

I wish to express my sincere thanks to Dr. Alka Singh, Principal, Vasanta College for Women, Rajghat, Varanasi for providing me all the necessary facilities to complete the project.

I place on record my sincere gratitude to my department colleagues Dr. Shashikala Tripathi, Dr. Meenu Avasthi and Dr. Rajesh Choudhary for their constant encouragement and valuable suggestions extended to me. My Sincere thanks to all the faculty members of my college especially Dr. Saroj Bageshwar, Dr. Ranjana Seth and Mr. Sanjeev Kumar for their cordial support.

A debt of gratitude is also owed to my colleague Dr. Manjari Shukla for editorial cooperation.

I am highly thankful to my publishers M/s Regency Publications, New Delhi for the publication of this book in a precise and beatiful form.

In closing, I wish to dedicate my work to my beloved mother Smt. Urmila Jha and wordless thanks to my husband Prem and my lovely daughters Arya and Aishwarya, without whom none of this would indeed be possible.

Dr. Bandana Jha

Preface

The whole idea, scope and panorama of Cinema involve in its domain an amalgamation of imagination, fantasy and reality. Artistry and the idea of Creation and re-creation are its tools. Cinema with its image, pictures and the range of innovative ideas has affected the society since time immemorial and to a greater extent it is affected by the society of various times and ages.

From the year 1913 to 2013, Cinema as a form travelled through a large number of spheres. When the country was under British domination and rule, it was Cinema which presented the idea of Freedom. When the country was going through the toughest times, it was Cinema that actually talked about ideals, aspirations, religion and talked about all the possible ways to lead a better and meaningful life. Cinema as a discipline was trying to become a medium for the masses, which could emerge as something, through which people get meaning and better understanding of their lives. With the concepts like Capitalism, Socialism, Independence, Livelihood etc. Indian Cinema was trying to create a new territory of meaning and expertise.

Crossing the borders, Indian cinema tried establishing itself on the world forum with the huge range of ideas and values, which were not only a part of Indian tradition and culture, but also a substantial and valid point of reference for the upcoming generation. It was a source of new learning for the world tribe.

Indian cinema chiefly focused on religion, spirituality, values because in the initial years of its formation, when the country was going through the British effect, it was important for the people of the nation to maintain their Indianness; and the best way to keep the Indian spirit alive was to present it through the lens of cinema by presenting the values of Indian heritage and culture in it. Initially focusing on festivals, cultural and social ethos of the times, the trajectory of Indian cinema later on moved towards Industrialization, focus on new machines and its effect on the Indian subcontinent in 1950s. It was the time in history of Indian cinema when themes like unemployment, alienation, stress, anxiety, depression, anger all got their exhibition in the hands of directors. Actors like Amol Palekar and Farooq Sheikh came to the silver screen with the expression of the conditions and plight of the young generation.

It was the time in the history of India, when the nation was officially independent, but it was going through the toughest of times. The realisation of self was required and the young generations of people were trying to create a niche for themselves. Indian cinema was playing a path breaking role in the realisation of these ideals and, it was during this very time that we could observe the impetus and potential of Regional cinema. The natural beauty of the country along with the cultural and historical details were presented and portrayed by the film makers. It was a platform for the better understanding and realisation of cultural competence. It touched every sphere of Indian sensibility so much so that made the youth to ponder on it, as well as gave them the solution to create a better and meaningful life for themselves. The credit to Indian cinema is also given, when we get to know that it actually operated as a bridge, filling the gaps created by religion, caste, creed and ethnicity in India.

The post modern world was also touched by the color of Cinema, sometimes through fashion and sometimes through passion. The spirit drawn from the western world for the Indian audience was quite doubtful, as it was unable to remove the orthodox shackles altogether and at the same time it was a medium to make the people of India aware of the world culture and ethos. Beyond this, the purpose of cinema was to make people realise about their respective 'Self'.

If we perceive the teaching and understanding of Bhratmuni's *Natyashastra*, it would be known to us that just like the realisation of Rasa(s), Indian cinema also gave us the taste to actually feel and interpret comprehensive idea of life. In short, cinema became life and life became cinema.

As the journey of cinema is taken forward, we reach to a point when the world started witnessing many new changes. Cinema was also affected and we observe that it started depicting a society with an altogether different set of values. Women, dalits, naxalites, gender roles, gay and lesbian subjects started reigning in the domain of cinema. The social change and its different parameters affecting the fabric of society created the cinema of new questions and values. Environmental problems, water pollution and problems, old age, handicap and films on specially gifted people brought forward the concept that Cinema was trying to touch all the lives in its best possible way giving the message of life and living.

After the 90s, Cinema became a multipurpose medium. It was not only the source of knowledge and wisdom, but also a platform to know latest fashion, music, dance, cosmetics, and the commercial world. The next question worth consideration in the understanding and analysis of cinema was to discern the distinction between aesthetic pleasure and communication. The formation and development of a film passes through three stages, from writer to actor, from actor to cameraman and from cameraman to the audience. There could never be any changes in this pattern of film making and analysis, as it is the way to the actual realisation of the idea which the film presents. The question arises that is the ultimate goal of a film maker through his/her film to reach the audience and provide them with only pleasure? Or is it something beyond this?

Another important sphere of influence which needs to be pondered is the position and role of the Protagonist. It is the protagonist who coming from the masses, becomes the representative of certain ideals and aspirations which guide, inspire and instigate the audience on different levels. He/she actually becomes the mouthpiece who plays the role of more than a character.

Diaspora is yet another element which has always drawn the attention of film makers. Indian cinema since ages has tried exploring its different facets, with possibilities as well as demerits. For the foreign audience, it is the Indian element of diaspora, or the expression of festivals, great grand wedding etc. that has given shape to Indian culture and ethos. Indian cinema became a powerful tool to understand the value of roots, which was represented by the visual images along with the auditory images.

The journey of hundred glorious years of Cinema shows so many ups and downs. It has now converted itself into a commercial industry. It is pertinent to discuss in detail that the purpose with which cinema began and the dais to which it has reached in contemporary times, needs to be updated as well as pondered upon. A new methodology needs to be developed to understand the paradigm of Cinema as it is that genre of human understanding which includes in its range and domain the fields of arts, language, technique, management, entertainment and social ethos etc. The whole idea of Nationalism many a time has got voice through cinema when it actually became the medium of political understanding and cultural diversity. The times have changed, and now the Indian cinema not only stands neck-to-neck with the Hollywood movies, but rather it has gained the potential and impetus to move far beyond it, thereby putting forward a promising future for the upcoming generations.

Dr. Bandana Jha

Contents

	Acknowledgement	***v***
	Preface	***vii***
1.	**Hundred Years of Indian Cinema: Crisis and Resilience** *Bandana Jha*	**1**
2.	**Confluence of Cinema and Politics: Tamil Filmland** *N. Sharada Iyer*	**5**
3.	**'The Film is Dead; Long Live the Cinema': An Economic Analysis of Digitalization of Cinema in India** *Anurag Dave*	**17**
4.	**The Cinema: Most Popular Audio-Visual Mass Medium to Influence Human Development as a Whole** *Anshu Shukla*	**29**
5.	**Dialectics of Representing Queer in Indian (Hindi) Cinema** *Saurabh Kumar Singh*	**39**
6.	**Indian Films and Plight of the Aged** *Anuradha Bapuly*	**49**

7. Satyajit Ray's AGANTUK: A Picturesque View of Society and the Art of Cinema **55**

Brihaspati Bhattacharya

8. *Cheluvi* and *Delhi Safari*: Movies Voicing Ecological Concern **59**

Purnima

9. Cinematic Journalism, Critic and Multiplexes **63**

Awadhesh Kumar Bhatt

10. De-colonizing the Screen: The Margins Acts Back **71**

Sayan Dey

11. Indian Cinema and the Commodified Women **77**

Bharti Rai

12. Gender and Caste Dynamics in Indian Cinema from 1930s to 2000s **83**

Sunil Kumar

13. Changing the Identity of Women in Indian Cinema: A Review Paper **91**

Ved Prakash Rawat

14. Contribution of Assamese Film Director Rupkonwar Jyoti Prasad Agarwala in Indian Cinema **103**

Bala Lakhendra

15. A Study of Female Portrayal in Satyajit Ray's Movies **113**

Sanjeeda Bano

16. Haider: Textualizing Tragic Flaw in 20th Century Indian Cinema **119**

Nikhil Pratap Singh

17. Iron Man of India on Silver Screen: Contribution of Cinema in Remembering the Forgotten Hero "Sardar Vallabhbhai Patel" **123**

Hemlata Yadav

18. Indian Cinema and its Globalization: A Filmy Twist **129**

Sunita Arya

19. Feminine Cinematic Constructs and Re (Thinking) Women in the Indian Cinema **141**

Manjari Shukla

20. The Inter-relation of Cinema and Literature **147**

Garima Singh

21. Analysing Historical Element in Indian Cinema **157**

Nairanjana Srivastava

22. Women and the Indian Cinema **161**

Amrita Katyayni

23. Impact of Corporatisation in Indian Movie Industry: An Overview **165**

Ranjan Kumar Bhattacharya

24. 100 Years of Indian Cinema: The Dream Continues **171**

Vibha Singh

25 Impact of Indian Cinema on Women: A Content Analysis **181**

Punita Pathak

26. Indian Cinema and Disabled Women: Beyond the Liberal Paradigm **185**

Suhasini Singh

27. Psychology and Films **189**

Gagan Prit Kaur and Richa Singh

28. Precarious Social and Political Issues in an Eternal Love Story-*Manjhi: The Mountain Man* **195**

Supriya Singh

Index **199**

Chapter 1

Hundred Years of Indian Cinema: Crisis and Resilience

*Bandana Jha**

In the movie *'The Mirror'* by Andrei Tarkovsky, a character reads out a letter written by Pushkin to another character, through which the readers get to know Pushkin's love for Russia (his country). Pushkin holds the opinion that even though at times he feels irritated with the state of affairs happening in his country still he never wants to change his country, his nationality or even the history which his ancestors have given him. Looking at Indian cinema, a similar feeling can be observed, especially when we hear the famous song of Raj Kapoor, *"Mera Joota hai Japani.... Phir bhi dil hai Hindustani"* making it clear that how much Indianness, values for an Indian. The Father of the Nation Mahatma Gandhi opinionated that it is very important to identify the true identity of Indianness and maintaining the identity is again a valid issue. For this matter, he says that our conscience should keep all its windows open so that different ideologies, beliefs and aspirations keep inspiring and motivating us. The only thing which should be taken care of is the speed of these winds of ideas, otherwise chances are, we too will be uprooted and then that will be a great loss.

Cinema has always been a platform that acted as a bridge between film makers and common man. The only art invented by science is the cinema.The relationship of Literature and cinema is quite complex as stated by Gurudev Rabindranath Tagore,

* *Associate Professor (Department of Hindi),*
Vasanta College for Women, Rajghat
Banaras Hindu University, Varanasi – 221 001
E-mail: bandana_jnu@yahoo.co.in

"The important thing in the cinema is the flow of images. Its visual movement should be so rich as to be able to fulfil itself without the use of words....The cinema is so far acting as slave to literature-because no creative genius has yet arrived to deliver it from its bondage." The way cinema uses narrative to come closer to the readers shows its easy way to connect and at the same time instruct and delight the audience.

Another dimension of cinema is the debate between myth and reality, and Indian cinema has shown this on various levels. Education for women, child marriage, dowry, corruption, criminalization of politics etc. had been the theme of many movies and in doing this cinema has emerged as a revolutionary kind of genre in itself. Basically Indian cinema is an ideal type construct which start with particular event but reaches to the general understanding of whole Indian Society. Famous film maker V. Shantaram made film 'Dahej' in late 50's become eye opener for Parliamentarian to discuss over dowry prohibition and finally 'The Dowry Prohibition Act 1961' enacted. Mani Ratnam used the ideal type approach in his film *'Bombay'* and *'Roja'* depicting terrorism and communal riots respectively and compel onlookers to think over the genesis of social problem in India. And the journey continues.

With the advent of Industrialization and Urbanization, there were so many changes that were observed in Indian society. There was the emergence of nuclear families, women started working for livelihood and many new changes entered the Indian subcontinent which gradually changed and affected the values of the society. Beginning from the portrayal of multiple roles to the establishment of Woman's Identity in society, Cinema played a pivotal role in giving the voice to woman, who was up till now considered the subordinate to Man in a patriarchal society. Cinema basically was becoming an answer to the questions that were perturbing and disturbing the psyche of half of the Indian population.

Initially beginning from the description and elaboration of Mythological tales, religious stories, the platform of Indian cinema brought Indian public to the theatres. Both the males and females were required to know the mythology of India for the values and culture, they were associated with. Portraying the Birth of Krishna, Killing of Ravana etc. were the subject matter of the movies and the biggest purpose of this was to make them believe in the power of God in the times of distress and disturbance. India was struggling to gain independence and the situations demanded a frame of reference which could inspire and motivate people and that was Indian Cinema. The saga of Satyavan-Savitri, Ahilyabai, Sati Parvati, Sati Sulochana, Shakuntala, Mohini Vir Bala etc. made their mark in Indian cinema. The woman who was living in the four walls of the house actually got a chance to realise her identity through these movies.

It is a truth well acknowledged that in earlier times, women in Indian cinema were always portrayed next to men, because the Indian society was still in the clutches of Post Vedic period, but gradually film makers introduced Indian women in their independent powerful forms with the standpoint that they can change the scenario of the world, if they are given the power and command. Shantarama's movies *Dunia na Maane, Padosi, Aadmi* depicted women characters in their empowered selves. Waheeda Rehman, Meena Kumari, Sharmila Tagore, Hema Malini and Rekha were the emerging stars of the Cinematic firmament who established their mark by being equal to the men of the times. Not only the costumes but, there was a drastic breakthrough in the thought processes of the times. In the modern times Kangana Ranaut through her movies *Queen* and *Tanu weds Manu* established the image of a new woman who was bold and brave to take her independent decisions. The character of Sridevi in *English Vinglish* also portrays the role of woman who is searching for her identity. A new edition of woman was coming to the forefront, who was educated, empowered and bold to take care of herself. She was creating the perfect balance between her home and work sphere and this new woman was re-defining the whole society in a new way.

School of Indian film making become one of the seven well established film making school across the world. Technically at each and every level Indian cinema during hundred years being influenced by Global Cinema at both Great and Little tradition level. Larger than life image melodramatic approach of Parsi Theatre gradually been replaced by Stanislavski's approach of film making.Fimstars like Amir Khan, Irfan Khan, Anupam Kher and many more practicing common man approach in film making at various level.

Indian cinema traveling through the period of hundred years portrayed independence, power of democracy, voting rights, life stories of marginalized people and their gradual development in a way that was unparalleled. Movies which were made throughout the ages ranged from expensive canvases to low budget movies. On one hand we had the great grand sets of Sanjay Leela Bhansali's movies and on the other, low budget movies like *Masaan*. Each film made by the film maker was portraying the culture, tradition and ethos of India in its own individual way. Indian Cinema a lethal soft power today reach out to Global audiences portraying Indian's colourful, vivid-diverse culture, secular, patriotic and peace loving images.

The role of Censor Board is also to be mentioned here as it is the medium that shows the collaboration of Cinema and Power (Democracy). Whether a movie will be tax full or tax free is decided by the censor board and it is the role of the board to establish a mark of Indian cinema so that on world forum it emerges as a powerful entertainment tool which has the qualities of instruction, morality as well as entertainment. Cinema is no more a typified/typical element but it has become a global phenomenon, which keeps motivating and inspiring people and making them aware of those values and ethos that they are looking up to through this medium of art. It cannot be denied that cinema eventually is growing and converting itself into a commercial commodity. As far as the idea of nation building is concerned, the role of story writer, director and producer is imperative, that too only if they take care of the values and standards which Indian cinema stands for.

Chapter 2

Confluence of Cinema and Politics: Tamil Filmland

*N. Sharada Iyer**

There is a growing interest in Indian cinema in the academic circle, though Hindi cinema traditionally regarded as representing Indian cinema continues to retain that privileged position, but focusing on the specific history of Tamil cinema generally referred to as Kollywood (the term being portmanteau of the word Kodambakam (Chennai, where the industry is based) and Hollywood), -more than any other cinematic tradition India has evolved, bears -the most vital connection with political and social development in the region. The social and production relationship associated with Tamil film at times becomes inseparable, undistinguishable from the social and organizational relationship involved in electoral politics.

The rich development of cinematic expression of political ideology, the collusion of political parties, and the emergence of political leaders from the film industry in one form or the other is not unique to Tamil Nadu alone, yet in Tamil Nadu the cinema politics nexus unquestionably represents the most vibrant and intimate connection between these two institution not only in India perhaps in the world. The State Cinema-politics nexus is a historic outgrowth of the institutional process that evolved during India's colonial past.

The party's involvement with film started around the time ofd India's independence, coinciding with spate of theatres construction and an upsurge in the popularity of touring cinema in rural Tamil Nadu The first silent movie **Keecchaka**

**Vice-Principal and Head, Department of English (Retd.)*
Vasanta College for Women, Rajghat
Banaras Hindu University, Varanasi – 221 001

Vadam was produced in 1916 by K. Nataraja Mudaliar, and the first Talkie, **Kalidas** a multilingual movie was released on 31st Oct. 1931 barely 7 months after India's first talking movie **Alam Ara.**

Annadurai, a protege of E. Ramaswam~~w~~y Naiker, popularly known as EVR an important member of the **Justice Party**, later broke away to form the Dravida Kazagam was convinced that it was possible to maintain a close relation between cinema and politics, and for the party to use media-cinema for propaganda. Annadurai knew that words have power, and they get their power they way they are used, they get powerful when they are spoken by people who are skilled in the art, that is the actors, who have the power to make it powerful so that the people are simply swept off their feet As the DMK gained in strength and visibility they successfully harnessed the power of cinematic celebrities to promote their political ideology of anti- Brahmin Tamil ethno- nationalism.

The rich development in cinematic expression of Dravidian ideology produced an exceptional diffusion between the area of film illusion and political reality for the spectators of Tamil Nadu. Such a socio-political environment provided the ideal condition for a number of people who were involved in both cinema and politics to be installed as charismatic leaders.

All the politicians or actors turned politicians right from C.N.Annadurai, Shivaji Ganesan, Karunanidi,Kannadasan Bharatidasan, S.S.Rajendran, N.S.Krishnan, M.R. Radha, K. Murosoli Maran, Nedunchezian, M.G.Ramachandran, Jayalalita, Rajinikant, Kamal Hasan Anbazagan, Vijaykant,Sarat kumar to mention a few who ~~who~~ have been in government or connected with it as party members have been intimately connected with films in one way or the other. After 1956 all the Chief Ministers of Tamil Nadu belong actively to cinema either as writers or actors, directors.

This connection between cinema and politics is not surprising, since **Regional Party, Regional Cinema and Tamil Literary Revival** have had a simultaneous growth and shared the same ethno-nationalistic ideology.

While Gandhiji was actively involved in independence struggle to free India from the British rule, the people of Tamil Nadu were divided between the desire to end the British rule or to fight the injustice of the indigenous caste system. Though nationalistic themes were popular in drama since 1920, but social themes too like caste system, anti- alcohol, women oppression dominated.

The first step towards it was the formation of **Justice Party**, a political organization —1917-1929 of which E.V.Ramaswamy Naiker was a prominent member. **The Justice Party** also known as **South Indian Liberation Federation** served as standard bearers of Dravidian ethno-nationalistic politics. Their political and cultural activities maintained a regular force to position South Indian Brahmins as cultural colonizers in Dravidian Land. The aim was to undercut Brahminical political power and access to British colonial bureaucracy.

In 1925 EVR formed **Swai Mariyadai Iyakham-SMI**- (Self Respect Movement). He was a member of the Congress ~~of the~~,but soon found it was dominated by the upper caste, moved away to form the D~~S~~ravida Kazgam in 1930 to widen their base in both rural and urban areas. Many of the members were rich landlords therefore not concerned with improving the condition of the workers. After EVR'S tour of Europe and Russia in 1932 he became an ardent Bolshevik. He re-formulated the SMI ideology " Capitalism, Superstition, Distinction and Untouchability must be ruled out " A powerful orator and vocal critic of caste Hinduism, he advocated intercaste marriages, and his demand was for a **Dravida Nadu** —A land of the Dravids.

In 1938 when attempts were made to make Hindustani the lingua franc there was a strong agitation —the agitation was organized and its view articulated by C.N.Annadurai, EVR'S protegee. The agitation shifted the Dravidian Movement from the internal conflict between Tamil caste hierarchy to a broader struggle over the politics of language and identity between the Northern and Southern.

Annadurai, young energetic artistically creative party worker, who had earlier acted in local theatres was a active member of **SMI**. He shaped theatrical performances into a propaganda vehicle for the Dravida Kazagam. He wrote, directed and staged his first major play **Chandrodayam** (1943). The flollowing year despite EVR'S misgivings he declared political theatre an official activity and worthy of party support. Annadurai broke away from EVR, and formed Dravida Munetra Kazagam,with members of the newly formed Party he was convinced to write and stage political plays. Hence from that point there was virtually no constraint to the closeness of Tamil popular art and political propaganda. Annadurai and the other leaders understood that performing art was a powerful tool for promoting Tamil ethno-nationality.

Tamil folk theatre companies principally performed plays from Sanskrit Literature —**Ramayan, Mahabharat** and the **Puranas**. These stories were steeped in Brahminical philosophy, and were vehicles from which Brahminical social conventions were maintained. They were very popular among the lower-caste and illiterate people when they were adopted for films

Annadurai, saw that the Tamil folk theatre companies principally performed plays from Sanskrit Literature —Ramayan, Mahabharat and the Puranas. These stories were steeped in Brahminical philosophy, and were vehicles from which Brahminical social conventions were maintained. They were very popular among the lower caste and illiterate people when they were adopted for films.

This was not lost on Annadurai, he envisioned a Dravidian ideological theatre, reproduced as cinema multiplying the effect the rural theatre group could attain. The DMK began working with cinema adapting an earlier political play. Murosholi Maran editor of '**Murosoli**' found that the early films were not successful as they were too heavy with political ideology and the script writers now learned to "select a good story and mingle it with doctrinal ideology thus mixing entertainment with party ideology."

Congress was disturbed by the growing popularity of politicalized Tamil cinema, their success at State Assembly elections in 1957- 62, using the cinema celebrities in the campaign. Kamaraj tried to dismiss it calling it a 'Party of Clowns' But it displaced the Congress Party which ruled unchallenged since 1950, for the first time a regional party headed its own State.However it was not the protest by political leaders and their demand for entry into temples that had its impact, rather it was because of the popular actors who came into into the forefront and focus. Now it came to be accepted, as MGR film star turned politician said "**Art and Politics are two sides of the same coin**" Congress had also used popular movie star like K.B.Sundarambal during political meetings initially but most of the members looked upon movie as cheap. Rajagopalachari considered cinema to be a source of moral corruption,hence the politicising of movies considerably decreased. Karunanidhi,on the other hand, in an interview said " They decried the cinema we used it."

Tamil Literary Revival—The missionaries believed or rather propagated that caste system did not belong to Dravidian ideology, but was brought by the Aryans and Brahminical social domination, South were using to keep them apart, to perpetuate their position of superiority. Dravidian literature had evolved independently of Sanskrit tradition. Robert Cadwell in **a Comparative Grammar of the South Indian Family of Languages** (1886) evolved a theory that Sanskrit was brought to South India originally by Aryan Brahminic Colonizers.

Local enthusiasm for the theory of and its egalitarian heritage sparked a **Tamil literary Revivalism** the last decade of the 19th century and early decades of the 20th century. Which promoted the study of Tamil history, literature, language. Members read and published hitherto neglected works of Tamil literature including twin epics like **Sillapadikaram** and **Manimekalai** (approximately 300 CE) **Tolkapyam** (a handbook of grammar) **Tirukural**. The discovery of these texts led to a public accusation that Brahminic interpreters of Sanskrit, had privileged Sanskrit texts—Vedas, Upanishad,Puranas, Epics over equally worthy Tamil poetry and philosophy.

The local scholar P. Sundaram Pillai re-interpreted **Ramayana** which is traditionally shown as a battle between good and evil, he said it was rather a battle between a Dravidian King and a powerful Northern invader. This was dismissed by the Brahmins as heresy, but decades later Sundaram Pillai's interpretation of the classic became a popular cultural vehicle among proponents of Dravidian organizations, defiled the image or Rama as a symbol of Northern cultural and political domination over the Southern States.

The revival also laid the foundation for political agitation and social reform within Tamil society, which became one of the facets of the growing Dravidian movement. Tamil Revival scholars highlighted portions of the re-discovered saintly and secular literature that powerfully argued against caste and gender oppression.

Their research added basic support for the basic Dravidian ideology that contended that the pre-Sanskrit society was fundamentally egalitarian. Thus the emerging Dravidian platform of social change was made indistinguishable from a return to a culturally distant and culturally mythical past From this perspective the path to social reform logically begins with the dismantling of Sanskrit influence on Tamil language and culture.

The writings of the late 19th century and early 20th century nationalist poets especially **Ramalingaswami (1823-74) Subramania Bharati (1885-1931) and Bharati Dhasan (1881-1994) Ramalingam** preached a simple religion devoid of ritual, dogma, social hierarchy, claiming that Shiva dances so that all caste religion principles and other doctrinal differences may disappear Bharati though a Smartha Brahmin called himself a Siddha, attacked the caste system in his poetry though his poetry permeated with patriotic and ethno-nationalistic feelings Though he spoke of India as one nation yet he had the deepest feeling for his Tamil Nadu—the land, its people, its culture. **Bharati Dasan**—disciple of Bharati identified Brahmanism as the root cause of repression and social hierarchy in South India.

The works of these poets written in Tamil and often set to music became a source of cultural and ethnic pride. **Ramayana and Mahabharata** were translated into many languages, making them available to the understanding of the common man. The poetry of these ethno-nationalists was adapted to the stage and performances by the drama companies and travelling artists and many were later adapted for the cinema. Politicians and partymen recited these at political meetings, and sang them at rallies and protest marches. Excerpts of these poems appeared in prints on the propaganda pamphlets, distributed to political parties, and social organizations that adhered to the ideology and aspiration of Dravidian movement.

Language as a Political Tool

The party articulated Tamil ethnic nationalism by presenting linguistic chauvinism and supporting performing art which it valued to be the expression of unique Tamil cultural tradition. DMK. leaders actively promoted efforts to expunge Tamil language of Sanskrit words that had filtered into its vocabulary through Hinduism and other contacts with the North. They adopted a high flung literary Tamil with the objective of investing status and dignity to Tamil and putting it in par with classical languages such as Sanskrit.

The popularity of a DMK leader was his power of oratory, especially in pure Tamil devoid of Sanskrit. The speaker impressed the audience with the power and beauty of Tamil in its purest form. And this style flowed in the cinema scripts and the heroes monologues.

Brought into the cinema in the form of a lengthy soliloquy by the hero. In the films produced in the 1940s and 50s Annadurai and Karunanidi scripted the heroes delivery in a court room or at a scene of injustice. Film courtroom scenes became political podium. The hero in the role of a lawyer, defendant delivered a long half hour emotion packed monologue staring straight into the camera lens.

These monologues created some of the most dramatic moments in the early Tamil films.When the DMK opted for films and introduced the Tamil language purity for its screen play Tamil films came to be perceived in literary terms. M.S. Pandian observes that the public awareness of the twin affiliation in cinema and politics of celebrities such as Karunanidu caused an expectation that films sculpted by these leaders would be full of political communication in a beautiful figurative literary Tamil For the audience these films were to be heard rather than watched. Murasoli Maran, said that Tamil Movies reflected the faces of both -the Past (demonstrating the rich language and culture of Tamil Language) and the Future (Social Justice) A.K. Neduncheyan —a former stage actor gained political prominence by transforming the melodrama of film scripts into political platform.

Karunanidi succeeded Annadurai after his sudden death. An accomplished journalist, by 25 he started writing screen plays for Tamil films. Karunanidi's literary ability gave him prominence and a public presence as a key proponent of DMK production of films, with M.G.Ramachandran who commanded a loyal following of politicalized Tamil movie goers.

These influence of the celebrities from the entertainment world was such that they soon dominated all the leadership position in the political group which they were affiliated to. The rivalry and conflict within the artistic sphere were translated into factions and conflicts within the party. Although Karunanidi was a prolific writer he could not match Kannadasan's literary ability. He wrote lyrics for five thousand film songs, 10 volumes of religious discourse, 4000 poems. Given the pivotal role in film music, Kannadasan also wrote lyrics to most popular songs for DMK propaganda films. He is also credited for introducing a classical literary tradition to contemporary film audience.The talent of Kannadasan was threatening to Karunanidi so he side-lined him, he left the party to join the opposite party along with Nedumcheyan. Karunanidi managed to gain the support of EVR. as well as Sivaji Ganesan and MGR. And got elected as Chief Minister of Tamil Nadu in 1996.

Regional Films

The advent of sound in cinematic technology undercut the competition from American and British films and simultaneously led to the diversification of Indian film industry into numerous regional films, that classified audience by their linguistic and ethnic affiliation. With the establishment of Sound Studios in Calcutta 1930, Madras 1934, the dependence of South on North ended. Madras began to take over the production of South Indian languages film Regional films were made in 29 languages. They enjoyed the luxury of playing on the ethnic specific issue, problem and their causes. During the period (1947-67) while Hindi film industry was experiencing the transitional period—from the studios to the independent producers Film studios assembled the physical and human capital they would need to articulates a distinct regional identity in the medium. As they did political party DMK. Engineered to project its message of political ethno- nationalism into the cinema screen and ultimately into power in the State of Tamil Nadu.

The meeting of capital, artistry, ideology, technical expertise and ethnic identity produced a powerful product, one more specific and personal than its counterpart in Bombay could have afforded to. A comparison between **Avvayar (1953) and Mother India** (1957) underscores the distinct agenda of Hindi and Tamil films. **Mother India** refers to the birth of a nation state, blurring any regional or caste identities that could muddle its universality. In contrast the Tamil classic opens with a dedication to Mother Tamil and a song of praise to the land of Tamil. The film celebrates the rich Tamil heritage through the life of Avvayar a saint poetess devoted to Lord Muragan. She lived sometimes between 100-250B.C.whose poems are still taught in schools. Though not explicitly political the radical anti-caste message, a key aspect of DMK ideology was none the less clear. Avvayar belonged to the lower caste and so were most of the film audience, hence the film greatly appealed to the masses.

Much of the success of the Tamil film industry was built on the stability of the Tamil film companies. This was provided by the huge **Production Houses—Gemini pictures and AVM Studio**, this was accompanied with the exiting new content and talent provided by the active involvement of DMK which was formed in 1947 which took the Tamil films to new heights. Till 1949 60 per cent of the film production in India was based in Bombay, and only 11 per cent in Madras. A decade later Madras claimed 46 per cent of the national film production overtaking Bombay which was now only 35 per cent.

Meyyapan started the **AVM Studio** in 1945 produced **Nam Eruvar (1947) Parashakt**i (1953), replicated the regional rhetoric of Tamil leaders.

Gemini Studio (1941) owned by **S.S.Vasan** made the studio self sufficient by opening the advertising wing, employing stars on long time contract. By 1958 it had its full **Eastman Colour Lab.** He was a writer of novels and script writing. **Chandralekha** (1948), a historical film on a grand scale, caused a sensation nation wide with its songs and dance sequence, lavish sets—dance on gigantic drums with hundred dancers set in a vast area. It was dubbed in several languages.

In Tamil Nadu the post- independence period was politically charged. Tamil Nadu was the first to elect a regional party DMK replacing Congress. Tamil ethno-nationalism of DMK permeated all ranks of Tamil Nadu films. The two most influential were Annadurai and Karunadi whose literary abilities and pivotal position not only gave them celebrity status not only in the film world, but also in the party. Both entered the field of theatre as actors and playwrights. Many of their plays were commercially successful and artistically notable films.

Velaikari (1948) established Annadurai and the theme of post-independence nationalist films. The peasant hero has to face many forms of injustice—exploited by the rich, the caste Brahmin, politicians and religion. The film plays upon religious hypocrisy, denounces superstition, exposes caste barriers that oppresses normal human social interaction.

Annadurai liberally borrowed plots, stories, scenes, events, costume,makeup from American films. He was inspired by Robert Riskin's films of Depression Era, which showed the Leftist ideals of distributional equality and equal opportunity.

Parashakti (1952) established Karunanidi as a script writer,in which Shivaji Ganesan and S.S.Rajendran founder members of the DMK made their screen debut A film showing the Tamil nationalist ideology of DMK. It was rated as a classic. The hero is presented as an angry atheist and politically committed. A story of a young women molested in the temple by the priest to whom she had appealed for sanctuary. Upon rescuing her the hero launches into a long monologue elucidating DMK. Political philosophy. The talk of various forms of exploitation they are subjected to by the high caste, the rich over the poor, the Brahmin over the illiterate and lower caste.Karunanidhi speaking about Parakshati said " Intention was to introduce the ideas and policies of social reform and justice....and bring up the status of Tamil Language as they were called for in DMK politics".

All the plays scripted by Annadurai and Karunanidi was acted by Shivaji Ganesan and MGR. Who were soon treated as celebrities. They grew so rich that they opened their own production companies.It also saw the beginning of Star System in Film World MGR and Karunanidi launched **Mekhala Pictures**, Shivaji started **Shanti Theatres,** later Kamal Hasan **Rajkamal Pictures.**

Shivaji acted in Annadurai's **'Shivaji Kanda Indu Rajyam.'** It established him not only as an actor but also brought him in closer contact with Annadurai and DMK. He played the hero in **Parashakti** too, which greatly raised Karunanidi's political career and the future of AVM. Shivaji soon distanced himself from DMK.

Shivaji's departure led to the rise of MGR as Tamil ethno-nationalist leading film icon.. Shivaji was a better actor, but MGR. once accepted by the DMK. remained a staunch loyalist. His growing popularity threatened Karunanidi position, he was sidelined, he broke away to form his own party **ADMK.**

1970s was a period of crisis and transition. Shivaji MGR.period was over. MGR. was getting more and more involved in politics. DMK.was at the helm of Tamil Nadu politics and it meant a heyday for film industry.

When Annadurai took over in 1967, he reduced the entertainment tax on locally produced Tamil language films. Which increased the profit and worked as an incentive. Annadurai's sudden demise, and Karunanidi coming into power had to face opposition and faction within the party. After the party broke up Tamil films became a propaganda machine for MGR, Karunanidi was closely associated with MGR. And in early days had featured in **Mantri Kumari** along with his actor wife Janaki, and had founded the **Mekhala Pictures.** During the conflict that ensued after the death of Annadurai, MGR campaigned for Karunanidi, ensured his victory, he was appointed treasurer. Threatened by MGRs popularity he sidelined him, and party's dependence on the actor for finance.Karunanidi repealed the prohibition law an act. MGR opposed on public health ground, when thrown out of party, he was confident of his popularity on the screen. He defied Karunanidi on the political stage, encouraged by the fact that people gave him the prime importance even when Karunanidi, Neduncheziyan Anbazagan were on the same platform. He organized his own fan club, where loyalties were inseparable from acting skill. He broke away from DMK to form ADMK. And was soon elected Chief Minister of Tamil Nadu.Of all the DMK attracted the greatest adulation More than two hundred thousand people attended his funeral in 1988, he was also conferred Bharat Ratna.

Jayalalita started her film career at the age of 13. She starred opposite MGR at the age of 17 and continued to be his leading lady in 20 films, in all she acted in 121 films. Her political mentor was MGR. The importance that was given by MGR created a lot of resentment and opposition by his party members. He made her a Rajya Sabha member with special powers, his representative to negotiate electoral alliances with Indra Gandhi.

After MGRs death his actress wife Janaki tried to form the government, but could not continue for a long time. Jayalalita became the Chief Minister after DMK was defeated in 1991. However her party fell to corruption and in 1996 DMK took over.

Karunanidi was grooming his son Stalin as young Commander-in-Chief—**Ilaya Talapati.** In the DMK.tradition he tried to boot his image through the entertainment media—T.V.rather than cinema.He launched his political career acting in day time soap opera. He was appointed Mayor of Chennai which was strongly resented in the party circle. His efforts to establish him as his successor caused a split in the party and Jayalalita came back to power.

Rajanikant having achieved celebrity status, his entry into politics was almost certain. He first expressed his interest by strongly supporting Jayalalita, but soon distanced himself because of the rampant corruption In 1995 election he stood by Karunanidi His support was instrumental in bringing Karunanidi back to power. Rajnikant was often referred to in all Karunanidi election campaign.

In 2001 when Jayalalita came back to power, Rajnikant took a nine day fast to press the cause of Krishna Cauvery dispute, which found great support from all political parties The clearest indication of his interest in politics was the release of his two highly publicised films, BABA 2002 and SHIVAJI 2007 and ROBOT. The theme of these films centered on the exposure and reform in politics which was growing highly corrupt.In these films he has made concerted efforts to emulate his predecessor Annadurai, MGR, Karunanidi and Jayalalita in the deployment of cinema as a principal tool of political communication. The film Baba closes with a suggestion that the hero -Rajinikant renounces the world to enter the world of politics out of necessity—the dearth of good leadership in the State. In Shivaji the hero—Rajinikant single handed fights the forces of corruption that tries to deny the people—of Tamil Nadu—access to education,health care has a near dead experience before he emerges with a new name Ravichandran to fight the enemy.

Karunanidi's son Stalin tried his way to cinema through T.V.. But Rajinikant felt T.V. Produced the industry. At the release of his 100th film **Shivaji**, the most expensive in the film in India's film history—174 million dollars,he arranged special screening of the film Karunanidi,Jayalalita, Chandrababu Naidu and Amitab Chandrababu Naidu extended primary membership to his Telugu Desam. What will Tamil Nadu entertainment generate by the way of political leaders will depend on Rajinikant and othe popular cinema celebrities like Vijaykant, main stream lead actor who has launched **Desya Muropokku Dravida Kazhayagam**, which is now placing itself as an alternative to mainstream Dravidian Party. In 2011 the Party became the official opposition in the Tamil Legislative Assembly, and Sarat Kumar another very popular hero forming the **Samathuva Makal Katsh**i, T. Rajendran a well known supporter of DMK broke away in 2004 to form **All India Latichiya DMK.**

The continued influence of Tamil film industry comes to the forefront when BJPs Prime-ministerial candidate Narendra Modi called on Superstar Rajnikant during the 2014 General Election, for as Annadurai said about MGR so is it true or more than true about Rajanikant.

"When we show his (Rajanikant's) face we get(any party he supports) we get 40,000 seats, when he (Rajanikant) speaks a few words we get four lakh".

Rajanikant made a curtsy gesture by describing Modi as **"a strong leader and good administrator"** BJP and the regional parties in alliance with BJP repeatedly played it in the election rallies, using it to their advantage, this only underlines the fact that the relationship relationship between Cinema and Politics in the State since the 1930s is growing uninterrupted.

The cinematic idols transforming themselves into political idols by associating themselves to political parties or forming their own has shaped the State politics. The common thread linking them is their cine influence. The reason that leads to their mass appeal is the character (the anti-establishment, Angry Man) they play in the movie and their cultural, ethnic and lingual connection with the masses. They have their image,they have their support, they have their ideology and ultimately the party support. The influence of cinema in the politics of Tamil Nadu has been significant. The role of 'STARS' in politics has made political astrologers read the influence of 'STARS'-favourable or unfavourable- in predicting the future of the State politics, Party and the leaders of those who seek to understand.

Books/Journals Referred to

1. Gopalan Krishna : "Tamil Nadu's Fascinating Connection Between Cinema and Politics" *Economic Times* 8 No. 13 Dec. 2008.

2. Hardgrave, Jr.Robert. L " Politics and Films in Tamil Nadu : The Stars and DMK" Asian Survey (JSTOR) 13.3 March 1973.
3. Jacob Preminda: Celliod Deites: The Visual Culture of Cinema and Politics in South India, 2006.
4. Prasad,M,. Madhava: "Cine-Politics: On the Political Significance of Cinema in South India" *Journal of Moving Images*, 13 Dec. 2008.
5. Sarah Dickey: " The Politics of Adulation : Cinema and the Production of Politicians in South India " *Journal of Asian Studies*. 52(2), 1993.

Chapter 3

'The Film is Dead; Long Live the Cinema': An Economic Analysis of Digitalization of Cinema in India

*Anurag Dave**

When we speak the word 'film' it refers to the celluloid form of cinema. Until recently, cinema that we used to experience in the dark room called theatre was a spectacle on the screen produced by a beam of light passing through a succession of images recorded on a reel of celluloid. This the audiences were experiencing since from the first theatrical screening of moving images by Lumiere Brothers at the Grand Cafe in Paris on 28 December 1885, to few years back. But three two years ago, in April 2013, Fujifilm, one of the only two major motion picture film manufacturers, discontinued the production of the celluloid medium.[1] With the other major manufacturer, Kodak, filing bankruptcy in 2012, analysts almost sealed the fate of film as 'dead'.[2] Therefore, in spite of its tremendous success and a long history, the film as we know will phase-out from our lives. The natural curiosity is that what the future of cinema is. The death of celluloid (film) is not the end of cinema, the future of cinema is digital.

Fujifilm in their official press release announcing the above mentioned closure, stated that the step had been taken 'in order to adapt to the recent rapid transition of digitalization in the shooting, producing, projecting and archiving processes...'[3]

**Professor, Department of Journalism and Mass Communication*
Banaras Hindu University, Varanasi – 221 005

This statement of the Company bears testimony to the rapid proliferation of digital technology of cinema over the traditional cinema. Digital cinema means any aspect of movie making in the digital domain, including capture, editing, distribution and projection. The basic idea that digital cinema works on is the use bits and bytes (strings of 1s and 0s) to record, transmit, copy and replay images, rather than using chemicals on film like in the case of the celluloid.

When digital camera shoots a scene, information pertaining to light and colour of each frame is stored by the camera in the form of string of numbers which can be realised on the screen in the form of pixels.

In the analog system, films worked on continuous gradations but in digital form pixels are independent from one another and work on data which is discrete in nature. This property of digital technology provides an edge to digital cinema over analog. Pixels can be easily manipulated by the computers and they can be copied repeatedly without any degradation of quality. Digital films can also be stored, transmitted from one computer network to another and retrieved without any information loss.

Shifting from transparent celluloid strip to a binary file is a paradigm shift. It is a shift from physical to virtual product and hence it has deep and fundamental impact on film making both as an art and business. It is affecting the whole ecosystem of film industry customers' behaviour and the dynamics between different parties within this system.

The present paper is an attempt to discuss these changes and their consequences in context of the Indian film industry.

The Indian Film Industry

India is a film-loving country. Films and cricket have earned the status of religion among a vast majority of the masses here. First motion picture was brought to India by the Lumiere Brothers in 1896. In 1913 the first Indian film ***Raja Harishchandra*** was made by Dada Saheb Falke. Since its first film, the Indian film industry has come a long way and in 2013 Indian cinema completed its 100 years.[4]

India is the largest film industry in the world in terms of number of films produced per year and the ticket size.[5] Over 1000 films are produced every year by the Indian film industry in more than 20 languages. Hindi cinema, which is popularly known as bollywood, is a part of the Indian cinema industry. India has a strong regional cinema and Telugu, Kannada, Tamil, Bengali, and Malayalam constitute large chunk its film Industry.

The estimated size of Indian film industry is INR 125.3 billion in 2013. Growth over the year is 11.5 per cent (INR 112.4 billion in 2012).[6] The following figure shows the growth of the film industry in India between 2005 and 2013.

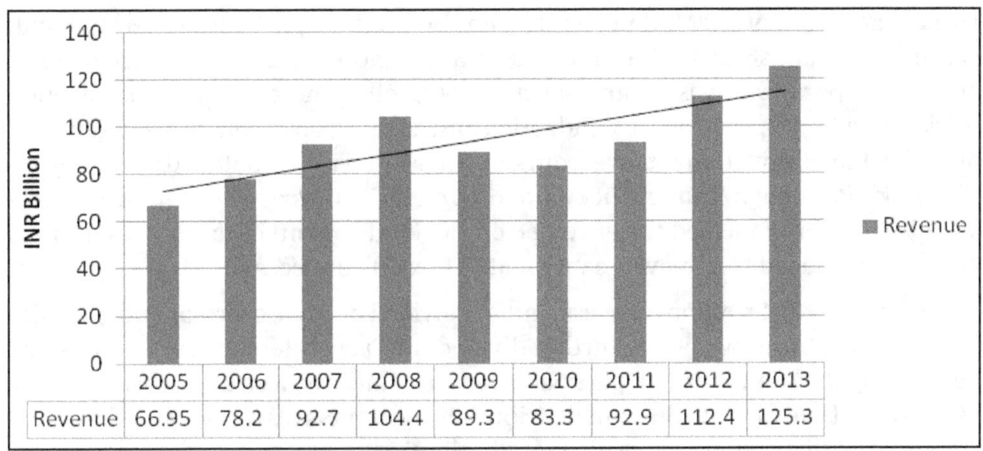

	2005	2006	2007	2008	2009	2010	2011	2012	2013
Revenue	66.95	78.2	92.7	104.4	89.3	83.3	92.9	112.4	125.3

Figure 3.1: Growth of Indian Film Industry.
***Source*: KPMG FICCI Frames.**

Despite its long history and huge size, till few years back Indian cinema was churning out low budget films where the average budget was half a million. Financial transparency was also not very much evident in Indian film industry till few years back when it was mostly funded by the diamond merchants and the underworld. From 2001 onwards, after declaration of cinema as an industry by the government, the fragmented Indian film industry is moving towards more and more organized form.

Value Chain and Film Ecosystem in India

The value chain within the film industry comprises production, distribution, exhibition and end consumers. In contrast to Hollywood, where studio system is too strong, Indian cinema experiences high level of fragmentation in all segments of value chain. A very few players like Reliance Mediaworks is present throughout the media chain. Few companies like Yash Raj are having presence in couple of parts of the value chain.

Figure 3.2: Film Industry Value Chain.

The Indian film production segment is highly fragmented with a large number of individual and corporate production houses and film funds. Around 400 production houses and nearly 30 corporate houses are involved in film production in India. Yash Raj Films, EROS, UTV Production, Dharma Production, Rajshree Production, Mukta Art are some of the major film production houses working in India. Along with Indian production houses, international corporate houses like

Disney India, Viacom18 Motion Pictures, Fox Star Studios, Reliance Entertainment, etc. are continuously driving the industry to adopt more professional approach. The growing corporatization is leading the industry to follow more structured production workflow with proper planning, budgeting and acquisition of content. A major shift of Indian film production is move from star driven movies to content driven movies. Films like Pan Singh Tomar, Vicky Donor, Queen, Gangs of Wasseypur, English-Vinglish, etc. have pushed the envelope on the kind of content that works in India and have managed to achieve unanticipated box office success.

In the film distribution business, India is divided into one overseas and six major domestic territories which are further divided into 11 sub-territories.[7] Distributers buy the rights of a film for a particular territory and recover their cost from the exhibition of the film. Again, film distribution segment is also fragmented in India with 15 to 20 distributers competing for distribution rights for a particular territory. In recent times, many large players are integrating production and distribution business with their presence in both the segments. This has led to a decline in the number of independent distributers.

In the exhibition segment, India is a significantly under-screened market. India has very low screen density of 8 screens per million as compared to 117 per million in USA.[8] Mumbai and Bangalore have a higher number of screens per million at 23 and 21 respectively, while cities such as Hyderabad and Chennai have only about 6.[9]

Digital Technology and Film Ecosystem

Digitalization of film technology is changing the traditional cinema business in India. Digital technology is affecting every aspect of film making process, from production and post production to distribution and exhibition. On one side digital technology is helping reduce the cost of distribution and opening up many revenue streams, while on the other side it is providing better cinematic experience to the consumers. The Figure 3.3 shows how Indian film industry moved towards the digital era along with its production value chain

Digital Technology and Film Production

Over the last few years, an increasing number of films in India have used the digital intermediate technology, whereby films are converted into digital format that helps in adjustment of image structure and provides more control over colour. Hence, there are increasing instances of uses of animation, 3D, VFX and computer generated graphics images. Now the standard production phases (pre-production, production and post-production) and the entire filmmaking process with them are changing. The increasing amount of digital effects is blurring the limits between principal photography and post-production. As a consequence, pre-production is no longer just the preparation of the shooting, but of post-production as well. It is also changing the content of Indian cinema by shifting from the single Masala films genre to different genres like Action, si-fi, super hero, horror, etc. where computer

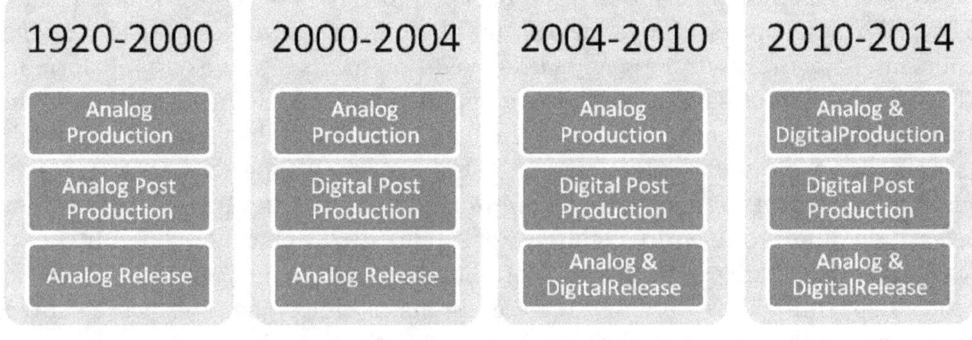

Figure 3.3: Evolution of Digital Era in India along with Production Chain.
***Source*: KPMG FICCI Frames.**

generated graphics, animation and special effects are more important. Digital technology is enabling producers to experiment with newer genres of cinema. In terms of production, digital videos are much cheaper than reel based production. There is virtually no processing involved before the editing stage. Filmmakers can go on taking takes and retakes without worrying about growing expenses due to wastage of costly reels. Filmmakers on a shoe-string budget can even reuse the tape multiple times. However, less cost pressure on directors means more room for creativity. They are *'moving beyond the cut'* and satisfied to see how their character would look on screen. The increasing number of films that are being shot in the digital format is paving the way for digital production, digital post-production, and digital release (DDD) structure. For instance, in 2009 Sathyam Cinemas and Real Image Media announced their first Tamil film production "*ThiruThiruThiruThiru*". The film was reportedly India's first end-to-end digital movie that was shot, colour-graded, and released entirely in the digital format.

Globally, digital production has come up more prominently after 2009 with Slumdog Millionaire becoming the first movie shot mainly in a digital format to be awarded the Academy Award for best cinematography.[10] Another significant use of special effect by using digital technology was the then highest grossing film of all times '*Avatar*'.[11] In recent time 3D films are doing better business and for 3D films, digital technology is essential.

Digital Technology and Film Distribution and Exhibition

The main impact of digital technology is on distribution and exhibition. One of the greatest advantages of digital technology is that it reduces the distribution cost of films considerably. The cost of any film produced in Bollywood is anywhere between INR 20 million and 600 million, depending upon the budget of producers. The cost of single print of any film is around INR 65,000 – 70,000, which remains constant. So, if the producer would like to have 500 prints it would cost him around INR 30-40 million.[12] This figure comes to around 20 percent for a big budget film in India and much higher than that for a small and medium budget film. Sometimes it is more than their total production cost. Therefore, small budget filmmakers create just 50 to 60 prints and even if a big filmmaker goes for 500 prints he could not release the film in the entire country. For a huge geographical area like India, at least 1000 prints are essential for 'carpet-bombing' with a new release. Therefore, typically in India films were first released in major cities. Then they were shifted to lower rung theatres and later on to B and C class towns. The whole process took at least five to six months' time and till the movies reached smaller towns, their markets were flooded with pirated copies of film CDs and DVDs. Hence, revenue from smaller towns was almost non-existent for the filmmakers.

But digital technology has a solution for this problem. The cost of per copy of digital print is just INR 3,500 – 5,000 which is significantly lower (almost one fifth) than physical prints.[13] Now films can be distributed through satellite technology or high speed optical fibre networks to geographically remote areas. This helps distributers to release films simultaneously at theatrical windows across the country. Hence, it reduces the scope for piracy and increases the revenue of filmmakers. In addition, digital technology allows theatres to store many films to their server at a time. Therefore, multiplexes are able to run different films during a particular period. Even the single screens can take the advantage of this by running multiple movies at different times.

The Table 3.1 explains how digitalization of screens is helping filmmakers to achieve wider release of films.

Table 3.1: Increase in Number of Screens at Time of Release

Film	*Year of Release*	*No. of Screens*
Hum Aapke Hain Kaun	1994	500
3 Idiots	2009	1000
Dabangg 2	2012	3500
Dhoom 3	2013	4500

Source: KPMG FICCI Frames.

Table 3.1 shows that the industry took almost 15 years (from 1994 to 2009) to double the number of screens at the time of release. But after that within three years (from 2009 to 2012) number of screen at the release increased 3.5 times and during 2012-13 it increased by 1000 screens. The growth of number of screens at release is the result of digitalization of film distribution and exhibition.

The wider release of a film is not just a tool in the hands of the filmmakers to curb the piracy, it is also helping them to recover their money at faster rate by reducing breakeven point. First week collection is getting prominence in Indian cinema. Wider release of films is increasing the first week collection. Total collections of successful films have reached a much higher level than earlier. In 2013, Chennai Express became the fastest film to enter the one million club in just 4 days of release. Same year, Dhoom 3 became the first film that collected more than INR 2 million in its first week of release. It is also reducing the theatrical life of films. It is also helping the filmmakers to experiment with newer genres of cinema since the investment in prints and copyright is minimal.

The main hurdle that film industry in India was facing in digitalization of cinema distribution was to convert the huge number of analog single screens into digital. This needs a good amount of investment for digital projector and installation of high-end computers. But majority of Indian cinema screens are not operating on high-end D-Cinema but they are using E-Cinema technology. E-cinema offers about 10 percent poorer quality in terms of the projected image but comes at about a third of D-cinema's cost.[14] Also, in most cases, cinema owners do not have to invest for costlier projector and infrastructure at once. All the logistic arrangements are borne by the technological players in return of revenue sharing arrangements. Like Real Image sells digital cinema system against a down payment of around 10 percent while UFO Movies collects a fee per show which is around INR 200 from the distributers and INR 250 from the exhibitors and retain the ownership of the system.[15] Important thing is that both the companies get the rights for on-screen advertising, in some cases a bigger revenue component than digital cinema solution. At present the revenue for exhibitors comprises 70 percent ticket sales, 20 percent food and 10 percent cinema advertising.[16] This proportion remaining unchanged, the industry is expecting the absolute volume will go up. Almost 90 to 95 percent of Indian cinema screens are digital now. Digitalization of screen also provides opportunities to the exhibitors to generate additional revenue by offering alternative content such as cricket matches, award shows, etc.

Another big challenge faced by the Indian film industry is lack of transparency in collection flow. Under-declaration of ticket revenue has an adverse impact on rightful revenue flow to all the stakeholders. This challenge is also addressed by the digital technology. Hence, computerized box-office ticketing provides the instant sales data that enables distributers for more scientific release strategies and maximise revenue collection. Online ticket booking is also growing in India. Online ticket booking also curbs the black-marketing and enhances the convenience of customers. Digital technology is changing the movie going habits of Indians. Released in 2014, PK became the first film in India to gross INR 100 crore from online booking.[17] It is the 25 per cent of total domestic revenue collection of PK. India's box office is estimated to sell 50 million tickets monthly, with an estimated 4 to 6 million being sold online. Online sales of niche Bollywood films like The Lunchbox and Madras Cafe stood between 40 to 70 per cent of the gross collections.[18]

Digital Technology and Alternative Distributions Platforms for Films

Apart from theatrical revenue, cable and satellite (C and S) rights and home video are the other two main revenue streams for the film industry in India. Cable and satellite revenue contributes almost 12 percent of total revenue of film industry in India. The total revenue from cable and satellite revenue was INR 1,510 million in 2013.[19] It is expected to grow further as the rise in pre-release and bundling of C and S rights are getting prominence in industry. One of the important aspects of larger theatrical release of film, due to digital cinema, is that the theatre–to–television window is reducing. The movies are being broadcast on television within the 60 to 90 days of their theatrical release. This is helping film producers towards better realization of C and S revenue. The following table shows the dates of film release and their TV premier

Table 3.2: Reducing Theatre-to-TV Window

Movie	*Date of Theatrical Release*	*Date of TV Premier*	*Days of Difference*
Agneepath	11th November, 2011	16th June, 2012	187 days
Kahani	9th March, 2012	3rd June, 2012	86 days
Ek Tha Tiger	15th August, 2012	11th November, 2012	88 days
Chennai Express	9th August, 2013	20th October, 2013	75 days
Boss	16th October, 2013	23rd November, 2013	38 days

Source: KPMG FICCI Frames.

Satellite channels are also launching strong marketing campaigns to mark the premier of movies.

Home video is another distribution channel of films. Home video consists of sales and rentals of movie DVDs and VCDs. But its contribution to overall film industry business in India is very low (almost 1 per cent in 2013). Physical distribution of 'Home Video' is declining but digital consumption of 'Video on Demand' (VOD) has the potential to become a significant contributor to the producer's kitty.

Traditionally, content distribution by the television mechanism works on passive participants who receive what the service provider offers. However, video on demand empowers the viewers with the flexibility in viewing content that they wishes to watch as per their convenient time. Industry is working on several different revenue models for VOD like Transactional (TVOD), Subscription (SVOD), ad-supported (AVOD) and sell-through (EST/DTO).

The number of DTH subscribers saw a growth of 18 percent in 2013. Therefore, pay per view is expected to grow robustly over the years. Phase 2 and phase 3 of

TV digitalization covered the smaller towns and cities, hence there is considerable monetising potential for regional pay per view service providers.

With the advent of faster networks like 3G and 4G, the content consumption on personal screen is expected to rise significantly in India. With 26 milion new subscribers in the first quarter of 2015, India is the second largest country in the world in terms of mobile users.[20] Mobile is also primary access device to internet. Therefore, its uses as entertainment device to watch video and gaming are expected to grow. itunes, Ditto TV (Zee), Box TV (Time Internet), BigFlix (Reliance), Lucup, Eros Now, Spull, hotstar (Star Tv), Amazon Instant Video, etc. are the different video platforms that providing video on demand in India.

Pay per view and Video on demand also aid the parallel cinema movies and independent filmmakers. Parallel cinema and independent film makers often struggle to find slots in the exhibition space and at the same time aggregators and content distributors are also looking to create their own content. Therefore, it's a win- win situation for both and new talented directors, who could produce movies with strong storyline, can use alternative platforms to reach the audience. The digitalization of cinema and advent of new distribution platforms are changing the traditional linear value chain of the film industry.

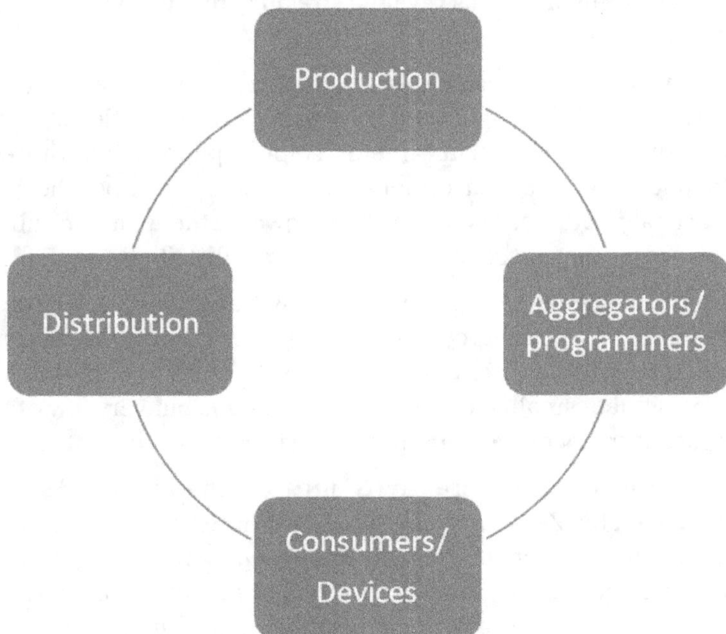

Figure 3.4: Changing Value Chain of Film Industry.

Several mainstream filmmakers are also exploring the new business model under the changing value chain. Kamal Haasan's Vishwaroopam was to be the first Indian film to release via direct-broadcast satellite (direct-to-home, DTH), but after protests of theatre owners this plan was dropped. Several filmmakers are releasing their films on Internet and reaching their audiences via aggregators' and internet video service providers. Ram Gopal Varma has started a new distribution system with his film *Anukshanam* by auctioning this movie through a website. In future, the digital technology may lead to new experimentations in film distribution and exhibition.

Discussion and Conclusion

Digital technology is changing the whole business process of film making from innovation in production and distribution to marketing. But digital is not just technology, it is applying digital mindset and building business strategy around that. It is not just to reach audience quicker but to be more targeted, experimental and collaborative.

Digital technology with proper business strategy can provide right kind of results to all the stakeholders of industry value chain. Manage print cost, reducing production time, better picture quality, more durability of films, flexibility in re-prints, curbing piracy, early recovery of investment, better viewing experience, alternative platforms to reach larger number of audiences, better marketing and increased monetisation of various revenue streams are the advantage enabling the industry by investing in technology.

Another benefit of digital technology is that it gives everyone a chance to tell their stories to the world. Digital technology is helping in democratization of cinema. In the past, one had to have money to rent cameras, sound equipment, editing equipment, etc. Now, anyone who has a smart phone and a laptop can shoot their stories and edit them practically for free. Then, they can showcase them on YouTube and other alternative platforms instead of being at the mercy of distributors and film festivals.

Digital technology has brought various new things and easier ways to make films but there are also some grey parts of it. Lower cost of filmmaking has over flooded the market with less serious work. After the advent of digital technology, Indian market is full of small and medium budget films but very few of them could make an impact as many of them are poor in research and content.

Technology has stuffed creativity up to some extent. As the famous cinematographer Peter Zeitlinger said once in a interview that "... *the moment when you started to see, immediately, the image that you were creating... this was the start of a very big disaster and destruction of the inner image and the inner vision, which you had to create with old technology on film, when you did not see what you did straight away. You had to see it in your mind. You had to create all [of] the world on the screen in your mind first; then shoot it, then everybody else did not know how it would be. But, nowadays, you look on the screen and this destroys the inner vision; and everything that constitutes creative visual work is becoming very hard.*"[21]

Similarly, activities like search for locations, creating huge sets, designing backdrop property and others of the ilk will gradually fade away as filmmakers increasingly shoot the actors against a green-screen with a high definition camera and fill in the background digitally. Naturally, the job of many creative people in industry like spot-boys, set designers, light-men, cinematographers, extras, etc. are under threat due to the digital technology. In due course of time we may have a situation when films need not be shot with the help of actors and actress; the whole film can be created with their images. Digital technology can lead to small crew approach for filmmaking and that can be the beginning of the end of their craft.

Footnotes

1. Discontinuation of Motion Picture Film production, April 2, 2013

   http://www.fujifilm.com/news/n130402.html

2. MICHAEL J. DE LA MERCED: *Eastman Kodak Files for Bankruptcy,* The New York Times, January 19, 2012.

   http://dealbook.nytimes.com/2012/01/19/eastman-kodak-files-for-bankruptcy/?_r=0

3. Announcement on Motion Picture Film Business of Fujifilm, September 13, 2012

   http://www.fujifilm.com/news/n120913.html

4. Wikipedia : Cinema of India

   https://en.wikipedia.org/wiki/Cinema_of_India

5. Emerging Markets and the Digitalization of Film Industry, UNESCO Institute of Statistics, 2013, p. 11

6. *The stage is set*: FICCI-KPMG Indian Media and Entertainment Industry Report 2014, p. 70

7. Ashok Mittal: *Cinema Industry in India: Pricing and Taxation*, Indus Publishing Company, New Delhi, 1995, p.54

8. *The stage is set*: FICCI-KPMG Indian Media and Entertainment Industry Report 2014, p. 67

9. *Ibid*

10. Helen Alexander and Rhys Blakely: The Triumph of Digital Will Be the Death of Many Movies; https://newrepublic.com/article/119431/howdigitalcinematookover35mmfilm

11. All Time Worldwide Box Office Grosses, http://www.boxofficemojo.com/alltime/world/

12. *In the interval, but ready for the next act*: FICCI-KPMG Indian Media and Entertainment Industry Report 2009, p. 115

13. *Ibid*

14. *Ibid*, 117

15 Rajesh Naidu: Digital Makes UFO movies OFS attractive, Economic Times Bureau, 24th April, 2015

   http://economictimes.indiatimes.com/markets/stocks/news/digital-play-makes-ufo-moviez-ofs-attractive/articleshow/47033769.cms

16 *The stage is set*: FICCI-KPMG Indian Media and Entertainment Industry Report 2014, p. 70

17. Boby Kurian and Anshul Dhamija: PK starts Bollywood's Rs. 100 crore online club, *The Times of India*, 31st January, 2015

    http://timesofindia.indiatimes.com/entertainment/hindi/bollywood/news/PK-starts-Bollywoods-Rs-100-crore-online-club/articleshow/46061158.cms

18. *The stage is set*: FICCI-KPMG Indian Media and Entertainment Industry Report 2014, p. 74

19. *Ibid*

20 Ericson Mobility Report: On the pulse of the networked society, June, 2015, p 5

21. http://cpn.canon-europe.com/content/interviews/peter_zeitlinger_digitals_dark_side.do.

Chapter 4

The Cinema: Most Popular Audio-Visual Mass Medium to Influence Human Development as a Whole

*Anshu Shukla**

Since its beginning with the film '*Raja Harish Chandra*' (1913), the cinema has remained the most powerful media for mass communication in India. Cinema has the ability to combine entertainment with communication of ideas. It has the potential appeal for its audience. It certainly leaves other media far behind in making such an appeal. As in literature, cinema has produced much which touches the innermost layers of the man. It mirrors the episodes in such a manner that leaves an impact on the coming generations. Cinema presents an image of the society in which it is born and the hopes, aspirations, frustration and contradictions present in any given social order.

It is hard to decide if films have a larger impact on the Indian Society or the latter has on the former. The most important contribution has of course been the entertainment. The emotional dramas with some great screenplays has been blockbusters. Many a times Indian cinema has remained a place where, as Manmohan Desai said, "people would forget their misery,....a dream where there is no poverty and where the fate is kind.." Films have also played an important role in the integrity of the nation. It was the only platform where people could see different cultures. At times when politics

**Assistant Professor, Vasant Kanya Mahavidyalaya, Kamachha, Varanasi*
E-mail: dranshushuklavkmbhu@gmail.com

was dividing the nation on regional basis Cinema showcased a superhit 'Sholay', directed by a sindhi, with music from someone of Tripura and main actors from Punjab, U.P, Gujarat, Tamil Nadu and Bengal, presenting the magic by a blend of talents from all across the country. Moreover, they have given the society the lectures on communal harmony cloaked under entertainment. Brothers separated by fate growing up in different religious families in Amar Akbar Anthony packed with high drama, or hindu guy marrying a Muslim girl in Mani Ratnam's Bombay, there have been remarkable cinema challenging the communalism in the society. Similarly across the time, from Achhut Kanya to Lagaan, untouchability has been questioned in a society which practices it since time immemorial. The female who was often neglected in major socio-economic aspects took the central theme in Satyajit Ray's classics. In a traditional Indian society where arranged marriages was a strict norm the movies somehow gave a complete different outlook to Man-woman's relationship. Even though sometimes exaggerated, the role of films in "teaching romance" can not be completely ignored. Today, as the business shifts from small towns to cities with the multi-screen mall culture, Indian films have changed their profile from farmer- centric backdrop to rich bunglows. It continues to impact society by showing exquisite locations, cars or bodies which remain an inspiration to the young who wants to be rich and is running faster than the other in the process of social capillarity.

Cinema has truly played a major role in changing our society. Patriotic movies make us remember to love our nation. Good comedic movies have treated many patients through laugh therapy. Adventure movies have given us a sense of adventure to explore new possibilities. There are many more! In our society there are many practices and traditions which are based on ignorance and which have withheld the progress of our society. Rigidity of caste system, untouchability, dowry system and purdah system have done enormous harm to our society. Cinema films can do a lot to eradicate these evils. They can be used for promoting national integration, Prohibition, intercaste marriages, family planning, eradication of illiteracy, etc. Such themes can help the transformation of our society. The cinema can be used as an instrument to help people get rid of obscurantism and also to guide them along the right path. It can help in remov"ing ignorance from our society. Not only this, several much needed social reforms can be introduced and brought about with the help of the cinema. The cinema exercises a great influence on the mind of the people. It has a great educative value. It can achieve splendid results in the field of expansion of education. There are certain subjects, such as science and geography, which can be more effec"tively taught with the help of talkies. Lessons on road sense, rules of hygiene and civic sense can be taught to the students and the " public as well in a very effective manner with the help of cinema pictures. Many successful experiments have been made in various countries on the utility of films as a means of education. Feature films have been produced for school and college students and students are being benefited by them. Cinema films have the power to influence the thinking of the people. They have changed the society and social trends. They have introduced new fashions in society. They may be described as pace-setters. They can create a direct impact on our social life. Films can go a long way towards arousing national consciousness and also in utilizing the energies of the youth in social reconstruction and nation-building by a skillful adaption of good moral, social and educative themes, and by introduction of popular sentiments, films can, to a great extent, formulate and guide public opinion.Because of their audio visual appeal cinema films are the most powerful means of publicity and advertisement. Small publicity pictures or skits when shown on the screen easily catch the imagina"tion of spectators. The cinema has so far remained unchanged as the most popular audio-visual mass medium, but now with the arrival of television and its impressive pace of advancement, the cinema can no longer afford the luxury of complacence. It has, therefore, to improve its performance and to maintain a high standard. In our country cinematography has been developed as an art and the film industry is an organised industry. It is a foreign exchange earner industry. Many Indian films have won international awards. Cinema has become a powerful vehicle for culture, education, leisure and propaganda. Contemporary research has also revealed more profound aspects to film's impact on society. In a 2005 paper by S C Noah Uhrig (University of Essex, UK) entitled, "'Cinema is Good for You: The Effects of Cinema Attendance on Self-Reported Anxiety or Depression and 'Happiness'" the author describes how, "The narrative and representational aspects of film make it a wholly unique form of art. Moreover, the collective experience of film as art renders it a wholly distinct leisure activity. The unique properties of attending the cinema can have decisively positive effects on mental health. Cinema attendance can have independent and robust effects on mental wellbeing because visual stimulation can queue a range of emotions and the collective experience of these emotions through the cinema provides a safe environment in which to experience roles and emotions we might not otherwise be free to experience. The collective nature of the narrative and visual stimulation makes the experience enjoyable and controlled, thereby offering benefits beyond mere visual stimulation. Moreover, the cinema is unique in that it is a highly accessible social art form, the participation in which generally cuts across economic lines. At the same time, attending the cinema allows for the exercise of personal preferences and the human need for distinction. In a nutshell, cinema attendance can be both a personally expressive experience, good fun, and therapeutic at the same time."

Movies are one of the best choices of recreation but along with that scientists and doctors have proven through careful studies and research, the impact of violence really depends on the personality and character traits of young adults and children. Achild or teenager who has been brought up in an abusive family and has been hit as a child is more likely to dash out at other people especially if they have just seen a very violent films.Film stars have eventually got a huge number of fan followers and the attitude portrayed by theheroes in a film will be followed by some of them also in their real-life situations. Unfortunately,not only the educated groups of viewers tend to follow the inappropriate mannerisms that these heroes portray in the screen. The worst part is the fans will copy the stunts performed albeit they will risk their lives. Nowadays, we usually notice that the winning formula for a successful cinema today is about bandit or rebellion, gangster, rowdy and other movies doing sinful actions unlike before that winning entries are about good manners, legends, ancient characters, culturalattractions and etc. On the other hand, there are films that will serve as your sources of information and knowledge. Research-based movies give you influence of research and inventing new things. A historical movie tells about the ancient times and their lifestyle which urges man to adopt or in some manner, influence from them. Classic movies give classic arts and lifestyle. These films are usually the sources of students for research purposes and it also serves as a means of broadening their knowledge about different things because it is more lively and perhaps, entertaining. How do people interpret history? One of the main sources of history are movies because authors knew that people watch and believe those featured in these films.

Cinema has perhaps the greatest potential to be the most effective mass media instrument. Besides proving cheap entertainment for masses, it can easily become a means of mass instruction and mass education. Cinema has certainly some clear advantages over other media. It combines primarily, both audio and video and is thus very appealing to the eyes and the ears. With the development of color cinematography, and stereophonic sound, it is certainly one up on other media. The moral values conveyed through the medium of cinema have a lasting effect on the audience. The audience also has a moral, emotional involvement in the course of events and the roles of various characters, their language and style of speaking does leave an impression on the spectators.

Movies have proved to be one of the best mediums of mass communication. One can escape in a wonderland and forget your worries for those brief three hours or be shell-shocked when you see the workings of terrorist operations or just get that good old feeling of being surrounded and supported by your loved-ones.

Movies have a great impact on the lives of peoples and mostly movies are produced according to the lives of peoples and due to this these they can impress their audience in both scene positive scene or negative scene. if a person gets impress from a character of a movie which is really calm and cool minded and a kind person and that person adopt the same qualities then this could be in positive scene while if a person gets impress from a really cruel criminal character so in this situation if that person start commuting crime so this would be called in the negative side of movies. Bollywood's boisterous masala fare elicits enthusiastic wolf whistles in cinemas in the East and West. On a more serious note, the Hindi movie industry has also had a deeper impact on Indian society. For example, the film *Baabul* (2006) raised the issue of widow remarriage, while *Kabhi Khushi Kabhi Gham* (2001) extolled the virtue of respecting elders. The widely acclaimed *Rang De Basanti* (2006) gave voice to youth angst about the nation's corrupt politics and politicians. Modern Bollywood directors like Madhur Bhandharkar and Prakash Mehra have raised awareness about the issues of the day through their movies. The films *Rann* (2007), *Corporate* (2006) and *Gulaal* (2009) exposed political and social controversies. Increasingly historians have moved away from a history that chronicles battles, treaties, and presidential elections to one that tries to provide an image of the way daily life unfolded for the mass of people: how they worked, what they did for fun, how families were formed or fell apart, or how the fabric of daily life was formed or transformed. Film has an important role to play in these histories. While traditional historical documents tend to privilege great events and political leaders, historians now use other records to discern the lives of "ordinary" people: census records, accounts of harvests and markets, diaries and memoirs, and local newspapers. Film is perhaps more like these records of daily life than it is like the documents that record great events. Attitudes about gender, class, and ethnicity, as well as heroism, work, play, and "the good life" are all portrayed in fictional films as they are in an era's novels, plays, and paintings. But as a form of mass visual entertainment, films reflect social attitudes in a specific and vivid manner.

Man has instincts, different thoughts flow which leave an effect on the minds. The person laughs with the films and tears with them. Scenes of 'Shaheed Bhagat Singh', makes people national-minded and sentimentally involved in the film show. The film dialogues are occupying places in our real life. Dialogues of Mugle Azam found place in the normal interaction of people for a long time. People talked and walked like the great king Akbar. In the same way, plays by Agha Hashat and Devdas by Sharat Chandra left a deep impact on the masses. In the same way, film 'Sholey' created an imending effect on so many.

Realism and Modernity are two words closely associated with cinema. It is always good and well groomed to see good subjects on cinema. They have a very positive and long-lasting effect on the minds whereas cheap and shabby movies affect the tender minds of audience very badly. The cinema exercises a great influence on the mind of the people. It has a great educative value. It can achieve splendid results in the field of expansion of education. There are certain subjects, such as science and geography, which can be more effectively taught with the help of talkies. Lessons on road sense, rules of hygiene and civic sense can be taught to the students and the ' public as well in a very effective manner with the help of cinema pictures. Many successful experiments have been made in various countries on the utility of films as a means of education. Feature films have been produced for school and college students and students are being benefitted by them. Cinema films have the power to influence the thinking of the people. They have changed the society and social trends. They have introduced new fashions in society. They may be described as pace-setters. They can create a direct impact on our social life. Films can go a long way towards arousing national consciousness and also in utilising the energies of the youth in social reconstruction and nation-building by a skilful adaption of good moral, social and educative themes, and by introduction of popular sentiments, films can, to a great extent, formulate and guide public opinion

One go to the movies expecting three hours of entertainment, some singing, dancing, action and comedy. But, there are a few times we feel a lot more than that. We feel a sense of having witnessed something historical, something that touches a deep chord. This is when we come across movies which leave a greater impact on the society. Some actually manage to change a couple of lives while some help to speed up pending justice, some fill you with emotional turmoil and some give your life a complete new direction. Cinema has a great impact on people and the stars are the biggest influences. We try to be like them, look like them and behave like them. We all want our life to be a perfect film story. Cinema plays an important role in our lives, even more than we notice. Some of the movies that led to a bigger social impact are.....

RANG DE BASANTI is the thought-provoking movie created a huge impact socially with the candle lighting sequence which is often used in real life even now by citizens for protesting an issue.The film left a social impact as many people came forward to talk about corruption and bureaucracy and their inefficiency in providing basic amenities. The film managed to strike the right chord and received huge success.

CHAK DE is one movie that played an important role in reviving popularity of hockey, especially women hockey in India. India talks about religion, sexism, India partition, regional prejudice, emotions and lot more through field hockey.

TAARE JAMEEN PAR movie beautifully captures life of Ishaan, a dyslexic kid who struggles everyday to do simple things of life. As simple as tying a shoe lace. It spread a message to all those families who want their kid to excel in everything – every kid is different and has different needs.Whenever parents see their child scoring low in exams, they blame it on his carelessness and ask him to pay more attention to his studies. The child is sometimes grounded, isn't allowed to watch tv or play his favourite video game so that he could concentrate more on his career. Hardly do we notice that it can be much more than just carelessness from the child's side.

3 IDIOTS is the revolutionary movie that gave a whole new twist to the Indian education system. The movie gives a message that education doesn't require money, uniform, big schools and colleges, all it requires is the strong will to study. The story also focuses on how the education system should look beyond high grades and should focus on what a kid wants to do.

SWADESH is the movie which focuses on the issue of brain drain and Indians moving abroad for greener pastures. The story revolves around the life of an NRI who works for NASA and how his visit to a village changes his life along with hundreds of other villagers. The movie inspired a lot of NRIs to come back to the roots and work for the country. The movie gives a message that a little help from the fortunate and educated ones can help the underprivileged to a great extent.

PREM ROG is the movie focuses on the sensitive topic of widow remarriage. Released in 1982,. At the time of a conservative India, when widows were boycotted from the community and were expected to spend the rest of their lives in misery, the movie comes as a breath of fresh air and portrays a better life for a widow.

In spite of touching on a sensitive subject, *OMG! OH MY GOD* movie received a great response from both audience and critics. India is a religious country. With 330 millions Gods to worship, it has become a business for some.Without being preachy and boring, the film teaches us how we should not look for God in idols and be blind-folded by those who try to play with people's emotions in the name of God.

The story of the movie *DAMINI* is of how a woman fights against society for justice. The film is considered to be the best woman-centric film ever made in Bollywood along with Mother India. The woman character portrays the role of a strong woman who fights against her own family for raping the house maid.

UDAAN was first Indian film to be part of Cannes' official section in seven years. Udaan tells the story of thousands of youths from India's middle-class families, who want to break free and follow their dreams.

The film *BLACK FRIDAY* is based on the 1993 serial bomb blasts in Mumbai which many believe were organised as retaliation for the Bombay riots which left over 300 people dead and more than 1500 people injured. The film has been appreciated by critics all over the world.

ACHHOT KANYA deals with the social position of Dalit girls and is considered a reformist period-piece. The story portrays a love story of a Brahmin Boy and a Harijan (Untouchable) girl. At the time when people were discriminated on the basis of their caste, this movie sets a good example of how every human being is equal and love knows no boundaries.

The movie *PAKEEJAH* focuses on prostitution as a career and changed the way people looked at the profession. It tried to show the inside world of sex workers and their lives and tragedies in a different era from today, when they were looked at very differently.

The movie *MATRIBHUMI* is based on the social issue of female foeticide, showcases the future of the country if we keep killing the girl child. There are still many places where a boy's birth is rejoiced while a girl child is killed. The movie revolves around the story of a girl who is married to five brothers. The movie portrays the glimpse of the cruel society and leaves a message of saving a girl child.

KYA KEHNA dealt with the taboo issue of pre-marital pregnancy and the views of society. No matter how much the country progresses, there are certain things which still cause raised eyebrows. And, pre-marital pregnancy is one of those issues. The movie focuses on this bold issue and spread a message of how unmarried pregnant girls should be given equal love, respect and support in the society.

DOR is the the story based on the lives of two women and how fate brings them together. The film beautifully captures the emotions of a widow (Meera) and a lady (Zeenat) who is trying to save her husband. The movie also portrays the life of a woman in India after the death of her husband and the difficulties faced by her.

VICKEY DONOR touched upon a less talked about topic of sperm donation. The film is a romantic comedy based on the backdrop of this sensitive subject and its implications. Producer of the film wanted to shed light on a serious issue still considered "taboo" in Indian society.

This powerful film *LAJJA* is based on the plight of women in India. The movie satirizes the honour with which women are placed in society and the restrictions on them. The four women's names (Maithili, Janki, Ramdulaari, and Vaidehi) being all versions of Sita, the ideal Hindu woman's name, is a message in itself. The film features some of the most powerful ladies of Indian cinema. The movie showcases victory of women against all the bad that society has done to them.

The movie *MY BROTHER NIKHIL* deals with the stigma associated with HIV/AIDS as well as the coming out of a closeted gay relationship. The film was highly appreciated world-wide. The film director stated that the film is based on true historical fact, and the standard disclaimer about fictitious content was just a compromise with the Indian government to gain permission to make the film.

Dealing with the social and cultural changes taking place in India shortly after independence, *MOTHER INDIA* had a powerful impact on the citizens of India. Nargis portrayed the character of the a widowed Indian woman who raises her kids with much difficulty. The movie focuses on the power of "good" as the mother kills her own son when he crosses the line and goes on a wrong path.

The film by Shyam Benegal *MANTHAN* traces a small set of poor farmers of Kheda district in Gujarat who had the vision and foresight to act in a way that was good for the society and not for the self alone. White revolution of India started in 1970, ushering in an era of plenty, from a measly amount of milk production and distribution. It was the first film in the world to be produced not by a single production house, but the farmers of the Gujarat Co-operative Milk Federation who contributed Rs.2 each for the production of the movie.

Conclusion

There are variable views about the effects of cinema on human development. For some the impact is negative on the other hand some percieves the positive impact of cinema. But ti is dam sure that cinema has touched almost every aspect of human development.

In our society there are many practices and traditions which are based on ignorance and which have withheld the progress of our society. Rigidity of caste system, untouchability, dowry system and purdah system have done enormous harm to our society. Cinema films can do a lot to eradicate these evils. They can be used for promoting national integration, Prohibition, intercaste marriages, family planning, eradication of illiteracy, etc. Such themes can help the transformation of our society. The cinema can be used as an instrument to help people get rid of obscurantism and also to guide them along the right path. It can help in removing ignorance from our society. Not only this, several much needed social reforms can be introduced and brought about with the help of the cinema.

References

http://youthvoices.net/discussion/how-do-movies-or-television-influence-people-s-behavior

http://www.enotes.com/homework-help/what-movies-effect-society-359147

http://cinemaroll.com/cinemarolling...movies-and-their-impact-on-society/

http://www.lemiffe.com/films-and-their-effect-on-society/

Chapter 5

Dialectics of Representing Queer in Indian (Hindi) Cinema

*Saurabh Kumar Singh**

In this article I will try to map the horizon of representations of queer identities like Gay, Lesbian, Hijra, and Transsexuals through providing numerous instances from Indian Cinema in general and popular Hindi cinema in particular. This paper will aim to show how the depictions of queer identities acquire a kind of subversive value and posit queer points of identifications. Different perspectives would be involved in analyzing the cases of queer portrayal in Indian cinema- from their non-existence to existence; from non-acceptance to acceptance of their identities. It will also aim to show how in the beginning we encounter stereotyped notions involved in the making of such cinema but at the same time witnessing the emergence of new wave of thought that treats the *subjects* with humanitarian perspective on compassionate grounds.

Indian society is largely conservative and the films dealing with the subject of homosexuality, centering on the problem of homosexuality, are in reality being made for a society where it is still deemed taboo to talk about. In this perspective the 1990s can be taken as a phenomenal period in the growth of Hindi cinema as it ushered into a world of transformed modern class film industry as it not only upgraded in terms of technology only but also in terms of making edgy and darker films instead of continuing the age old repetitive themes of love, friendship, honour, clash between

**Assistant Professor, Deparment of English,*
Vasanta College for Women, Rajghat
Banaras Hindu University, Varanasi – 221 001

the forces of good or bad and black and white. But the contemporary Indian cinema has undergone substantial changes over the last couple of decades. Some Indian film directors have attempted to deviate from the typical romantic movies to try and delve into controversial and even taboo topics such as homosexuality. It is the time when despite public outrages, representations of sex and sexuality including the portrayals of queer sexuality find 'a room of one's own' somewhat in open manner.

The well known critic Gayatri Gopinath draws our attention to the film like *Fire* which provided us an altogether new vantage point to interpret a road between homosociality and homoeroticism: for example when mythological characters (turned upside down) like Sita (Nandita Das) and Radha (Shabana Azmi) get involved in erotic foreplay like massaging the feet and oiling the hair. It can be safely affirmed that *Fire* opened up new ways of reading films using an interpretive strategy. It is very significant because homosexual couples in Indian society who despite of their love for each other can't come out in a society which disapproves of such relationship and the impositions of heteronormativity. Heteronormativity is an agenda of heterosexists which exhibits the cultural bias in favor of opposite-sex relationships of a sexual nature, and against same-sex relationships of a sexual nature. In a democratic and pluralistic country like India, it is equally sustained by constitutional law that abuses human rights and limits fundamental freedoms such as is enumerated in Section 377 of the Indian Penal Code (IPC). The credit for this goes to Lord Macaulay, who drafted Section 377 of the IPC in 1883 which states that whosoever voluntarily has carnal intercourse against the order of nature with any man, woman or animal shall be punished with imprisonment for life or imprisonment of either description for a term which may extend to ten years or liable to fine. The ludicrous and debatable phrase in this 133-year-old law is 'carnal intercourse against the order of nature.' Who is to decide what is 'against' and what is 'for' the law of nature? Aren't the laws of nature about sexual relationships themselves subject to the changeability with time, space and person? Perhaps yes.

A queer reading involves the strategies to read a movie text which may have homo social elements and can be interpreted as the homoerotic. In 1960s to 1980s the concept of homosociality and homoeroticism was usually applied to dosti, yaari or male bonding which has been reinterpreted through the lens of queer perspectives. Critics like Gayatri Gopinath, R Raja Rao, Hoshang Merchant, Ruth Vanita, Shohini Ghosh, and Ashok Row Kavi have tried to interpret certain film narratives like *Dosti* (1964), *Anand* (1970), *Namak Haraam* (1973), *Sholay* (1975), *Dostana* (1980) and etc. to understand the instances of homoerotic texts. According to Ghosh the heterosexual love interests in some of these movies seem to be secondary. He points out that Hindi cinema hardly ever uses sexually explicit scenes to convey love and friendship. Somewhat both of them use same devices. They have used the plot of friendship, love and sacrifice in numerous ways. In some of these male bonding movies one male protagonist would give up his beloved to his friend, thereby establishing a love between homoerotic friends as superior to love between heterosexist lovers.

During the last twenty years or so Indian cinema has been showing strong convictions to portray the curious cases of queer identities in somewhat sexually explicit manner. There can be many ways to characterize and categorize queer identities in cinema, but my study will primarily revolve around three categories in which films have incorporated queer characters and queer plot. The first is in the form of eunuch (hijra) as queer, the second is in the form of homosexuals (gay) as queer, the third is in the form of lesbians as queer. However, it is unavoidable fact that many a times these broad categories turn out to be blurred and overlapped.

The queer as eunuch has been playing a significant role in the making of cinematic plots. There are different types of portrayals of eunuchs in Indian cinema, such as transsexuals, homosexuals and hijras. They are usually reduced to the objects of derisive comedy or disgust. Traditional Indian cinema portrays them as stereotyped. Most of them have been the brunt of crude jokes. Many actors cross-dressed with deliberate crudity so that they are not mistaken for a woman but a eunuch to evoke laughter. However, it has not been in practice for a long time. The mind set of many film makers started to change and it resulted into the portrayals of different sides of the eunuchs which helped them, slowly but steadily, be socially recognized and accepted.

In Indian society, the term eunuch is broadened to include homosexuals, sexually abused men, hermaphrodites (intersexed), men who are sexually impotent and emasculated men. The term eunuch in India refers as much to a societal role as it does to one's anatomy. This is because men who are different, whether they are homosexuals, impotent or hermaphrodites, "do not feel comfortable to express sexual identity in the normal society because they will not be accepted society as it is not the norm" (Hindocha Eunuchs in Indian Cinema). The only place eunuchs can freely express themselves and be normal in their own way is if they join the hijra community. Many men turn into hijras, "because their families have disowned them because they were infertile; and because of that, they have no choice but to behave like women" *(ibid)*. Some of them ran away from home because of the undesired marriages with females. None of them can think of a life where they are forced to marry females and have children by them. So they are left with no options but only way out is to cut off their manhood and become hijras. This is the only community, which will accept them and let them live their lives the way they want to.

The men who are sexually abused from a younger age turn to the hijra community because that community has the same level of empathetic understanding. And in this community they feel comfortable and are initiated into a society that accepts and sustains them. The society helps them to understand their place in the world. It gives them as sense of belonging and a sense of individuality. In India hijras are a religious community renouncing male sexuality and identifying with the creative power of Mata Bahuchara (the Goddess hijras believe in). In the West, hijras are generally known as hermaphrodites or eunuchs. The difference between the hijra and the eunuch:

"... is that hermaphrodites are born hijras. This is because they are people 'whose genitals are ambiguously male like at birth' and eunuchs are made hijras, because it refers to emasculated men. The force behind the words hermaphrodite and eunuch is impotence and impotence is central to the definition of the hijra as not man. The role of hijras is deeply rooted in Indian culture that it can accommodate a wide variety of temperament, personalities, sexual needs, gender identities, cross-gender behaviour and levels of commitment without losing its cultural meaning." (ibid)

In the beginning eunuchs were seen merely as invaders of homes where women have given birth to a male child. In order to bless these male babies eunuchs were called upon. Hijra community has been portrayed as the generalized category of gender and sexual deviancy. This has resulted in the fear of extorting money from passengers in trains and at traffic red lights. But the filmmakers like Santhosh Sowparnika in *Ardhanari*, Santosh Sivan in *Navarasa* and David Atkins in *Queens! Destiny of Dance* have initiated new attempts to finally take the 'hijra' community seriously although they started to appear on celluloid in the late 70s in films such as *Amar Akbar Antony*. In 1990s various filmmakers tried their cameras to make the films like *Sadak* by Mahesh Bhatt where the eunuch has been portrayed as main villain. The same was also seen in the movie like *Murder 2* where the villain is homicidal murderer but a married straight man castrated because he hates women. According to me the portrayals of hijra as murderer is totally misleading because a community which is already forced to live a life of marginality and utmost disgust must be given proper representation. The community which is not given the status of a human being must be given their due respect and dignity. *Tamanna* happens to be one of those films which portray a hijra as a true human being. The film is about Tikoo, his friend Salim and the adopted daughter Tamanna. Tikoo in order to make his/her daughter happy does everything which is required by so called normal human being. He dresses himself like a normal man. And never lets her true identity out in the presence of Tamanna. Inspite of this among normal human beings he is not accepted as normal as others. The climax of the movie is the revelation of Tikoo as a hijra to Tamanna and the daughter and the emotional drama which follows hereafter. According to Ruth Vanita, "the film uses the trope of closeting and outing, which are relevant to homosexual people in India today who often lead double lives, but not as much to hijras who usually publicly display their difference" (184). In this movie the director Mahesh Bhatta has attempted to break the stereotypical notions of society about hijras. He has drawn our attention to issues like parenthood, friendship, and many more aspects of hijra community. He successfully delivers the positive message that hijras are successful parents and friends and can rear a child like any other normal human being, because they too can offer *vatsalya* love even though they cannot conceive child biologically.

Darmiyan: In Between (1997) directed by Kalpana Lajmi is a fantastic film. The film has all the characteristics of what makes a film work. It is sorrowful, classy, and entertaining. Set in the Bollywood scene in the 1940s, it deals with issues such as alcoholism, eunuchs, depression, and failure. The film features Kiron Kher whose character, Sardari Begum, plays actress Zennat Begum, a person who has everything she could possibly want in life including fortune and fame. Unfortunately, Zeenat´s happiness is shattered when she finds that her son, Emmi (Arif Zakharia) is a eunuch. She avoids him at all costs and neglects him until Zeenat´s mother steps in and adopts the child. Emmi finds the love and care that he needs with Zeenat´s mother, and eventually Zeenat loses her No. 1 position in the film industry to Chitra (Tabu) along with her lover, Indar (Shahbaaz Khan). All of this pushes her to alcoholism and forces her into depression because she simply cannot cope with her failure. She begins to reject the people who love her and is scared to love again. Meanwhile, Emmi tries to help his troubled mother and shows her that he has confidence in her. He adopts an abandoned child but is forced to give her to Chitra because of society's cruel ways. Finally, Emmi returns to his mother's home and tries to help make what's left of her shattered life more peaceful. Other notable movies which represent hijra include *Bombay* (1995) *Appu* (2000), *Shabnam Mausi* (2005), Shyam Benegal's *Welcome to Sajjanpur* (2008) and Marathi film *Jogwa*(2009).

In India, queer as homosexual more or less has been taken not only a Western phenomenon but also that has been taken as a fashion by the wealthy and elite upper class families. In most of the movies homosexuals have been shown as somewhat exposed to modernity and Western culture. These movies portray some typical aspects like they all are settled in urban settings, they can speak good English, have good jobs, and well educated. These homosexual entities have evolved and adopted a lifestyle specific to their own sexuality. If we try to make a generalized portrayal of homosexuals in cinema, they can broadly be defined in two categories: First non-serious portrayal and second serious portrayal. One of the earliest examples of casual, non-serious and comic portrayal of homosexual identity is the depiction of Paintal dressed as a woman in *Rafoo Chakkar* (1975). Apart from this *Mast Kalandar* (1991) portrays a homosexual character Pinkoo who is the spoilt son of the main villain. He also is seen as the bad guy but quite comically flirts with men to get their attention. *Kal Ho Na Ho* (2003) engages with the portrayal of funny gay sub plot involving the two lead heroes that turned out to be a new initiator in the ongoing debate of queer as gay. The story involves three friends Naina, Aman and Rohit. Both Aman and Rohit are heterosexuals who like Naina. The twist in the ongoing tale occurs when Rohit's housekeeper Kanata Ben mistakes them to be in gay relationship which shocks and disgusts her. The mistaken gay relationship and the shocked mindset of Kanta Ben have been used to bring about enough humour in the movie. In this sense it would not be an exaggeration to say that it shows society's paranoia over queer as gay.

What could be a possible response of an Indian mother after knowing about her son's sexuality, it can be seen from *Dostana* (2008) chiefly focuses on the reactions of an Indian mother when she comes to know that her only son is a gay. This cinema tackles the issue in non serious way. The heroine tells the mother that love is blind- to which the mother replies that "But not that blind that one cannot tell the difference between man and woman!" In order to bring about humorous note thee mother blesses the homosexual couple as, "Jite raho! Phulo! Phalo! – Khair, choro!" (May you two live long and have many children! – Well, forget the latter!). The title of the film hints at friendship but it culminates into a pretended gay relationship to meet certain ends. The treatment of the sensitive issue is one of utter mockery which might be taken as the standpoint of general human mentality.

Other notable movies which somewhat continues the representations of homosexual sexuality in certain stereotypes are Parvati Balagopalan's *Rules - Pyar Ka Superhit Formula* (2003), Madhur Bhandarkar's *Page 3* (2005) and *Fashion* (2008), Anurag Basu's *Life in a... Metro* (2007), Reema Kagti's *Honeymoon Travels* (2007), and Karan Johar's *Student of the Year* (2012).

As far as the representation of homosexuals in serious manner is concerned, the movie *My Brother Nikhil* (2005) based on the real life experiences of Dominic D'Souza, directed by Onirban emerges as the most important. The movie is about the rejection and the marginalization of once state swimming champion but HIV positive Nikhil. His marginalization operates at two points: personal and public. The first one involves his rejection and throwing out from the home by his parents and the public humiliation begins when he enters a into swimming pool and others leave, and further got arrested by police and imprisoned in rat infested sanatorium. The film challenges and breaks certain notions homosexuality and masculinity. Nikhil is a well reputed swimmer/athlete which goes against the grain that homosexuals cannot indulge in heterosexist masculine job. In spite of the fact that he is a gay, women are more attracted to him which inverses the idea about gay and masculine sexualities. Most importantly the relationship between Nikhil and Nigel is more of an emotional bonding than that of sexual bonding. Onirban's another masterpiece is *I Am* (2010) which, so far, happens to be the only film dealing with homosexuality and winning national award. One of the four stories *I AM* **Omar is about the plight of homosexuals in this country. Here** Omar a struggling actor meets Jai from Bangalore, a corporate man. They flirt and have dinner together and then have sex at a public place in the car. Finally it is revealed that Jai is only a bait for a sex hustler and the sadistic cop to make money.

Sanjoy Nag's *Memories in March* (2010) deals the issue of homosexual love on more compassionate grounds. The movie accepts homosexuality as a normal fact of life. Although it occurs as an initial shock to conventional mother Deepti Naval when she for the first time gets to know the alternate sexual preference of her beloved deceased son for a bald man (Rituparno Ghosh) over Raima Sen. She personally visits the office of her son to collect his keepsakes but when she comes to know about the special bond between her departed son and Rituparno, she wishes she had known about her son's sexual preferences before, so that she could have consulted her psychiatrist friends. But slowly and slowly the mother begins to accept the relationship as she discovers a caring, warm, and sensitive person as her son's companion. They both begin to understand each other quite empathetically as they both share shared memories, shared grief, shared love, and poignant revelations soaked in lyrical narrative and prolonged silence sequences. What we find is the emotional bond among the mother, her son's lover, and the girl who loved her son. This certainly cannot be the compensation for the void created by the departed soul but it does help a lot in wreathing the scattered beauties of ife in one string.

Chitrangada: The Crowning Wish is another path breaking film directed by Rituparno Ghosh inspired from the *Mahabharata*. The film is about a cinematographer (against his father's wishes to be an engineer) Rudra Chatterjee, who challenges social conventions no every now and then. He is making his team to stage Tagore's *Chitrangada* and meets Partho, a drug addict percussionist. This meeting culminates into serious love affair. They want a child to adopt but they cannot as a child cannot be adopted by same sex lovers. So Rudra decides to go for a gender change to be a woman. The movie comes out with a message that, 'Be What You Wish to Be', even if this wish involves the change of one's gender. This movie might be seen through different perspectives. One might call it a film that holds a mirror to progressive society that is still fumbling about how to handle homosexuality. You might call it a film that educates without being preachy about same sex relationships. By merging myth with reality, this movie throws up a lot of questions, answering a few while leaving the rest open to interpretations. How difficult is it for parents when they come to about alternate sexuality of their only son? In this connection mother of Rudra remarks, "I gave birth to this body, which is yours... I have a right to know, whatever goes on in this body. I have a right to know, if it is changing, transforming...".How difficult is it for a gay to be termed as a diseased body to be cured by doctor? Equally tormenting and traumatic is the feeling that they will never be allowed to adopt a child despite the fact that biologically they can never have a living product of their love?

Aligarh (2016) directed by Hansal Mehta recounts the true story of Dr Ramchandra Siras, a Marathi professor and poet in Aligarh University. Few months short of his retirement, Siras becomes the victim of a sting operation — wherein he's videotaped making love to a young *rickshawwallah Irfan. The sting is* conducted by self-appointed moral guardians and custodians of a society that believes it is entitled to expose and shame what they deem as inappropriate and corrupting. Hansal Mehta understands the damage such occurrences can do to one's psyche. He vividly recalls how a part of him has died with this incident after he was invaded by a mob. Perhaps it might be the reason that he captures Dr Ramchandra Siras's horror, humiliation and alienation with a brutality. The movie talks more about individuality than the sexuality. It has been portrayed through sadness engulfing his saggy eyes and grey hair. He is portrayed almost like child clinging to his briefcase as children cling to their teddy bears. In Hindi cinema, "where homosexuality is an object of derisive gags or caricature, the portrayal *Aligarh* offers is refreshing and respectful. But it's much too multifaceted, at times for its own good, to be acknowledged for just that." (Sukanya Verma *Aligarh*) Other remarkable movies representing homosexuality are *Bomgay* (1996), *Mango Souffle* (2002), *The Pink Mirror* (2003), *Tedhi Lakeer* (2004), *Teen Deewarein* (2003), Marathi film *Thang (*2006), *Touch of Pink* (2004), *Stag'*(2001), *Water* (2005), *Yours Emotionally* (2006), *Piku Bhalo Aachhey* (Bengali, 2004), *Happy Hookers* (2006),*I Can't Think Straight* (2007), *68 Pages* (2007), *Luck by Chance* (2009), *Dunno Y.. Na Jaane Kyun* (2010) and *Bombay Talkies* (2013),

The queer as lesbian identity, though has not got ample space, yet compared to cinema dealing with gay relationship, had accrued more controversy and ruckus. It might be the possible reason behind serious lack of films dealing with lesbian relationships even in times of a steady rise in gay visibility in mainstream Indian cinema. This apparent privileging of gay visibility over lesbian might have to do with the fact that Hindi cinema is fearful of shaking the roots of our cultural heritage by depicting bahu and betuyas in transgressing roles, thus shattering the very pillars of customs and rituals of patriarchal Indian society. Apart from the master texts like Deepa Mehta's *Fire* and Karan Razdan's *The Girlfriend* the filmmakers of Indian Diaspora like Ligy Pullappally's *The Journey,* Mann Katohora's *When Kiran Met Karen,* Nisha Ganatra's *Chutney Popcorn,* Sonali Gulati's *Sum Total* and *Out and About* and Pratibha Parmar's *Nina 's Heavenly Delights* and *Flesh and Paper*, a short movie on Indian lesbian poet Suniti Namjoshi, have dared in significant ways to portray lesbian women. Though the portrayals of lesbian women in these films are not directed towards any acceptance of alternative sexuality, but these representations further the process to reinforce negative stereotypes associated with lesbianism within the conservative Indian societal norm.

Fire (1996) directed by Deepa Mehta happens to be one of the first and foremost movies to depict a lesbian relationship starring Shabana Azmi and Nandita Das. It is a poignant portrayal of complicated relationships by fine artists. Here, two women Radha and Sita come together to fulfill their passions not out of choice but due to the lack of acknowledgement from their spouses. The naming of the characters has led the Hindu fundamentalists to create ruckus over the release of the movie and eventually ended as a ban for promoting religious insensitivity. But in spite of these obstacles this film makes visible the invisible lesbian community but it also reclaims and validates it. In this connection Gayatri Gopinath notes how the film produces a complicated relay between female homosociality and female homo-erotic practices it erotically charged up certain mundane activities such as the protagonists oiling each other's hair or just cooking. By explicitly crossing the divide between female bonding and sexuality it opened up a new way of looking at things (Bandopadhyay, 2007:17).

Girlfriend (2004) directed by Karan Razdan is about the story of Tanya (Isha Koppikar) and Sapna (Amrita Arora) as housemates who have been friends since college. Their relationship at some point becomes sexual because one night they get drunk. Once, when Tanya returns from a business trip, she discovers that

Sapna has fallen in love with a man, Rahul (Ashish Choudhary). She becomes jealous and schemes to break their relationship. It has been shown that Tanya as a child is sexually abused and this incident results into a lesbian attitude. The movie simply pathologises this sexual deviancy of Tanya and her whole beahaviour has been seen as 'abnormal'. The portrayal of this lesbian relationship was advertised with titillating pictures, infused with a storyline that defied logic and cause and effect relationship. It has resulted into a movie which is a mockery of true lesbian identity; a painful masquerade which ironically was found to be offensive by politico religious fundamentalists. The girlfriends are least interested in arguing the case for lesbians or for relationships of similar nature. Nor did it bother to probe into the psychological or emotional connotations of the woman-to-woman relationship, reducing it to a crudely put together soft-porn thriller. The movie simply turned out to be a movie on so called lesbianism as political strategy to arouse the audience to come to theatre for box office success. However, the film has done one good thing: it has made people aware that such lesbian relationships do exist though in utter ugly, unimaginative and derogatory manner.

If we look at the status of India as far as rules and regulations regarding homoerotic relationships are concerned, an initial amendment in Section 377 was brought on 2nd July 2009 Chief Justice Ajit Prakash Shah and Justice S. Murlidhar in which the honorable court located the rights to dignity and privacy within the right to life and liberty guarranted by Article 21 (Under the Fundamental Rights to Freedom) of the constitution and held that criminalization of comsensual gay sex violate these rights. Thus India officially became the 127th country in the world to decriminalize homosexuality. But this status could not remain for longer time as the judgment of Delhi High Court was overruled by the Supreme Court of India on 12 December 2013 holding that amending or repealing Section 377 should be a matter left to Indian Parliament not the judiciary. On 2nd February 2016, the final hearing of the curative petition submitted by the Naz Foundation and other came for hearing in the Supreme Court. The Court maintained that 8 curative petitions submitted will be reviewed afresh by 5 members constitutional bench.

The representation of queer in Indian cinema has more or less been evolutionary in pattern. These representations in early phase were primarily indirect and and presented them in ambiguous relationship without making any clear statement. They simply hovered upon the continuation of certain stereotypes. The evolutionary movement involved somewhat direct statements and representations. It could be possible only because of radical economic, social and political changes. But in the whole evolutionary process a major amount must be credited to growing understanding of audience. At the same time these films have played at least some part in creating awareness about homosexuality in Indian society either through controversies and opposition or through sensual depiction of homosexual relationships in movies. The award of best feature Film in 59th National awards to the movie *I Am* might be taken as a big leap towards receiving, understanding and acknowledging homoerotic (queer) films. Though few of the recent films have shown same-sex desire among Indian men and women, its acceptance in Indian society still has a long way to go. In the IPC it is still like a pendulum between legal and illegal status. But the best part is that we have travelled a long way as far as representations of queer identities are concerned. Perhaps the right time has come when we should come out together and talk, should come out together and question, should come out together and live and should come out together and love.

Works Cited

1. Hindocha, Nishma. "Eunuchs in Indian Cinema." *Queering Bollywood*. Web. February 16 2016.

   <http://connectmedia.waag.org/media.opencultures.net/queer/data/indian/euunchs_in_bollywood.html>

2. Bandopadhyay, Sibaji. "Approaching the Present, The Pre-text: The Fire controversy." *The Phobic and the Erotic*. Ed. Brinda Bose.Kolkata: Seagull. 2007. Print.
3. Vanita, Ruth. *Lovers' rue: Same sex marriage in India and the West*. Pakgrave Macmillan. 2005. Print.
4. Verma Sukanya. "Aligarh is a refreshing and respectful take on homosexuality." Rediff.com. 26 February 2016. Web. February 29 2016.

   <http://www.rediff.com/movies/report/review-aligarh-is-a-refreshing-and-respectful-take-on-homosexuality/20160226.htm>

Filmography

1. *Fire*. Dir: Deepa Mehta. 1996. Starring: Nandita Das, Shabana Azmi.
2. *Girlfriend*. Dir: Karan Razdan. 2004. Starring: Ishaa Koppikar, Amrita Rao, Ashis Chowdhury.
3. *Kal Ho Na Ho*. Dir: Nikhil Advani. 2005. Produced by Karan Johar. Starring: Shah Rukh Khan, Saif Ali Khan, Priety Zinta, Jaya Bachchan.
4. *My Brother Nikhil*. Dir: Onir. 2005. Starring: Sanjay Suri, Juhi Chawla, Purab Kohli.
5. *Murder 2*. Dir. Mohit Suri. 2011. Starring: Emraan Hshmi, Jacqueline Fernandez, Prashant Narayan.
6. *Tamanna*. Dir. Mahesh Bhatt. 1997. Starring: Paresh Rawal. Pooja Bhatt.
7. *Darmiyaan: In Between*. Dir. Kalpana Lajmi. 1997. Starring: Kiron Kher, Arif Zakariya, Tabu.
8. *Mast Kalandar*. Dir. Rahul Rawail. 1991. Starring: Dharmendra, Anupam Kher.
9. *Dostana*. Dir. Tarun Mansukhani. 2008. Starring: John Abraham, Abhishek Bachchan, Priyanka Chopra.
10. *Memories in March*. Dir. Sanjoy Nag. 2010. Starring: Deepti Naval, Rituparno Ghosh, Raima Sen.
11. *Chitrangada: The Crowning Wish*. Dir. 2012. Rituparno Ghosh. Starring: Rituparno Ghosh, Jisshu Sengupta.
12. *Aligarh*. 2016. Dir. Hansal Mehta. Starring: Manoj Bajpai, Rajkumar Rao.
13. *I Am*. 2011. Dir. Onir. Starring: Rahul Bose, Arjun Mathur.

Chapter 6

Indian Films and Plight of the Aged

*Anuradha Bapuly**

As the demography of India is changing due to better health care and life expectancy, the study of the condition of elderly in India becomes of utmost importance. Due to demographic transition, there has been a continuous growth in the population of the aged not only in India but also all over the world. India is the second largest country in the world both in terms of the total population and the proportion of the elderly in the population (**see Figure 6.1**).

Ageing scenario in India shows that the number of people above 60 years will be increasing in the coming years and by 2020, 11.1 per cent population will be in this bracket and by 2040 this will increase to 17.5 per cent and in 2050 the population above 60 years will be 21.3 per cent. In absolute numbers, by 2020, 14,15,23,000 people will be above the age of 60 (Bose,Shankardass and Kapur, 2004). Due to population ageing and transition from agricultural economy to market economy, joint family type to nuclear family, modernization, rabid western education without ethical values, increasing professional involvement of women, decline in traditional Indian cultural values and a growing sense of materialism and self-centric approach have weakened the intergenerational relations and strong familial obligations. As a result of changing social structure, negative values of the younger generation towards the elderly and compulsory retirement of the elderly from economic activities will contribute a great deal in the emergence of old age as a social problem in the country. The declaration of 1982 as the International Year of the Aged by United Nations and

**Assistant Professor,*
Department of Sociology, Vasant Kanya Mahavidyalaya,
Kamachha, Varanasi – 221 010

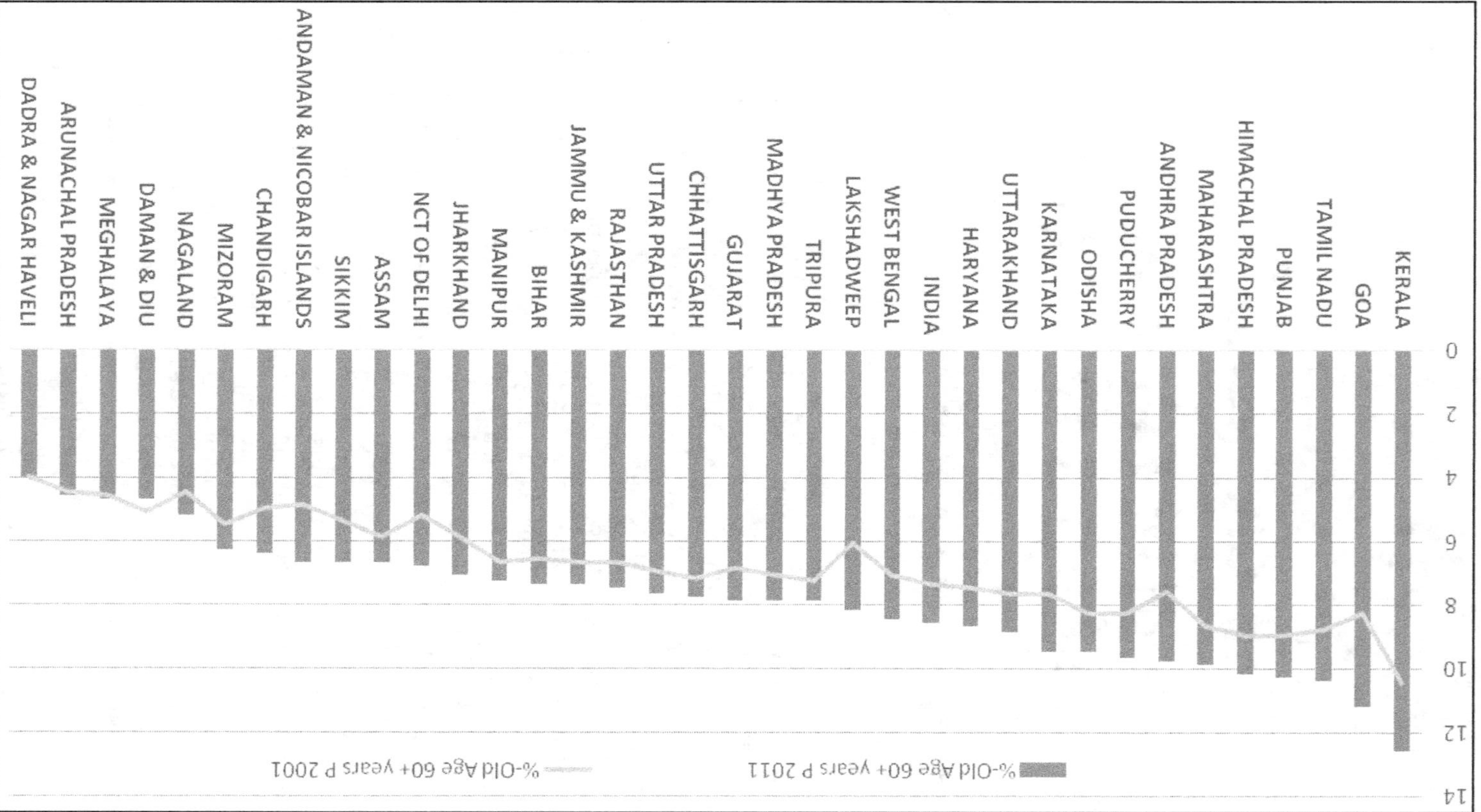

Figure 6.1: Percentage of Elderly (60 years or more) to Total Population, India, States and UTS, Persons, Census 2011 and 2001.

the Year 2000 as the National Year for Older Persons by the Government of India shows the seriousness of the problem of old aged(Joshi,2006).

There is a need to promote systematic study on older persons. The study of Gerontology and the Sociology of Ageing are still in their infancy in India. The increasing population of the aged throughout the world has attracted the attention of Social Scientists, Demographers and Policy makers. Amid this backdrop, the objective of the present paper is to analyze the portrayal of condition of the aged through Indian Cinema. Cinema is a medium which has a mass appeal. Over the years it has successfully projected different issues that are prevalent in the Indian society.

Cinema is a rich medium which showcases the prevailing social norms. It is reflection of the society which has very powerful impact on people. The cinema is the prime form of entertainment which has always addressed universal issues (Dasgupta,2009). India which has become a powerhouse of cinema has seen a rise in number of movies that have portrayed the life of an elderly person andthe challengesfaced by him in fast changing Indian social structure.

The journey of Indian Cinema began with *Raja Harishchandra*, made by Dada SahebPhalke in the year 1913. It was a silent movie and it took 18 more years for the first talking movie to be made in India. Though *Alam Ara* was released on 14th March 1931, which was the first Indian talking movie, Indian cinema has since then moved in leaps and bounds. Cinema has gained popularity across Indian society during the early 20th century. With the mass production of camera films, production of movies became cheaper and gained access among the masses. New theaters were opened in the big cities and people started visiting this places as new art form had arrived which people could identify with.

Since then, movies have been made on mythological, historical, sports, nationalism, family values and also prevalent issues that were prevailing the contemporary society. Issues like untouchability, child marriage, casteism and communalism were denounced in the movies. Movie making made forays into every part of the country. Be it Bengal, Kerala, Assam, Tamil Nadu or Mumbai, movies became a medium of expression for people from every region.

After the success of *Alam Ara*, new production houses came into being. These production houses made sure that every aspect of film making is properly looked after and the films are distributed to every region of the country. These production houses became house hold names and the actors and directors became celebrities. Production houses started taking up subjects that affected people in their day to day life.

In the year 1957, a movie called *Mother India* was released. Even through the subject was about peasants and it was set in the rural backdrop, the movie became an instant blockbuster. The movie, which was directed and produced by Mehboob Khan, captured the journey of a woman who raised her family single handedly after her husband died and left his family with sufferings and a loan to repay. Radha (the protagonist), raises her twosons through hardships an gains respect from the whole village. In the end, Radha kills her son to save the daughter of the money lender whose acts had destroyed her family. The film portrayed a self-respecting elderly woman who did not think twice before killing her own son to save the honour of the village. Nargis had played the role of Radha so convincingly that it became the catch phrase so that whenever an elderly woman took a stance against the popular belief she is referred to as 'Mother India'.

M.S. Sathyu came up with a gem called '*Garm Hawa*' in the year 1973. GarmHawa tells the story of a generation of Muslims who are torn between India and Pakistan just after the partition of India. The protagonist played by BalrajSahani is the patriarch of the family who fights a battle of uncertainty inside his family where the majority wants to move to Pakistan as they feel that Pakistan is the land of opportunities and India is unsafe for Muslims and outside with the society which is agitating against the formation of Pakistan. When almost everyone in the family leaves for Pakistan and the Protagonist, his wife and his octogenarian mother are looking tostay back in India.This movie broadly showed the patriarch of the family as a very strong willed person.

Mahesh Bhat's *Saaransh*, travels through the life of an elderly couple, B.V. Pradhan and Parvati Pradhan, who have to fight against the apathy of the system and the bureaucracy in everyday life and their zeal to fight for their belief. Here too the protagonist is an elderly man who single handedly takes the onus of fighting against the corrupt system.

Just like *Mother India, Deewar* portrayed mother as a strong character who would not support the wrong and take the righteous path. Traditionally in the Indian context where we have had the concept of joint families for centuries, mothers have played an important part in shaping the family values. There have been many instances where a widowed woman has brought up her family with little or no support from outside.

In Satyajit Ray's *Agantuk*, the protagonist Manmohan Mitra (played by UtpalDutt) goes through a phase where his intentions are doubted and his actions are looked upon suspiciously. Manmohan is visiting India after 35 long years and he wants to meet his only surviving relative Anila before he sails off. Anila and her husbandSudhindra start to suspect that the person who calls himself as Manmohan Mitra might be an imposter whose main intention is to claim a share of the inheritance. The conflict increases and this makes the guest so uncomfortable that he suddenly disappears. Even though Anila and her husband manage to win Manmohan's confidence back, this does not happen in real life too often as we are torn between false ego and distrust towards an elderly person.

The Malayalam movie '*Thinkalaazhcha Nalla Divasam*' tells the story of a son (played by Mammootty) who wants to sell his ancestral house and send his mother off to an old age home so that he can buy a flat in Bangalore. Even though the son is doing well financially, he does not have any remorse to send his mother away to the old age home as his brother and sister become mute spectators. This movie highlights the problem that the elderly parents are facing due to nuclear families and migration of children, who have no affinity towards their parents or ancestral village, to cities and far away land.

In recent times, a movie called *Piku* has effectively portrayed a few aspects of aging such as BhaskorBannerjee's struggle with ill health and loneliness,his relationship with his young unmarried daughter andhis life in a Cosmopolitan city. The movie revolves around their conflicting ideologies while being fully aware that they are each other's only emotional support. While Piku is successful professionally, she is struggling to play the role of an ideal daughter. Even though Bhaskor loves his daughter, his care for her sometimes becomes too intrusive.

Indian cinema has dealt with the issue of neglect shown by kin through couple of landmark movies like *Avtaar* and *Baghban*. Both these movies ended with the protagonists winning against all odds. These kinds of movies bring in a positivity among the elderly that their most important asset is their experience which will ultimately take them across the winning post. These movies also highlighted the need for a social security net which can safeguard them during hardships and the torment that elderly people have to go through when their children start abusing them and even evict them out of their own property which took them a lifetime to build.

Nana Patekar enacted the title role in *Natsamrat* (directed by Mahesh Manjrekar) which tells the story of a person who has gained great fame as a theatre artist, but his children feel embarrassed by their father's behaviour. GanpatBelwalkar, the protagonist, goes through a phase of rejection by his kin post retirement. His life is torn apart after his wife's death. The movie depicts the dependence of the husband and the wife on each other quite sensitively. This Marathi movie was commercially successful and critically acclaimed.

The year 2015 saw the release of the Bengali movie '*Bela Sheshe*' which was based on the life of an elderly couple. Soumitra Chatterjee plays the role of BishwanathMajumdar (owner of a successful publishing house) who decides to divorce his wife of 49 years, Aarti Majumdar. This decision of Bishwanath comes as a shock to his kids and their spouses. Unable to understand the motive behind this decision, the kids try different ways to find out the reason. Through the course of the film it is revealed that Bishwanath wantsAarti to be independent so that she does not go through any hardships when he leaves this world.

These kind of movies deal with the problem and prospect of graceful ageing and how the societal perspective can be changed through Indian cinema. In olden days the aged embodied wisdom and maturity and thus they were valued and honoured both in the family and in the society. Elder care was not a problem(Suryanarayana,1998). But in modern era, it is a very common trend in domestic and institutional settings that mostly the older persons are living as abused or unwanted human beings. Social exchanges are slowly shifting towards economic exchanges. Under the scenario, the elderly are exploited by the family and society (Thara Bhai,2009). It shows an urgent need to sensitize people and change their negative attitudes to the aged and ageing, which causes irreparable harm on their health, status and dignity.

References

1. Bose,Ashish, Shankardass, and Kapur,Mala (2004). Growing Old in India:Voices Reveal Statistics Speak, Delhi: B.R. Publishing Corporation.
2. Joshi, Arvind Kumar (2006). Rural Aged: Living Arrangements, Problems and Care in A.K. Joshi (Ed.) Older Persons in India, Serials Publications, New Delhi, pp.68-85.
3. Dasgupta, Susmita (2009). The Hindi Commercial Cinema in the Days of Globalisation in Sociology of Globalisation: Perspectives from India, Edited By- SakaramaSomayaji and GaneshaSomayaji,Rawat Publications, New Delhi, pp.250-263.
4. Suryanarayana, M. (1998). Changing Status in the Family Life of the Rural and Tribal Aged, Paper Presented at the Regional Conference of Help Age India, Madras.
5. Thara Bhai, L. (2009). Ageing: A Conceptual Clarification in the Backdrop of Globalisation, in Sociology of Globalisation: Perspectives from India, Edited by- SakaramaSomayaji and GaneshaSomayaji, Rawat Publications, New Delhi,pp.264-275.

Chapter 7

Satyajit Ray's AGANTUK: A Picturesque View of Society and the Art of Cinema

*Brihaspati Bhattacharya**

In our Indian tradition, Lord Brahma is the creator, *i.e.* the God of creation. He is the one who creates and has made the world into existence and same is the case about a film director too; he is the "*Brahma*" of his creation, *i.e.* film. He is the lone responsible and can be treated as an almighty of his creation as it is said by revered *Acarya Anandavardhana* in his *Dhvyanyaloka*:

Apare kavyasamsare kavirekh prajapatih |

Yathasmai rochate vishvam tathedam parivartate ||

Here, director can be referred as *kavi*. He make us believe his thought and we react and feel accordingly; we cry, we laugh, we sob, we blush, we do everything and most importantly we live into it completely. In the history of cinema, there are very few directors who have marked their presence timelessly and are beyond the limit or boundaries of nation, religion and time.

Satyajit Ray is one of the paramount figures in the list of such immortal directors. He was born on 02nd of May 1921 in the city of Kolkata into a Bengali family prominent in art and culture and was nurtured accordingly with the cult of rich art and cultural perspective of Bengali society.

Assistant Professor (Department of Sanskrit),
Vasanta College for Women, Rajghat
Banaras Hindu University, Varanasi – 221 001

Bharat-ratna Satyajit Ray won 32 national awards which is, indeed a record and is the only Indian filmmaker and internationally next to Chaplin to be awarded an honorary degree by Oxford University. He was widely recognized in the cinema fraternity by his very first movie, *Pather Panchali* which garnered him 11 international awards. Satyajit Ray had a tendency or capability to depict time or society as a character. His most of the films have nature or society as a principal character. His last movie was *Agantuk: The stranger*. This film is a mild satire set on the backdrop of social structure of urban society in the era of 90's when liberalization and globalization were knocking at India's door. The amalgam of right and wrong, virtuous and non-virtuous, etc. blends that particular era and *Monomohan Mitro* (the Agantuk) helps us to revive that era on silver screen. The story revolves around a *mama* (maternal uncle) *Monomohan Mitro*, her niece *Anila Bose*, niece-in-law *Sudhindro Bose* and their rise and fall of emotional expediency.

Sudhindro Bose is a guardian of neo-urban Bengali family with his son and wife comprising the family. At a sudden morning, while Sudhindro his having his tea along with a cigarette, her wife receives a letter of her name from abroad without sender's address and Sudhindro, unwillingly eager to know about that letter.

What was there in that letter?

Well, the letter was of Anila's *mamaji* (maternal uncle), who left his family 35 years ago while Anila was a baby of 2 years; hence, she has only heard about his *mama*. After a period of 35 years, he informs her niece about her arrival in Kolkata and expresses her desire to live with her niece Anila and her niece-in-law for a fewer days wishing all goodwill to them in the letter.

Sudhindro becomes extremely conscious and refers the sender as a thief or an impersonator and he says

"He is expecting, *na na,* extorting traditional Indian hospitality. Oh! Ki odbhut (How strange)..!! "

Also, he confirms his doubt over the absence of sender's address in the letter and states how is it possible for a person being secluded from his native place since long, to write such a classic bangla and connotes a sentence for instance

"*asha kori shaami opotyo loiyaa shukhe aacho (I hope all is good with you and your family)..*"

Loia is an integral word of old classic bangla, the bangla in which which *Kobi Robindro, Acarya Bibhutibhushan, Pandit Vidyasagar* etc. used to write.

Along with this, Sudhindro is also unpleased as their Durga Pujo holidays will be strained on stranger maternal uncle's arrival (as he is arriving on 17th, Saptami of Durga Pujo) and Anila is in a dilemma between the right and wrong, *i.e.* it would be non-virtuous to unwelcome her uncle and also (the unrecognized face of her uncle) she has never saw her uncle before so how can she be sure that the person going to live with them for a fewer days is her uncle only? But, later Sudhindro and Anila resemble the thought to welcome their uncle and Sudhindro comes out with a solution and suggests Anila to check her uncle's passport as soon as he arrives and to seclude all worthy items of their house so that the risk of their theft would be minimal and so as Anila does too, she secludes two antique idols made up of bronze in the almirah at her uncle's arrival and welcomes her uncle whole-heartedly. This whole hearted welcome overwhelms Monomohan Mitro, the uncle and while having the lunch e appreciates *lengcha*¸ a sweet predominantly found at all Bengali houses. He says-

"aj mone holo banglae fire eshechi (Now, here I am in Bangla).."

The vast and varied knowledge of mamaji exhilarates Anila's 9 year old son and he enjoys his *dadu's* (grandfather) company which further darkens the mist of Sudhindro.

Here are four main characters through which Satyajit Ray depicts the picturesque view of the society by his cinematic art. They are- Sudhindro, her wife Anila, Mamaji and the urban society of 1990.

Sudhindro represents the society of neo-urban Bengali family which has induced itself with the touch of liberalization and globalization and has a sense of professionalism through which he measures sentiments professionally. He speaks Banglish (Bangla-English) where English terms and usage have a dominance which inculcates the feeling of sophistication in him.

Anila, equally talented as Sudhindro is a housewife, an avid reader of English novels and believes in the values, goodness and has a great sense of hospitality for family members. She is affluent in Bangla and use of other language is rare in her sentences. She often has friendly discussions with her husband on various issues where being unsatisfied, contradicts her husband too.

Monmohan Mitro, the stranger is somewhat mysterious in his behavior too. A die hard traveler, who for the sake of travelling left her house and after 35 years he is coming back to stay with her niece's family for a fewer days and has an intrinsic plan to name her property after Anila. He sends the letter to her without sender's address and stays a bit rude to Sudhindro's queries and has a vast knowledge of world affairs which often surprises Sudhindro and Anila. He is a true native cultural man loving the food, reciting and quoting Bengali writers, poets, etc. Might be there is a sense of loneliness in him which he has to remove, hence; he is in a quest of a fewer days stay at her niece's house to assimilate his 35 years long distance from his family. He has a literal flow of Bangla in his sentences whereas Sudhindro has a flow of English.

Urban society of 1990, it is the society of adolescent neo-urban culture induced with a soft touch of liberalization and globalization which sometimes has a situation of pendulums' to and fro culture, *i.e.* it was the initial stage of decentralization where families or the family values started shifting their thrust from the concept of joint family to that of nuclear family. Hence, it shifted its base on sole identity and economical values.

Conclusively, these all four have something blank in them and it is the crux of life- the blank, and life is all about making a balance of sentiments and filling that blank in us and hence, Satyajit Ray concludes his *Agantuk* with an unending end. This was his film after which he became the *Agantuk* of immortal world.

References

Agantuk: The stranger, movie, Satyajit Ray.

Dhvynyaloka, Acarya Anandvardhana.

Satyajit Ray, Wikipedia, Internet.

Chapter 8

Cheluvi and *Delhi Safari*: Movies Voicing Ecological Concern

*Purnima**

Indian Cinema has recently seen works which have voiced their concern for environment and its protection. Movies like Karnad's *Cheluvi* and *Delhi Safari* have openly voiced their concern for degrading environment. *Cheluvi* is a voice for protection of trees where *Cheluvi* the protagonist who has power to convert into a tree gets deformed when she is ill-treated as her branches are cut when she takes the shape of a tree. By humanizing the tree the movie raises sympathy for the mute trees which are felled relentlessly. Similarly the movie *Delhi Safari* an animated movie speaks for animal rights in present scenario of deforestation where animals are poached, hunted and captivated and they have nowhere to go with decreasing forest cover and the loss of their natural habitat. In the movie the animals present their plea to the government with the help of a Bollywood parrot who can speak in human tongue and the movie presents the pangs of the animal world which cannot present its problems as they do not have the guift of language which human beings have and in turn are denied the rights as they can't speak for their rights. This paper aims at bringing out the eco-consciousness that these movies spread and how these movies become the spokesperson for the silently suffering environment.

The magical world of folklore has a strong impact on our psyche and in a light mood grave moral lessons can be transmitted to the receptive mind of the

**Assistant Professor, Department of Englishm*
Vasanta College for Women, Rajghat
Banaras Hindu University, Varanasi – 221 001

audience. Karnad has achieved double goal in *Cheluvi* by retelling the folklore and creating environmental awareness.*Cheluvi* derives its story from the folk-tale tradition and with a magical narrative, makes us realize about the environmental problems. Tree has life and it is giving us free air and oxygen and our return to it is that we are mercilessly killing it. *Cheluvi* is the story of a young woman whose family lives in poverty but the girl is guifted with a magical power which enables her to metamorphose into a flowering tree. One day she confides her supernatural ability in her sister and together they go deep into a forest. When her sister pours a pitcher of water over *Cheluvi* she turns into an incense bearing tree that grows exotic flowers. *Cheluvi* instructs her sister to carefully gather as many of the flowers as she can without breaking any of her branches. After collecting the flowers her sister pours another pitcher of water over *Cheluvi* who then regains her original human form. Karnad retells a Karnataka folk-tale, dubbed in Hindi, usually told by women while feeding children or putting them to bed, a time when other women would also be present. It is the way myths are kept alive in oral story telling in idea.

A young woman, *Cheluvi* (Kulkarni), living in abject poverty with her mother and sister, can turn herself into a tree yielding an endless supply of blossoms of sweet-smelling white flowers as long as they are picked very carefully and the branches of the tree are not broken. As breaking of the branches would damage the tree and in return deform the girl *Cheluvi*. The son of village headman(Karnad), Kumar (Prashant Rao) enchanted by the scent of the flowers, marries *Cheluvi* and they enjoy her flowering in strict privacy. During Kumar's absence, the headman's young daughter Shyama (G. Yakkundi) forces *Cheluvi* to disclose her secret. Unable to comprehend the delicacy and beauty of the event, the children destroy the tree, leaving *Cheluvi*'s body as a mutilated tree-stump. In the end, Kumar disconsolately leaves carting off the *Cheluvi*-stump. The folklorist A.K. Ramanujan pointed out that in Sanskrit and in Kannada the same word is used for 'flowering' and 'menstruation'. In this way the movie can also be admired with an ecofeminist perspective where woman and environment are seen as closely associated with each other. Women are closer to nature and fertility of women can also be connected to fertility of nature. Art direction is provided by Jayoo and NachiketPatwardhan, they have beautifully connected the tree and.her human form. By using the technique of magic-realism. Fabula is used to make the audience believe in the story of *Cheluvi* and how we are insensitive to the life that is there in trees. A large number of trees that are being cut for commercial use and for construction work is degrading the environment. Writers have always voiced their concern for environment and iitsprotection. R.K Narayan has also portrayed man's disregard of nature in the short story "The Axe", Narayan spells out his concern for nature in the lines, "They are going to build small houses by the score without leaving space for a blade of grass...." ("The Axe" 21). Rapid deforestation has taken away the natural habitat of animals and birds. There have been incidents in recent years when wild animals, tigers and leopards have entered into human surroundings. The truth is that these animals are not encroaching on our land but we are encroaching upon their land. The animals who don't have the guift of language like us, how would they raise their voice against our atrocities towards them? Kahlil Gibran beautifully puts down the pathetic state off nature in ink, he writes:

"I heard the brook lamenting like a widow mourning her dead child and I asked, "Why do you weep, my pure brook?"

And the brook replied, "Because I am compelled to go to the city where Man contemns and spurns me for stronger drinks and makes of me a scavenger for his offal, pollutes my purity,, and turns my goodness to filth.."

And I heard the birds grieving, and I asked, "Why do you cry, my beautiful birds?" And one of them flew near, and perched at the tip of a branch and said, "The sons of Adam will soon come into this field with their deadly weapons and make war upon us as if we were their mortal enemies. We are now taking leave of one another, for we know not which of us will escape the wrath of man."(71-72)

Man has become a devil not harnessing but harassing nature for material profit.

The movie Delhi Safari narrates the story of a journey undertaken by a leopard cub, his mother, a monkey, a bear and a parrot when the forest they live in is on the verge of destruction. The parrot is not the natural inhabitant of the forest but his help is needed by the group because he can communicate in human tongue as he is a pet of a Bollywood actor and the wise owl suggests that he might be helpful in taking his plea to the Parliament. Builders have encroached upon their forest and the animals are in a state of deprivation. They are facing threats of poaching and deforestation is snatching away their natural homeland. The animals decide to go to Delhi and protest in front of the parliament and ask the parliament some very simple yet pertinent questions. They ask: "why has man become the most dangerous animal? Doesn't man understand that if the forests and the animals don't co-exist with humans, the balance of the ecosystem will be endangered? Jim Corbett in his book *Man- Eaters of Kumaon* writes: "A tiger's function in the scheme of things is to help maintain the balance in nature and if, on rare occasions when driven by dire necessity, he kills a human being or when his natural food has been ruthlessly exterminated by man he kills two percent of the cattle he is alleged to have killed, it is not fair for these acts a whole species should be branded as being cruel and bloodthirsty."(xii-xiii) We fail to realize that it is we who are snatching away the "natural food of these predators. The film starts with Yuvraj 'Yuvi', leopard's cub saying that he lost his father Sultan due to the human interference but doesn't want to lose his home at any cost. He becomes the leader of his group and the animals unite for democratic justice and peaceful protest. In the recent years wild elephants and leopards have entered the human settlements. It is an established fact that animals striking into the human settlements as a result of decreasing natural food and habitation of these animals and if animals are not given their democratic rights they will turn violent against humans. The film carries a flashback of the morning with Yuvi and Sultan playing in the forest while his mother, Begum enters. The leopard family enjoy their companionship but their happiness doesn't last for long. A whole lot of bulldozers enters the forest and is cutting trees. Begum manages to escape, but Yuvi and Sultan are trapped by the bulldozers. In a bid to save Yuvi, Sultan catches Yuvi in his mouth and tosses him to Begum. Yuvi is saved but Sultan is killed by a human wielding a shotgun, making the whole forest a large enemy of the humans. A talk happens of Bajrangi, a monkey (saying that he would beat out the wits of those men, and asks whether anyone knows anyone who knows language of humans. An old wise white owl pipes up, saying he knows someone. Yuvi meets the owl the next day, and asks about the animal who could take the animals' message to humans. The white bird says he is Alex who lives with a film director Vikram. Bajrangi, Bagga the bear and Yuvi go and kidnap the parrot and convince him to go to Delhi with them to talk to the parliament. After a few good and bad experiences on their way, they follow the map to Delhi. Begum tells that no one is going to Delhi after listening to a tiger's story as soon after she sees the ghost of Sultan which encourages her to undertake the journey and the group proceed to Delhi. They finally reach Delhi and tell their message. The media telecasts their story, in the beginning the parrot falters but later he is able to bring the pathos of animals before the human world. With the help of an animation movie, the movielight- heartedly spreads its message to a wider audience. The message is given and though it chooses children as their audience, the movie is clearly voicing the muted animals whose rights are not granted because they cannot speak for their rights.In the last scene it is shown the jungle is saved and all are happy. Perhaps that is the kind of end we all would like to have and not an end of species extinction or violent attack of animals on human settlements.

References

Cheluvi. Dir. GirishKarnad 1992. Film.

Cheluvi. Web.<en.wikipedia.org/wiki/*Cheluvi*>

Corbett, Jim. *Man Eaters of Kumaon*. New Delhi: OUP 2012. Print.

Delhi Safari. Dir. Nikhil Advani 2012. Film.

Delhi Safari. Web.<en.wikipedia.org/wiki/Delhi_Safari>

Gibran, Kahlil. *The Wisdom of Kahlil Gibran*. New Delhi: UBSPD 2012. Print.

Narayan, R.K. "The Axe". *Images: A Handbook of Stories* Ed. M.M. Lukose. Madras: Macmillan India Limited 1986.Print.

Chapter 9

Cinematic Journalism, Critic and Multiplexes

*Awadhesh Kumar Bhatt**

The crisis of cinematic journalism has recently been a topical issue in many countries. In India, too, it has been claimed that arts pages, previously dominated by aesthetically oriented critics, have been shrinking and become more news oriented and entertaining. In this article, we explore the change of structures, values and ideals of arts reporting as friction between two opposing paradigms, the aesthetic and the journalistic, and analyse how the changes are reflected in the contents of the cultural pages and in the self-image of arts journalists. The research data of this case study consist of the arts pages of the biggest national newspaper, HelsinginSanomat, and of various internal planning documents related to its management. In addition to a longitudinal content analysis, we also employed theme interviews with and observation of cultural journalists. The results show a change of paradigm in arts journalism, with the consequence that the previously autonomous department has become an inseparable part of the news organization, increasingly adapted to meet the challenges of news journalism.

Arts criticism arts pages cultural in the United States the full-time and cinema critics job has been a casualty of the economic crisis facing American newspapers. Consequentially, in most American cities there are fewer reviews than ever being published, and a dearth of criticism has developed. However, the internet has

**Ph.D. Scholar Musicology,*
Faculty of Performing Arts
FPA, BHU, Varanasi
e-mail: ak_bhatt@yahoo.com

also fostered the creation of theatre reviewing web sites that are filling this void in criticism. In this article I discuss the creation of these web sites, their reception, and their challenges through the lens of my position as managing editor of one of these sites, Indian Film Association. I also discuss the unresolved issues that face and other cinema reviewing web sites, including questions of authority, quality, ethics, and identity. Finally, I make recommendations to bloggers, theatre artists, and traditional media writers that should foster high-quality criticism on the internet.

The advent of the internet has changed cinematic criticism and made the economic model of the full-time cinema critic in the United States increasingly unviable. Whereas in the 1992 most large Indian cities had multiple cinema critics working for local media outlets, today only few Indian cities have at least one full-time cinema critic working in traditional media: Delhi, Mumbai, Banglore, Kerla, Chennai.

Therefore, the number of cinema reviews has decreased and the cinema critic profession is endangered. In this Indian city, far from the major cultural centers of the nation, a group of online non-professional writers has created a surge of cinema reviews. Consequentially, reviews are being written for cinema companies that have never been reviewed before and cinema criticism is experiencing a local Renaissance.

One site at the center of this increased reviewing activity is, which is an organization of civilian internet writers? (to use terminology) that in 2012 published 532 reviews far more than any other media outlet in the states. The purpose of this article is to explore cinema reviewing web sites using as a case study to explore the creation of these sites, their reception in the local cinema community, and the unique struggles they face.

Just as the industry of journalism is evolving, so is the portrayal of the media in film. In the 1930s, screwball comedies like It Happened One Night and Meet John Doe featured newspaper reporters who run into moral slip-ups but emerge as heroes in the end. In the 1970s, movies like All the President's Men por-trayed newspaper reporters as determined, hard-working people who will stop at nothing to expose wrongdo-ing, while films like Network began addressing broadcast news and the dangers of becoming too consumed with ratings. Today, the portrayal of journalism onscreen is still evolving as new media moves to the forefront of reporting. Scholars like Matthew Ehrlich (2004) and Howard Good (1989) have devoted much of their careers to the study of journalism in film. However, often the most recent movies these scholars address are 2003's Shattered Glass and 2005's Good Night and Good Luck. Though there is a wealth of scholarship sur-rounding older journalism films, there is little research on films reflecting modern trends in journalism, perhaps because these films are just now emerging.

There are countless films depicting newspapers, magazines, television and media ethics cases. Films only recently began exploring current journalism trends, such as the advent of the Internet and recent struggles with shield laws and confidential sources. Based on a general knowledge of current journalism films and exist-ing scholarship about trends in past journalism films, it is hypothesized that journalism movies now typically fall into three categories: films depicting modern developments in the profession (like State of Play, which exam-ines the conflict between traditional print media and online journalism), more nostalgic films that hearken back to the media's glory days.

This study does not determine cause and effect. Whatever the motivation behind these onscreen por-trayals of the media, journalism films enter into "a cinematic public sphere that could be used to communicate ideas and shape public opinion". Without interviewing the filmmakers, one can only specu-late the reasoning behind the way journalism is portrayed in film, and without interviewing the audiences that consume those films, one can only speculate how these portrayals have influenced how viewers feel about the media. However, through a qualitative content analysis, observations can be recorded and analyzed that paintan overall picture of how the media are being portrayed onscreen today, adding to the wealth of scholarship about media portrayals onscreen pre-2005. This overall picture of the media onscreen likely influences audi-ences to some degree. According to film historian Steven Ross (2002), movies are "partly a reflection of what [audiences] are. And what they are is no less influenced by what they see". Regardless of the reason-ing behind these portrayals, observing and analyzing the media's representation onscreen says something powerful about how the media are viewed in society today.

Media and Ethics in Film

One researcher at the forefront of journalism in film scholarship is Matthew Ehrlich, whose book Journalism in the Movies details the overall portrayal of the media in film throughout history. Ehrlich deals primarily with films in the "journalism genre," or movies in which the main plot is about journalism or the main characters are journalists. Ehrlich notes the contradictory nature of the portrayal of the media onscreen, say-ing "The movies have portrayed journalists both as upstanding citizens and heroes and as scruffy outsiders and villains". Ehrlich addresses the negative portrayals of journalism in film in his article "Facts, Truth and Bad Journalists in the Movies." According to Ehrlich, many real-life journalists would likely say many onscreen journalists exercise inappropriate and unprofessional behavior. However, he says "'bad journalist' characters actually have helped shore up the press's preferred self-image, either by seeing through lies and pretense to the truth or by paying the price for not telling the truth. Ehrlich also says that by examining the profession in this way, journalism movies can be seen as "a culture thinking out loud about itself'. This idea is the primary focus of Ehrlich's article "Thinking Critically about Journalism through Popular Culture." In this article, Ehrlich argues that people can be educated about the media profession by studying journalism "more broadly as a practice and institution by analyzing movies as a long-running commentary on the press".

In "*The Bollywood Version: Movie Portrayals of the Press,*" acknowledges that many film portrayals of the press are negative, but like Ehrlich, he chooses to look at the larger picture of the overall portrayal of the media in film. He uses films like Five Star Final, His Girl Friday, Meet John Doe, The Green Berets, and Network to exemplify the characteristics often portrayed in journalism films and offers key phrases to describe the character of the reporters in these films: "*manipulate public opinion,*" "*increase their wealth,*" "*essentially sociopathic characters,*" and "*must resort to the equivalent of spying*". Above all, Zynda upholds Ehrlich's argument that journalism films hold the press accountable, saying "*As the press serves as a watchdog on government, so Bollywood, likewise on behalf of the public and with a like commercial basis, keeps an eye on the press*".

Nostalgia in Film

While some modern journalism films explore recent trends in the profession, others hearken back to a significant period in journalism history and rely on a sense of nostalgia in their storytelling. In Recycled Culture in Contemporary Art and Film, examines the use of nostalgia in film overall. As an example of the quintessential nostalgia film. Though it was produced in the 1970s, the film takes place in the early 1960s, which is reflected in everything from the neon sign-style open-ing credits to the music to the way the characters speak. Dika says "American Graffiti invokes that historical period directly, eliciting a sense of regret and confrontation with it". In "The Tube is Flickering Now: Aesthetics and Authenticity in Good Night and Good Luck".

There is a great deal of scholarship surrounding journalism in film, but most of this scholarship ends with 2005's Good Night and Good Luck. There is very little research on journalism films that have been released in the past five years, a hole in the scholarship this study aims to fill. Nostalgia in film and media ethics in film have also been studied in the past, but not in recent journalism films. Some scholarship exists surrounding recent trends in the media like the rise of online journalism and issues with shield laws, but as these issues have only recently begun being portrayed onscreen, there is virtually no scholarship surround-ing their use in film. This study takes existing scholarship on journalism in film, media ethics in film, nostalgia in film and current trends in journalism and applies it to recent journalism movies that do not yet have much scholarship surrounding them.

With the hypothesis and secondary research in mind, a series of open-ended research questions were developed to answer for each of the ten films:

What is the primary type of media depicted in the film (newspapers, television, radio, magazines)?

When and where does the story take place?

How are the time period and location in which the story takes place portrayed on screen?

Are the journalists honest in their newsgathering practices?

What kinds of relationships do the journalists have with their sources?

What kind of relationship do the journalists have with their co-workers and superiors?

How is the journalist's personal life portrayed?

Are any modern trends in journalism portrayed onscreen?

If so, are there any tensions between these new trends and old ideals?

What do the journalists look like (race, gender, age, size, how they dress)?

Each of the ten films was then viewed, and each research question was answered for every film. The notes on each film were compiled, and based on the data for each individual film, the researcher attempted to place the films into the three hypothesized categories. The data for the films in each category was analyzed for trends and common themes, and that data in each category was also compared to the other data in the ten-film sample as a whole.

Findings and Analysis

Overall, the films did fall into the three hypothesized categories, with the ethics category containing the most films. State of Play and Nothing But the Truth fell under the current issues category; The only anomaly in the study was Superman Returns, which was not as easily definable because while the Daily Planet newspaper and journalists Clark Kent and Lois Lane played prominent roles in the story, journalism was not the primary focus of the film and was used less than in the other films. However, the film does raise a few ethical questions about journalism and could therefore be considered part of that category, but this film does not place the same emphasis on ethical issues in journalism as the other films in that category. For the most part, however, journal-ism films today do either deal with current issues in journalism, nostalgic portrayals of journalism, or ethical dilemmas in journalism.

Current Issues in Journalism

Although there are a number of current issues in journalism affecting the industry today, such as the struggle between print and online media, only two of the ten films in the sample focused primarily on current journalism trends - State of Play and Nothing But the Truth. Though the two films share a few similar themes, they focus on different issues for the most part. State of Play, a suspense film about a jaded newspaper re-porter and a fresh-faced politics blogger who team up to investigate a corporate conspiracy, heavily emphasiz-es the struggle between print and online journalism. In the film, there is clearly a hierarchy at the newspaper involving print and online media.

Nothing But the Truth, while presenting both sides of the issue, seems to be arguing in favor of legal protection for journalists when asked to reveal confidential sources and a federal shield law. The movie cites significant events in media history involving confidential sources like, arguing that without confidential sources, reporters would have never been able to break those stories and communicate that information to the public.

While these two most recent journalism films address some of the most important issues facing journalists today, it seems journalism films in the other two categories resonate more with audiences. However, perhaps the fact that the two most recent journalism films deal with current issues in the industry is an indication that upcoming journalism films will follow the same path. Both films in this category are also about newspapers, indicating that newspapers are the type of media facing the most challenges today.

Media Ethics

The highest number of films in the sample fall under the media ethics category, which is not a sur-prising statistic given that most of the existing surrounding journalism in film addresses ethical situations onscreen. Good argues that journalism movies focusing on ethical situations often foster negative stereotypes about journalists, saying "Bollybood has given us reporters corrupted by cynicism, ambitions, and drink, careless of others' lives and reputations, and ever reluctant to let the truth stand in the way of a good story". As indicated in previous scholarship, this study also found that most ethical situations presented in journalism films often focused on negative characteristics, actions or decisions of the journalists. The majority of the journalists depicted are corrupt or unethical in some way, while the protagonist is usually either the only ethical reporter in a sea of unethical ones, or an unethical reporter who rises about the rest to become a heroic and honest journalist. This type of portrayal has been discussed in journalism in film scholarship before. Good emphasizes this idea in one of his books, saying "every year brings yet more journalists to the screen, sometimes to play the hero, sometimes the villain, and sometimes something of both" (2008, p. 5). This study found that three types of ethical situations were most often presented in the films - deception or unethical reporting practices, most often involving relationships with sources, and questionable choices in personal relationships and home life.

Given Zynda's observation that reporters are most often portrayed onscreen as "confident, aggressive people who are young, attractive, and single", it is not a surprising finding that romantic relation-ships often find their way into journalism movies. Perhaps the most glaring example of an unethical relation-ship in the sample is in the comedy Scoop.

While some of the journalist characters in the films in the ethics category emerge as heroes, for the most part the films reinforce the notion that the portrayal of the media in journalism movies "is usually not very favorable; despite an occasional All the President's Men, the films are more like Network in their critical and even cynical view of journalism". It is also worth noting that the primary journalist characters in the films in this category are all women. In all of the movies in this category, including Super-man Returns, it is female journalists who engage in unethical relationships with sources and fill the role of the workaholic reporter whose personal relationships and home life suffer. On the opposite end of the spectrum, the films in the nostalgia category are all centered on male reporters and their roles as heroes fighting against a corrupt or illegal entity. While some of their flaws are shown, the same emphasis is not placed on them as is placed on the flaws of the female reporters in the films in the ethics category, partially because the histor-ically-based situations presented in the films in the nostalgia category are not as conducive to emphasizing these negative traits.

Several key ideas about the portrayal of journalism in film emerge from the findings of this study.

While journalism films cover a wide range of subjects, they often can be categorized into groups of films containing similar themes. In the case of this study, it was found that modern journalism films are most often focused on current issues in journalism, nostalgic portrayals of journalism, and media ethics. These are certainly not the only categories of journalism films, but they are the categories that emerged from the journalism films of the past five years.

It could be that audiences do not find as much entertainment value in stories that explore struggles in the media industry, and any media professionals who watch journalism films may not want to be reminded of the current tensions they face at work when they watch movies. In the coming years, as these current issues within the industry develop, movies will likely start to feature trends like online journalism more prominently.

Other journalism films utilize a more nostalgic portrayal of the media, focusing on real-life events in media history and capturing the essence of the time period through costumes, hairstyles, set design, and the coloring of the film. Though the flaws of some of the characters in the film are shown, the protagonists are portrayed as heroes in pursuit of the truth and looking out for the public's best interest. These portrayals of the media are very positive overall and therefore likely more appealing to audiences than films portray-ing current struggles in journalism. Though those films portray journalists as heroes, many more questions are raised about their actions and a lot of emphasis is placed on negative tension. In more nostalgic films, particularly the three from this study focused on the time periods and prominent, audiences are likely attracted to the role of the journalist as investigator and crusader in a time they recognize as a high point in journalism history.

The majority of the films in the study fall under the ethics category, which is not surprising given that films focused on ethical dilemmas have been continuously prominent since the earliest days of journalism films. The ethical questions raised in these films likely appeal to audiences because they present an excit-ing conflict. Though they often perpetuate negative stereotypes about the media, most of the films show the evolution of a character from practicing unethical reporting tactics or tackling ethical dilemmas between their personal and professional lives to finding themselves and finding a more honest personal and professional outlook. According to Ross, "in addition to entertaining people, films can often provide a mechanism for discussing some of the most important ideas of the day". These films raise questions and incite discussion while simultaneously featuring stories audiences can find pure entertainment in, which is likely part of their appeal and part of the reason this category of journalism film has stayed strong through the years.

Although this study does not determine the cause and effect behind the portrayals of the media presented in these films, which could not be achieved without interviewing the filmmakers and audiences, it does paint a picture of the images of the media being presented to moviegoers today. Further studies could analyze the films individually and dig deeper into the media portrayals within each film rather than dealing with multiple films in broader categories. However, this study does present the overall image of common portrayals in modern journalism films and uses observations about the films and existing scholarship to draw comparisons between the films.

According to myself, however the movies choose to portray journalists, "Bollyboodhas reproduced myths in which the press is always at the heart of things and always makes a difference". Themedia play the important role in society of communicating information to the masses. Journalism films com-municate ideas to audiences about the industry that provides them with the information they receive every day. The ideas presented in journalism films reach a mass audience and likely affect viewers' thinking about the media to some degree. For this reason, it is important for media professionals to have an understand-ing of how the industry is being portrayed in popular culture. The media are constantly evolving, and as the industry continues to change, so too will the image of journalism in film.

References

Blood Diamond. (2006). Dir. Edward Zwick. Perf. Leonardo DiCaprio, DjimonHounsou, and Jennifer Connelly. Warner Brothers Pictures, DVD.

The Devil Wears Prada. (2006). Dir. David Frankel. Perf. Meryl Streep, Anne Hathaway, and EmilyBlunt. 20th Century Fox, DVD.

Frost/Nixon. (2008). Dir. Ron Howard. Perf. Frank Langella, Michael Sheen, and Sam Rockwell. Universal Pictures, DVD.

Dika, V. (2003). Recycled Culture in Contemporary Art and Film: The Uses of Nostalgia. Cambridge:Cambridge University Press.

www.screen.com

Chapter 10

De-colonizing the Screen: The Margins Acts Back

*Sayan Dey**

In the recent times the globe has been debating a lot over the innumerable 'posts' which has been ideologically, bio-graphically and geo-politically enunciated for the sake of defining and re-creating a world beyond the matrices of colonialism or the most current phenomena of coloniality. Unfortunately in most of the cases our effort of disentanglement have proved to be a major failure because our strategies and attitudes have failed to nurture the options which would enable us to think outside the colonial space and untie us from what eminent Argentine de-colonial critic Walter Mignolo terms as 'tyranny of abstract universals.' As a scholar I believe that human expressions forms an integral medium to de-link oneself from the western-centric ideologies as physical and verbal actions forms an integral part of our discourse. The characterization and representation in the Indian movies have undergone consistent ideological and thematic transformations since the last century. The journey has been characterized with multiple contradictions and symbiosis but at the end it has more or less tried ensure the evocation of an Indian version of cinema and cinematography with trans-cultural and trans-national representations underpinned in it. The empire has written enough to us and it is time for the margins, the colonized, the barbaric representations to act back and my paper will explore the multifaceted ways in which the Indian movies has been

**Research Scholar, Department of English,*
Vasanta College for Women (Affiliated to BHU, Varanasi),
KFI, Rajghat, Varanasi – 221 001
E-mail: sayandey89@yahoo.com

fighting hard to dislocate the global/colonial ideologues from its productive sense and its creative lens, inducting the indigenous, native elements in the process.

Introduction: Decolonization

Ramon Grosfoguel, Associate Professor from the University of Berkeley in his essay "A Decolonial Approach to Political-Economy: Transmodernity, Border Thinking and Global Coloniality" analyzes the global socio-epistemic shift since the inception of colonialism in the following manner:

> We went from the 16th century characterization of 'people without writing' to the 18th and 19th century characterization of 'people without history,' to the 20th century characterization of 'people without development,' and more recently, to the early 21st century of 'people without democracy.' We went from the 16th century 'rights of people' to the 18th century 'rights of man' to the 20th century 'human rights.'
>
> *(Grosfoguel 7:2009)*

The above statements reveal how the juridical face of colonialism have radically modified itself in the 21st century globalism which Peruvian sociologist Anibal Quijano entitles as a system of 'modernity/rationality' (Coloniality and Modernity/Rationality 1:2007). During the 16th century the rise of Eurocentric colonialism, under the canopy of *la mission civilisatrice* (the civilizing mission) and geographical navigations successfully interrupted the global south mostly the Americas, Europeanizing and Latinizing them as what we know as Latin America. Mostly history drafts colonial history in the language of outright physical violence yet its roots lies in the multi-dimensional epistemological and gnoseological constructs which empowered and enabled colonizing powers to reign over the natives.

As we understand the systems and the philosophies of knowledge being imposed upon us it is also very crucial to see how the globe continuously functioned from one version of western centrism to the other and for that we should also invade into the process of commodifcation and marketization of the ideologues. According to British social anthropologist John Rankine Goody, the world still lingers within the hellenocentric typologies. In his essay "The Theft of History" (2006) Goody records that the classical antiquities of '*polis*, democracy, freedom, economy, rule of law, art, *logos*' (26-27:2006) continues to reign the world even in the present day. Elaborating his ideas about the 'philosophy of sale' Brazilian law critic Boaventura De Souza Santos in his essay "A Non-Occidentalist West? Learned Ignorance and Ecology of Knowledge" (2009) resorts to the story of "Sale of Creeds" (190:1905) drafted by ancient Greek rhetorician and satirist Lucian of Samosata. Zeus along with the assistance of Hermes offers various schools of Greek philosophy established by different philosophers for the purpose of sale. The 'merchandize' is put on display and every buyer has the right to ask about the value and the contribution of the philosophy in an individual's life before purchasing it. But the philosophies as commodities do not have the rights to question their masters about it. They should function as according to the whims and fancies of their respective masters. This is how the native, indigenous traditions of the Global South and the Far East where trafficked and marketed by the colonizing fathers.

Descartes' *Cogito, Ergo Sum* (I Think, therefore I am) is regarded as the inception point of all modern philosophies and theoretical phraseologies but according to Argentine-Mexican writer and philosopher Enrique Dussel the Descartian cogito map was long preceded by the Eurocentric *Ego Conquiro* (I conquer, therefore I am). It is the philosophy of conquering new lands as already mentioned earlier in the essay which ultimately enabled them to cross and intervene through the borders of other existential disciplines. But modern philosophy has consistently failed to locate its locus/loci of enunciations because of its 'point zero' existence as denoted by Columbian Philosopher Santiago Castro-Gomez in the translated version of his essay *"La Hybris del Punto Cero. Ciencia, raza e ilustración en la Nueva Granada (1750-1816)"* (2005). According to him the 'point zero' is the situation which hides the points of inceptions of different strategies and actions this confusing and captivating the colonized natives. This is what led to the creation of the modern version of meta-coloniality as said by Zimbabwean decolonial critic Sabelo Ndlovu-Gatsheni. Gatsheni in his essay "De-coloniality as the Future of Africa" (2015) states that the judicial-political nature of colonialism have withdrawn its institutions long time and has replaced it with the institutions of meta-coloniality which transcends far beyond the physical existence and persist in the realm of abstractness. In order to de-structuralize this realm of abstractness the first thing we should undergo is to come out from the clutches of what Spanish Liberal Philosopher Ortega y Gasset terms as 'orthopedic thinking' (Graham *Theory and History in Ortega y Gasset* 154:2001). I re-structuralize the perspective as 'orthopedic existence.' It is important for us to disenfranchise ourselves from the static clutches of conceptual and analytical thinking. The superfluity and the naturalness of human persistence has to be restored and this is only possible through what eminent Argentine semiotician as 'critical border thinking.' Deriving the term from Chicana thinkers like Gloria Anzaldua (1987) and Jose David Salvidar (1997), Walter Mignolo (2007) through his essay "De-linking" describes that instead of thinking of accessing the centre it is crucial for us to enunciate and emancipate pluri-versal epistemes and pluritopic hermeneutics at the very borders of existence.

In the upcoming section I wish to elaborate the perspective of de-coloniality and border thinking within the contours of arts and aesthetics especially in the arena of the Indian stage and screen performatives.

Decolonizing the Screen

In order to internalize the evolution and the growth of Indian cinema we need to trisect our discussion frame into the following sections:

- ✰ The transition of Indian Cinema from the hands of Western techniques, acting and thematic influences towards indigenous socio-cultural, spatio-temporal and eco-political emancipation.

- ✰ The pan-Indian and global growth of regional movies and its fragmentation in the hands of pandemic commercialization.
- ✰ The influence of Indian theatre forming a backbone in several of the current Indian movies.

A meticulous analysis of the above mentioned points will enable us read Indian movies from a de-colonial perspective. Well commencing with the first point the first light of influence on the Indian movies where thrown by the Lumiere Brothers who in the year 1896 shot their very first movie in Bombay. History took a slightly different turn when Harishchandra Bhatavdekar alias Save Dada, the popular still photographer, largely influenced from the Lumiere Brothers ordered a camera from England and shot a simple wrestling match at the Hanging Gardens which was screened in the year 1899 and is considered to be the first motion picture in the history of Indian cinema.

The first reformation came in the platform of Indian cinema is the production of the silent movie by Dadasaheb Phalke named *Raja Harishchandra* in the year 1913. The silent film was a massive commercial success and it encouraged Dadasaheb to supervise and manage multiple film productions from 1913-1918. It was indeed a tumultuous time in the arena of Indian politics. On one side India is experiencing its struggle for colonial disentanglement from the hands of the Britishers and on the other hand a section of the Indian army has been forcefully christened in the British army to participate in the First World War. Thus it was an extremely difficult time for the practitioners of arts and aesthetics to continue with their creative ventures and it is very much visible in the fragmented situation of Indian cultural productions of that time. Despite this situation the development of Indian movie was a great step ahead which transcended itself from a mere element of thematic and technical mimicry towards re-constituting the lost fragments of Indian history and myths. The welcoming of the Hollywood movies created a special significance in the cultural cauldron of the educated Indian class yet the majority of the population banked on the national and the regional productions that appealed to a larger mass.

The first ever talkie movie directed by Ardeshi Irani was *Alam Ara* in the year 1931. It was another significant break in the Indian cinema and was a very crucial step towards disenfranchising the Indian movies from Eurocentric, hegemonic ideologues. The prospect of decolonizing and pluriversalizing Indian socio-cultural, mythological and historical elements where further encouraged through the development of regional movies. The first Bengali feature film was *Nal Damayanti* produced by J.F. Madan in 1917. In the south the first feature film was *Kechhaka Vadam* which was made by R. Nataraj Mudaliar of Madras. The first Bengali talkie movie was Jamai Sasthi screened in 1931 and was produced by Madan Theatres Limited. Apart from Bengali and South Indian movies there were innumerable productions in Oriya, Punjabi, Gujarati, Marathi and many more. Especially in Marathi *Ayodhyache Raja* was the first talkie that was produced in their respective language in the year 1932.

The journey continued unhindered and in a better way after 1947 when prominent directors especially from the segment of Bengali cinema like Satyajit Ray, Bimal Roy and after the 1960s we find a galactic evolution of Ritwik Ghatak, Mrinal Sen and others. Their films thematically ranged from the socio-cultural taboos of dowry, foeticide, patriarchal domination, rural-urban conflict, modern-tradition conflict to the problems and the grievances of the common men and women. What was remarkable was the settings of their movies which mainly remained centered in the hinterland of Indian geography. It was popular step which was hailed pan-globally as it was for the first time that Indian socio-cultural underwent a collective effort to dismantle the 'colonial ideographic approach towards well outlined nomothetics' (Mignolo "Prophets Facing Sidewise" 116:2005) so that the common mass is able to come out of the western-centric, enunciated, generalized and orientalized version of Indian history and myths towards a liberalized, particularized, individualized version of Indian history.

As De Souza Santos in his article "World Social Forum and the Global Left" (2008) mentions that the history as enunciated and emancipated through the colonial discourse has been a specially chosen segment of the native history which satisfies the ethics, typographies and the grammatology of the western ideograph (24). Thus the primary step of decolonization is to identify and excavate the 'past of the past' (De Souza Santos 31) which remains submerged under the uni-ethic and uni-ethnic elements of the western-centric discourses. But the re-creation and re-emergence of the Indian indigenous history and myths through cinema and cinematics have suffered a major setback due to the massive commercialization of Indian cinema which has ultimately evacuated constructive thematic and conceptual propagation and has resorted to blind, dull mimicking of the western themes and most importantly their digital inputs which ensures a smart production output. Digitization of Indian cinema using multi-dimensional, artificial paraphernalia quite successfully bridges the gap between illusion and reality thus deceiving the receptive and analyzing capability of the Indian audience and this element is of great concern. This is not only enslaving Indian cinema within the capitalist entitlement of the "100 Crore Club" but also marginalized the regional movies which cannot incur massive production cost unlike Bollywood.

It is this degradation which ultimately prompted me to formulate the third section which is the conclusion of my essay and it records how theatres has been influencing the Indian cinema in the modern times and its future need to protect its indigenous values.

Conclusion

The commercialization of Indian cinema has caused what Kenyan decolonial critic Ngugi wa Thiong'o terms as 'social decapitation' (Re-membering Africa 65:2009). The root has long term being separated from the body and the connectivity needs to be restored. Recently as an anti-thesis to vibrant commercialism it is being observed that in terms of acting, camera and thematic constructs Indian movies have been following the footsteps of theatre. Even movies like *Oh My God* and *Haider* which has been adapted from a Gujarati play named *Kanji Virudh Kanji* and latter an adaption of Shakespeare's *Hamlet,* has been encrypting multiple theatrical techniques like a play within a play or the musical drama imitating the Dumhal dance of the Wittal Tribe in *Haider*. These are the few instances which represents how Indian movie is transcending from a pure generalized global platform towards the individualized, particularized and most importantly localized versions of expression which were absolutely debarred during the colonial era and current within the ethical persuasion of the comprador bourgeoisie who enjoys the advantage of influencing and imposing the majority with their uni-directional ideological designs. The journey of decolonization has already begun and the margins have enunciated their critical border thinking and have started acting back.

References

Anzaldua, Gloria. *Borderlands/La Frontera: The New Mestiza.* San Francisco: Spinsters Publications, 1987. Print.

Castro-Gomez, Santiago. *La Hybris del Punto Sero. Ciencia, raza e ilustracion en la Nueva Granada (1750-1816).* Bogota: University of Javeriana, 2005. Print.

Dussel, Enrique. *Beyond Philosophy: Ethics, History, Marxism and Liberation Theology.* New York: Rowman and Littlefield Publishers, 2003. Print.

Goody, J. *The Theft of History.* Cambridge: Cambridge University Press, 2006. Print.

Graham, John T. *Theory of History in Ortega y Gasset: The Dawn of Historical Reason.* United States: University of Missouri Press, 1996. Print.

Grosfoguel, Ramon. "A Decolonial Approach to Political-Economy: Transmodernity, Border Thinking and Global Coloniality." *Kult 6 – Special Issue.* Roskilde University, 2009. Print.

Mamdani, Mahmood. *Define and Rule: Native As Political Identity.* USA: Harvard University Press, 2012. Print.

Mignolo, Walter D. "Delinking." *Cultural Studies, 21(2).* 2007. Print.

Paul, Sanchita. "History of Indian Cinema." 2005. Web <http://www.mapsofindia.com/my-india/history/history-of-indian-cinema>

Quijano, Anibal. "Coloniality and Modernity/Rationality." *Cultural Studies, 21(2).* 2007. Print.

Saldivar, Jose David. *Border Matters.* Berkeley: University of California Press, 1997. Print.

Samosata, L. *The Works of Lucian Samosata.* Oxford: Clarendon Press, 1905. Print.

Santos, Boaventura De Souza. "A Non-Occidentalist West? Learned Ignorance and Ecology of Knowledge." *Theory, Culture and Society, 6(8).* New York: Sage Publishers, 2009. 103-125.

Santos, Boaventuro De Souza. "The World Social Forum and the Global Left." *Politics and Society, 2,* 2008. Print.

Chapter 11

Indian Cinema and the Commodified Women

*Bharti Rai**

In the perpetuation of gendered equality, our attention is easily drawn to the discourses with high visibility such as culture, customs, traditions, conventions and rituals etc. But areas of low visibility escape unnoticed. But such areas of low visibility are the areas that have the utmost potential to damage. Cinema, language and education are some such areas where there is deeply embedded a politics that is played so covertly that it does not look like politics. Cinema is a potential tool that disseminates the ideology of the mighty through its creations. Indian cinema is not an exception in this regard.

Dadasaheb Phalke, the Father of Indian Cinema, is credited for the inception of Hindi cinema with his movie "*Raja Harischandra*" in 1913. That was an era when women did not choose to step across the threshold willingly into a restricted zone of Cinema to them. With the gradual leap of time, attitudinal transitions took place and by the 1930s, Devika Rani, Zubeidaa, Mehtab, Shobhana Samarth – out of passion for acting, tried their hands at it. These women were not into it because they were need-driven rather they were in the celluloid world because they were dream-driven. And thus a metamorphosis of Indian Cinema took place with female actors acting as females and not men acting out female roles. Suraiya, Meena Kumari, Madhubala and Waheeda Rehman, changed the face of Indian cinema and heralded

**Research Scholar,*
Department of English,
Banaras Hindu University, Varanasi – 221 005
e-mail: bhartibhu@gmail.com

a new era of Indian Cinema. *Achhut Kanya*", "*Jeevan Prabhat*", "*Nirmala*", "*Alam Ara*", "*Zarina*", "*Chitralekha*", "*Parineeta*", among others, are some of the movies with woman-centric themes of that era. The same theory applied to the portrayal of female characters as well. To start with, women who chose the unconventional profession of acting were looked down upon as prostitutes or women who were "easily available." Although, later movies like *Mother India* were made in which Nargis Dutt played a more challenging and substantial role, the basis of the portrayal remained the same.

The conditions of women at that time were still better in terms of remuneration, status and roles as the leading ladies of that time were on par with their male counterparts. But the question that haunts is, are women enjoying the same status in the 21st century as they enjoyed in 20th century? Are they standing on the same pedestal as that of male actors in today's world of Cinema?

The ethos and ideology of any culture is best projected in its Cinema. The various aspects of a movie are its characterization, its plot, music, lyrics etc. character being of paramount importance. The audience and the films have always been involved in a two dimensional interaction where one is the manifestation of the other. The cinema projects what the audience wants to see and the audience always welcomes the movie which projects their sub-conscious, their repressed desires and their consciousness. The main stream cinema has always been welcomed by the spectators because of an affiliation of the taste whereas women-centric movies (even if a hit at box-office) have always been a 'deviant'.

The ideal woman in the decades till 1980's was depicted to be submissive and shy, dependent and fragile, usually clad in a sari, whereas the famous vamps of Bollywood donned bold outfits. Women who dressed in a style more influenced by the West were usually considered to be morally degraded. If we look at the 1970s or '80s, the favourite vamps of that era like Bindu, Helen or Aruna Irani were some of the first women to smoke, drink or engage in pre-marital sex onscreen, unlike other actresses. Such activities were a sign that the women characters had questionable morals, though when a male actor did the same onscreen he was seen as being macho. The actresses on the other hand would not even dare to do so as they were expected to be docile, shy and dependent women because these were the virtues of a "well-cultured" Indian woman.

But today the roles that woman play on the screen have undergone multitudinous changes. "Men act, women appear. Men look at women; women watch themselves being looked at." The above quote suggests very succinctly the position of women in the realm of the 'look', including within the mainstream Indian 'Cinema. Consider the first part of the statement, "Men act, women appear". In Indian cinema, women have been relegated to the passive position in film after film, as "bearer, not the maker of meaning", merely an appendage to the man, the wielder of power".

As Laura Mulvey writes in her seminal article, "Visual Pleasure and narrative Cinema," "in their traditional exhibitionist role, women are simultaneously looked at and displayed, with their appearance coded for strong visual and erotic impact, so that they can be said to connote to be-looked- at ness". The woman displayed has functioned at two levels; as erotic objects for the characters within the story, and as erotic object for the spectator within the auditorium. As in the songs, using the device of the show girl or dancer, the two looks are unified, so that the gaze of the audience and male characters in the film are combined neatly, providing both with a sense of control and passion. This also extends to most other visual representations of women with men, be it a photograph in an advertisement of a condom, or a love scene in a film, whether mainstream or pornographic, even if the woman is shown in an amorous pose with a man, the real display is for the spectator of the representation.

What Budd Boeticher says about the narrative cinema in the west also applies here: "What counts is what the heroine provokes, or rather what she represents. She is the one, or rather the love or fear she inspires in the hero, or else the concern he feels for her, who makes him act the way he does, in herself the woman has not the slightest importance." (17) The stories played out on the screen are the men and their conflicts, their, dreams, their aspirations, their tragedies, their revenge, their desires and their heroism. The women exist only in relation to the men, as their mothers, their wives, and especially their lovers. It is hard to find even one story revolving around a single unattached woman and of course there is the worship of youth and 'beauty'. We rarely ever see a woman act independently, make her own decisions, question authority or even are a working woman unless her mother is on her death bed, or the father crippled, and definitely never once she gets married! Traditionally, women have been reduced to being a mere spectacle in tile movies, pretty faces commodified for their beauty, with hardly any dividing line between beauty contests and acting in films. Women's specially constituted role as spectacle, as the subject of the Look, is especially evident in the song and dance numbers which are such an important part of the publicity and the selling of a film. In fact there is an entire genre of songs, called 'item numbers,' in industry parlance, which generally have a showgirl or dancer performing, and a predominantly male audience watching, that are deliberately inserted into the film, often without any direct connection with the rest of the film, to attract audiences.

There is literally a dearth of woman-centered movies in our film industry today. Even if someone tries to break this stereotyped image of woman and produces a woman centered film, the movie has a sad predicament. Even if the movie is a super hit at box office, still the turnover is far less than a hit movie with male protagonist. Let us have a look at a comparative analysis of some Bollywood block blusters.

Another factor that exposes the gender discrimination rampant in Indian Cinema is the remunerations these actresses receive for the equally hard work done by male actors. Top male stars, such as the three Khans – Salman, Shah Rukh and Aamir – and action star Akshay Kumar, earn around 400 million rupees ($6.7

million) per film on average, apart from a share of the profits, according to industry experts.

Movie	*Year*	*Studio(s)/Producers*	*Language*	*Worldwide Gross*
PK	2014	Vinod Chopra Films	Hindi	792 crore (US$120 million)
Bajrangi Bhaijaan	2015	Salman Khan Films/ Kabir Khan Films	Hindi	626 crore (US$92 million)
Baahubali: The Beginning	2015	Arka Media Works	Telugu and Tamil	600 crore
Dhoom 3	2013	YashRaj Films	Hindi	542 crore
Prem Ratan Dhan Payo	2015	Rajshri Productions	Hindi	431 crore
Chennai Express	2013	Red Chillies Entertainment	Hindi	423 crore
3 Idiots	2009	Vinod Chopra Films	Hindi	395 crore

This is Bollywood's year of the woman. Some of the biggest hits in India's prolific movie industry this year have female leads in female-oriented stories.

In this summer's surprise hit, "Queen," Kangana Ranaut is the spunky heroine who embarks on her honeymoon alone after she is jilted the day before her big fat Indian wedding. In "Mary Kom", Priyanka Chopra plays a female Olympic bronze medal-winning boxer. Previously, women were relegated to playing the male lead's girlfriend, sister or mother in subservient roles reflecting the traditional dominance of men in Indian society. But for all their box-office success and newfound prominence, Bollywood actresses are asking: Where is the money?

A-list actresses such as Deepika Padukone and Katrina Kaif get paid a tenth of that per film. When Padukone recently signed a movie deal for 70 million rupees ($1.1 million), it generated a buzz since it was one of the highest amounts paid to a female lead.

Now, the question is what can be done to change this lop-sided and unbalanced perspective that the majority of the spectators and the film makers hold. This gendered discourse of cinema is so congested with discriminations at all levels that it is a herculean task to shift the loci of the disparities. All these disparities and prejudices converge at the point of the mindset, the ideology of the film makers as well as the spectators. The two dimensional dialogue that goes on between the consumer and the producer, where in the object of commodification is woman, needs a revolutionary change. Woman is not just an object of gaze. We need to understand that she too has dreams and aspirations and she too has her share in all the trials and tribulations which a man has. It is a high time to realize and dismantle the identity of a woman as an object of sexual gratification and shift the focus from woman as being-of-flesh to a human being.

References

Ashis, Nandy. *The Secret Politics of Our Desire.* Delhi : Oxford University Press, 1998.Print.

Bagchi, Amitabha. *Women in Indian Cinema.* [Online] 1996. [Cited: 7 2012, 22.]

Bamzai, Kaveri. *Bollywood Today.* New Delhi: Lustre Press, Roli Books,2007.Print.

Bill Nichols, ed. Movies and Methods. Berkley: University of California,1985. Print.

http://www.cs.jhu.edu/~bagchi/women.html.

Jain, Jasbir and Rai, Sudha. *film and feminism essay in Indian cinema.* Jaipur and New Delhi : Rawat Publication, 2002. p.6.

Kavoori, Anandam P. and Punathambekar, Aswin. *Global Bollywood.* New York : New York: New York,University Press, 2008.Print.

Lakshmi, Rama. In India's Huge Marketplace, Advertisers Find Fair Skin Sells. Washington Post. January 27, 2008.

Mulvey, Laura. *Visual and other Pleasures.* United Kingdom: Palgrave Macmillan, 1989, Print.

Chapter 12

Gender and Caste Dynamics in Indian Cinema from 1930s to 2000s

*Sunil Kumar**

India is the largest film producing country in the world and Bollywood, the main centre of film production in India, is known world over for its musicals. Cinema provides in-depth information about the various things of the past as well as the current happenings. Cinema is closely related to the life of common man and the principle that define human society. The understanding of cinema lies in culture. The components of meaning in cinematic articulation are inseparable from various social, intellectual and cultural developments. This paper aims at drawing a trajectory of how Indian cinema has grown in its portrayal of caste and gender issues over the decades. A rear view would reveal that Indian cinema's first decade both before and after Independence did respond quite strongly to the socialist nerves as issue of caste became a part of the popular film narratives like in *Achhut Kanya* (1936) and *Sujata* (1959). The 1960s however, saw cinema narrowing down its concerns to the socio-economic confines of the upper -middle class people. It never occurred to any filmmaker to portray a Dalit protagonist fighting against social evils. However, the parallel or the new wave cinema did make efforts to bring the lower caste subjectivity on the big screen. The social questions like of caste- based gender violence and feudal exploitation gathered remarkable momentum through films like

**Junior Research Fellow*
Department of English,
Banaras Hindu University, Varanasi – 221 005

Shyam Benegal's Ankur (1974). The latter part of the paper deals mainly with films belonging to the later decades of the twentieth century and portrays the change that a Dalit woman's persona has gone through over the decades. The stereotypes are done away with; and the rebelliousness and the fighting spirit among rural Dalit women, which is a novel phenomenon has been explored in these offbeat films, namely, Shekhar Kapur's Bandit Queen (1994), Jag Mundhra's Bawandar (2000), and Priyadarshan's Aakrosh (2010).

Caste is a very touchy issue in Indian society. First time the issue of caste was raised in the Film *Achhut Kanya* made in 1936. The issues of caste were seldom highlighted by the Indian film directorsin films but they never took this issue on a serious note. Many films after *Achhut Kanya* were made but there is hardly any film portraying mainstream actor as a dalit protagonist. Change in the leadership and transfer of power from strong leaders of upper caste to leaders coming from poor background gave a lot of strength to dalits and other socially backward caste

If historical evidence is to be believed, the Dalits and the Adivasis were the original dwellers of this country. Today Dalits comprise a little more than one-sixth of India's population, which amounts to some 160 million people, and live a contingent existence, shunned by the society because of their rank as Dalits – the lowest caste of the India's caste system. And within this class of Dalits, the worst affected are the women, who constitute almost half of India's 160 million Dalits, comprising about 16 per cent of India's total female population, and 8 per cent of the total population. They are weighed down by the triple burden of the oppressive hierarchies of caste, class and gender. While they have to bear the brunt of poverty and the social stigma of caste with the Dalit men, they also have to withstand the patriarchal power which makes them vulnerable not only to domination by the upper castes, but also by the very same Dalit men. Hence, they become the sites also of the sexualized forms of oppression. Dalit women have to face the paradox of being regarded as polluted and untouchable and yet get exploited in the most intimate sphere of social relations. It is through this subaltern lens that I want to review Indian cinema in this paper. The accustomed supposition that cinema's intent is to produce narratives to satisfy the entertainment acumen of the people should undergo an essential scrutiny. Films as being the most potent forms of artistic expression cannot be considered sans their politico-ideological objectives. However still, when one looks at the century-old Indian cinema from a Dalit perspective, only a handful of senile, obscure examples come to the fore. Caste, despite being a persistent and acceptable fact of Indian reality is often cast away by the Hindi filmmakers.

Achhut Kanya (1936)

Hindi films may have boasted of a reformist *Achhut Kanya* (1936), the love story of a Dalit girl and Brahmin boy very early on in its life but there have been few Dalit stories and characters down the hundred years of its existence. Franz Osten's

Achhut Kanya, both because of a modern and a critical look at the traditional and rudimentary social practices of Indian society and because of its polished film style, is still considered to be one of the high points of Indian cinematic accomplishments. The controversy that was generated by the portrayal of the love affair between a Brahmin boy, Pratap and an Untouchable girl, Kasturi, is wrapped up within the film through the pivotal dialogue of "*Tum Brahmin ho, main acchut*" (You are a Brahmin, while I am an untouchable); as if that is a decree writ in stone and cannot be challenged. This emphasizes the degree of fear and the feeling of defeat that is engrained in the mind of a Dalit girl who has lost all her assertive power under the debilitating effect of the caste system. What we see in *Achhut Kanya* is not a triumphing love cutting across caste barriers and culminating in a union but a subversive, inhibited and a controlled transgression by a Dalit woman that ultimately ends in a personal tragedy.

Sujata (1959)

Another Incident of controlled transgression is seen when Indian cinema returns to the issue of caste, untouchability and a possibility of an inter- caste marriage, in Bimal Roy's *Sujata* (Well -Born) in 1959. This is a film that tugs at our heart strings with its portrayal of the pain and dilemmas of an untouchable girl growing up in a Brahmin family. The untouchable girl ironically enough is named Sujata, meaning well born. She is the infant girl who is the sole survivor of a trolley coolie's family that has succumbed to cholera. And since her family belongs to low caste no one in the locality is willing to take care of her, except Upendra, a progressive Brahmin who despite repeated objections from his wife Charu, refuses to let go of the girl and brings her up as her own daughter, of course sans education. The twist in the tale arises when Adhir, a well educated Brahmin boy originally chosen as a prospective groom for their real daughter Ramaa, falls in love with Sujata. The shock caused by this development puts off Charu so bad that while one of her diatribes against Sujata, she falls down the stairs and loses a lot of blood. And when a need for blood transfusion arises, the only blood group that matches with that of Charu is that of Sujata. She comes to Charu's rescue with her blood and Charu finally learns that blood has no 'caste' and accepts that Sujata is as much her daughter as Ramaa is. The film closes with the suggestion of an acceptance of Sujata's marriage to Adhir with the parental sanction of both families. If Achhut Kanya and Sujata are to be compared, one has to agree to a certain degree of liberalism that has seeped into the society and the cinema at large within the course of twenty-three years, which is the time gap between these two films. All the more, while in Achhut Kanya, Kasturi is hardly given any voice throughout the movie and ultimately sacrificed for the endorsement of tradition, Sujata's silence is turned into a near assertive voice when she saves her adoptive mother with her blood.

Ankur (1974)

Similar agency can be seen in the character of Lakshmi in Shyam Benegal's 1974 film *Ankur* (The Seedling). Although this film cannot be considered a product of mainstream cinema, it very powerfully brings out the feminist conception of identity and burden in a feudal society where caste dominates. In this film Surya, the Zamindar's son gets increasingly attracted to Lakshmi, the Dalit woman employed to take care of his house. Disconcerted by her loyalty to her deaf- mute good -for nothing husband and miffed by her snubbing of his advances, Surya wastes no time in removing Kishtaya from the scenario. On being caught one day stealing toddy (palm wine) from Surya's farm, he is made to sit on a donkey backwards and paraded in the village with his head shaven. Due to the humiliation incurred, Kishtaya runs away abandoning his wife. Surya, his head full of the romantic fantasies of Hindi cinema, tells Lakshmi that he will look after her now; and Lakshmi yields to him out of economic necessity. However, their brief affair is unexpectedly terminated as soon as Saru, Surya's wife, who has heard rumours of this liaison, comes and dismisses Lakshmi from the job. By this time Lakshmi is pregnant with Surya's baby and Surya, fully aware of the shame and humiliation that the birth of an illegitimate child will bring upon him, desperately tries to persuade Lakshmi to have an abortion, but she doesn't concede, since having a child had been her devout wish, which she has not been able to accomplish with her impotent husband. Meanwhile Kishtaya returns and is overjoyed to learn that she is carrying what he believes is his child, and he innocently hands over to her the money he has earned while he has been absconding. Boosted by a fresh hope and confidence, and aware of the urgent need to provide for his wife and upcoming child, Kishtaya goes over to the farmhouse with the intention of asking Surya for work. Surya, anxious at seeing Kishtaya approaching the house with a stick, misunderstands the latter's purpose and beats him black and blue. Witnessing this from the hut, Lakshmi runs to her husband's rescue, and let loose an outburst of curses at Surya, who makes a quick and disgraceful retreat to the house. In the final scene of the film, a young village boy is shown as hurling a stone at Surya's house. This act of brazenness coupled with the blood -red screen that ends the film advocates the anger and frustration felt by the peasants towards the long- exploiting feudal dynasts. Interestingly, the liberalism of thoughts that we witnessed in the character of Upendra in Sujata, is absent in the character of Surya, despite both being University educated men. This goes to show how deeply the caste- based sensibilities are ingrained in the Indians, that education being the most potent weapon of development also fails at its feet. The protagonist of Ankur is a Dalit woman Lakshmi, and the story is the drama of herself -empowerment in the face of feudal caste- based oppression. Benegal takes her two-fold marginalized status and turns it around such that, her position with respect to her gender and caste gets reordered as more powerful than that of Surya. He does this by allowing Lakshmi, as well as other female villagers an agency to assert themselves by speaking out. Lakshmi indeed, despite being a subaltern, empowers herself at every turn. She not only speaks up for herself alone but also for her deaf- mute husband. Thus by the end of the 70s, Dalit women had achieved some minimal levels of expression in Indian cinema. And with the passing of a few more decades of development and upliftment programmes, there have been changes, if not in the living conditions of Dalits but in the level of antagonism and the level of a will to fight against oppressors. This transformation is witnessed more in women than in men as they are at the receiving end of stronger modes of oppression.

The decade of 80s unfortunately seems to be a decade that was silent on the issue of Dalit feminism. But in the following decades, there have been caste based films in Indian cinema, although extremely few, which have chosen to give some sort of voice to the Dalit women. Examples include Shekhar Kapur's internationally- acclaimed *Bandit Queen* (1994) and Jag Mundhra's 2000 film *Bawandar* (The Sandstorm), both based on real life incidents.

Bandit Queen (1994)

Bandit Queen through Phoolan Devi's life has very poignantly portrayed the intersection of caste and gender in the everyday life of rural north India. Through a representation of caste based segregation in villages, Phoolan's child marriage and the endless torture by her paedophilic husband, her exploitation at the hands of upper caste Thakurs and subsequent humiliation when she's paraded naked in front of the entire village in the presence of villagers as passive spectators; Kapur has attempted an indictment of the gender and the caste hierarchies present in the rural areas of India. The latter half of the film deals with the dramatic killing of the Thakurs by Phoolan Devi in the infamous Behmai massacre, when this brave woman chose to take justice and her destiny into her own hands. She takes revenge from all those who saw her being paraded naked in a mutilated and raped condition, and did not come for her rescue. The largest massacre in the history of free India by a group of bandits raises Phoolan to the highest pedestal of notoriety, and has the entire nation snarling for her blood. The film then recounts the rest of the story, leading to her much awaited and broadcasted surrender before 8,000 people, in Bhind.iii Kapur's representation of repeated rapes that sparked off a sharp public debate, also demonstrate that the construction of the boundaries of gender is always entwined with the politics of caste. Phoolan Devi is repeatedly assaulted not just because she has defied hegemonic social norms by leaving her husband but because of a caste based construction of sexual accessibility where upper-caste men often assert violent sexual authority over lower- caste women. Dalit women's activists echo the notion that Dalit women are hit the hardest in everyday life and during caste clashes. However, the Indian government has time and again failed to prosecute cases of rape. Beginning with the lodging of the First Information Report (FIR) at the local police station through to the judge's opinion, should a case reach that far, women in India are faced with daunting obstacles in prosecuting cases of rape. And if the woman is poor, belongs to a low caste and lives in some rural area, it becomes all the more difficult to get any action done. And those who are indeed able to pursue cases of sexual assault have to in the process battle inescapable biases with the police, the doctors and the judges. One of the cases that illustrate a typical example of the influence of caste bias on the justice system is Bhanwari Devi's rape case where "rapists were acquitted on a Judge's reasoning that 'an upper-caste man could not have defiled himself by raping a lower-caste woman'."iv This judgment sparked many protests and the case was taken up by many women's rights organizations in north India. Within a decade of the incident, a cinematic representation of the same was directed and released by Jag Mundhra by the name of *Bawandar* (The Sandstorm, 2000).

Bawandar (2000)

Bhanwari Devi, the protagonist of this film was a typical illiterate village woman before she joined, under the influence of social worker and activist Shobha Mathur, the Rajasthan Government Women's Development Programme (WDP) called Sathin in 1985 as a grass root worker. This organization worked primarily against caste based discrimination and orthodox practices like child marriages in villages. In April 1992, she reported the child marriage of the one year old daughter of Ram Karan Gurjar to WDP authorities, due to which the police came to the village and created an intervention. As a retaliatory measure, the Gurjar (high caste landlord) family gang -raped Bhanwari in the presence of her husband on September 22 of the same year. When she approached the police, Bhanwari was told that she was too old and unattractive to merit the attentions of young men. Even after undergoing a whole lot of trouble in getting her case heard, she ends up disappointed with the trial judge acquitting the accused on the reasoning that "rape is usually committed by teenagers, and since the accused are middle- aged and therefore respectable, they could not have committed the crime. An upper- caste man could not have defiled himself by raping a lower- caste woman". Her case has been reproduced on the screen in a fairly meticulous manner by Jag Mundhra. Here, a Dalit woman's body becomes a most prominent site of exploitation when she is gang raped by four upper caste members of the same Gurjar family in what forms the most disturbing scene of the film. The film through this sequence reinforces the idea of the Dalit body as being something that can be easily used as a site for vindication, can be easily abused, tortured, and then disposed off. What's commendable is that despite this traumatic experience, she pulls herself together and convinces her husband to file a FIR report and pursue the case further. However, Sanwari (name changed in the film), can still not be seen as an iconic figure of Dalit women's emancipation since all her efforts and her persistent plea for justice goes in vain. In this context, the scene which shoots the court trial becomes extremely overwhelming because while being cross -examined, Sanwari gets raped again, and this time verbally. She's asked inappropriate questions with implicit sexual connotations which are aimed at embarrassing her and proving her to be a woman with no moral standards. Though Sanwari did not break down at all and in fact exhibited a sheer eloquence through her curt replies, the accused were all set free. The judge pronounced what could be some of the most shocking remarks that were ever made in a judicial statement. The film borrowed the same words of the judgment which translate as "Bhanwari Devi was a Dalit and so, her rapists, upper caste men, could not have possibly raped her." The film Bawandar nevertheless was critically acclaimed and Nandita Das, who played Sanwari was applauded for her performance. However, this film too like Bandit Queen was of a controversial nature. It was censored by the Central Board of Film Certification, and given the 'Adult' Certificate with a recommendation of five cuts. There were also concerns that the film might end up annoying the Gurjar community, to which the accused belong. The Government was worried about the film leading to caste -based contention. However, despite the controversies regarding its distribution, the film Bawandar did very well in showcasing the caste-based victimization of Dalit women especially in rural landscape.

Aakrosh (2010) directed by Priyadarshan where, while dealing with honour killings in a pocket of Uttar Pradesh where the law and the police play havoc instead of implementing order and peace, the caste-schism is also played out between the two investigating officers, namely Pratap Kumar and Sidhhant Chaturvedi who are brought in to investigate the mystery behind three young men who have gone missing. Pratap is a Dalit while Siddhant is from an upper caste and the two often fall out because their perspectives on the oppression are different. The high stakes failed when the film turned out to be a box office disaster.

There are many similar films playing the Dalit card in Bollywood but even if the means are good, the end does not justify the means. In other words, the technical brilliance and artistic excellences are neatly undercut by the pretentious hypocrisy presented in the narrative. Vidhu Vinod Chopra's *Eklavya* (2007) is an example in which 800 camels were reportedly used in an action sequence in *Eklavya*. This spells out the film's true agenda – glamour and chutzpah. *Eklavya* presented the radical and "new" Dalit in the shape and form of a bold police officer Pannalal Chauhar who not only asserts his Dalit identity but also bristles against the caste based feudal oppression that still pervades in parts of Rajasthan.

Conclusion

The inclusion of dalits as protagonist or as major characters in Hindi film industry is a very touchy issue. The fact that Bollywood produces near about one thousand films every year but there was just a handful of films highlighted the issue of caste. It was only during seventies and eighties, when directors like Shyam Benegal, Adoor Gopalkrishnan, Govind Nihlani, Prakash jha started making films which highlighted socially relevant issues. Though opinion is somewhat divided on whether casteism has been dealt with adequately in the films or not, almost everyone agrees that in the film industry caste has always been exiguous. One of the objectives of cinema as a potential medium of communication and a propagandist tool is to construct social realities. But, one can say that since the major stakes in the film industry are held by upper castes, their films often portray a very supercilious image and way of life. The traditions shown in the films are for instance, very Brahminical. The marriage ceremonies shown pertain to the Brahminical traditions with the priest given the supreme position in all customs, and the lavish weddings with great pomp and show completely discount the feudal nature of Indian society and the denial of Dalits to have wedding processions in villages. Never the less, cinematic representations can indeed function as a medium of deconstructing caste binaries if they are allowed to grow without any restrictions. Therefore, I feel that there is a need to expand the horizon of Indian cinema in terms of content and subject matter so that an appropriate picture can be placed in front of the mass audience. There is also a need to create a space for the marginalized groups, and more so for marginalized women, who have remained in a vacuum by virtue of their marginality since time immemorial.

References

Bandhu, Pranjali. "*Dalit Women's Cry for Liberation*". Gender and Caste. Ed. Anupama Rao. New Delhi: Kali for Women. 2003.Print.

Chakravarty, Sumita, S.: *National Identity in Indian Popular Cinema* – 1947-1987; OUP, Delhi, p.112, 1996.Print.

Kashyap, Smriti."*Bandit Queen Review*". Fullhyd.com.

Human Rights Watch. (1998). "*Attacks on Dalit Women: A Pattern of Impunity*". Broken People: Caste Violence against India's "Untouchables". New Delhi: HRW. Print, pp. 167-155. 1998.Print.

Chapter 13

Changing the Identity of Women in Indian Cinema: A Review Paper

*Ved Prakash Rawat**

In the journey of 100 years, Indian cinema has come a long way and so the women character. Showing many shades, the portrayal of women not only touched the lives of the audiences but also showcased the strength, beauty and complexity that define a woman. The present paper also reported that from film and television to radio, magazines, literature, newspapers, the portrayal of women is stereotypical and distorted. Male superiority and female inferiority are repeated constantly in mainstream of Indian films. In the early phase of Indian cinema women were represented as absolutely pure wives through the epical characters or sometimes they visualized as ideal girlfriends, self-sacrificing mothers, sisters and daughters or they were immoral prostitutes, cabaret dancers, and strippers. In the present day, the typical Indian woman, item number and individualism share an almost symbolic relationship. These three ingredients have become the major part of Indian cinema. Gone are the days when stories were written about the shy village girl or ethical beauty, these are the times for rebellious lovers and sexy and confident business women who rule the roost in cinema and also in real life. The portrayal of women in cinema is slowly becoming real, no longer a figment of imagination. The characters have become close to reality, if not the reality itself. In recent times

**Associate Professor, Department of Psychology,*
Vasanta College for Women (Affiliated to BHU, Varanasi),
KFI, Rajghat, Varanasi – 221 001

we have seen some remarkable films where the woman is not merely eye candy or a supporting character but the main hero that drives the story. Hindi cinema, mainstream or otherwise boasts of several talented female filmmakers who make the cinema have not restricted themselves to mere women oriented themes but also for other valuable subjects.

The view that humans are social creatures was expressed perhaps most clearly by the sixteenth-century English poet John Donne who wrote "no man is an island, sufficient unto himself". We influence others and are influenced in turn by them. Obviously males and females differ biologically in their genitals and other aspects of anatomy and in their psychological functioning. Many social Psychologists separate psychological **Identity** or **self-concept** into two parts namely **personal identity** and **Social Identity** (**Brewer and Brown,** 1998; **Ellemers, Speares** and **Doosje,** 2002; **Verkuyten,** 2005). Our personal identity is the part of our psychological make-up that distinguishes us as a unique individual. Our social identity refers to our sense of ourselves as a member of the various families, Kinship, religious, national, and social groups to which we belong. We might refer to this part of our identity by saying, "I am a Hindu... I am a computer engineer....I am an Indian......I am a teacher....I am a film actress/actor or I am a woman/man.... and so on.

Social change is change in established pattern of social relations, or change in social values, or change in structures and subsystems operating in society. Social change may be partial or total, though mostly in partial. Total change hardly ever happens. **Percy Cohen** (1979) has said that one might also distinguish between minor changes and major or fundamental changes in a society. Change in the core or strategic features of a society or a social system may be defined as major change. The status of women has been the central concern of many reform movements before and after independence.

In the 60 years since Independence, Indian cinema has gone through a lot of changes including a shift from classic mythological blockbusters to Bollywood type remakes of Hollywood's successful films. **Women** in the Indian film industry have played an important role in the success of individual films. Their roles however have changed overtime, from being dependent on their male counterparts to very independently carrying the storyline forward. Before referring to the changes, it is relevant to understand the importance of Indian Cinema in the world today. According to studies and surveys with available records, Indian films are screened in over a hundred countries and watched by nearly four billion people worldwide. The Indian film industry is considered to be the largest film industry in the world with over 1000 films produced each year in more than 20 languages where Hollywood produces less than 400 films per year.

Bollywood, a part of the Indian film industry located in Mumbai, can be called the national film industry as it produces the most watched films in Hindi language.

Mumbai has been the largest film centre in the world, although Calcutta and Madras in India compete vigorously. The Bollywood film industry has derived its name from the American film industry, Hollywood. It is one of the most popular and successful industries and amazes most people even though half of the cinemas are found in the southern part of India.

One questions arises then why Mumbai chosen as a center and how did it became so popular? Well the reason lies in the fact that Mumbai was appropriate as the centre of importance for the Indian cinema industry. It had modern port; a city with European influences and pretensions minimal to Indian history and society. In addition it appeared neutral to the religious passions of South Asia, the great Hindu-Muslim clashes. All races and religions lived in Mumbai in relative harmony. It was in Mumbai that English drama and poetry flourished. A number of Western ideas that were English-stimulated synthesized with the Indian ideas. Thus the demons, avatars, gods and spirits of three thousand years of Indian mythology mixed and came into contact with contemporary Western, Marx, ideas and icons.

The first women to act in Indian films in the 1920s were women of mixed British, European and Indian origins referred to as the "Anglo-Indians". Since they had hybrid origins, they were deemed separate from the women of pure Indian origin (**Ganti, 2004**). There was a stigma associated with Indian women acting and in the context of this social stigma, when Indian women began to act, directors, in order to conform to social norms might have been pressured to portray Indian women leads as characters that lives within the confines of society even in the films. In Indian cinema, this is probably the beginning of the idea of having to necessarily cater to audience needs and conform to existing value systems.

Ganti (2004) reported that in the very early days of cinema when Phalke was beginning to make films, women were not willing to act due to the stigma attached to public performance. Acting, singing or dancing for an audience was associated with prostitutes and courtesans, and so were outside the boundaries of decent society.

According to Manusmriti which had a profound effect on shaping the morals of Indian society, a female should be subject in childhood to her father, in youth to her husband, and when her husband is dead, to her children...women were given no kind of independence...She is told to be cheerful, efficient in the management of household affairs, fastidious in cleaning utensils, careful with expenses... these norms governed the lives of women in traditional India and they find clear articulation in Indian cinema, especially in popular films (**Gokulsing and Dissanayake, 2004**).

Braudy and Cohen (2004) reported that in the early phase of Indian cinema women were represented as absolutely "pure" wives through the epical characters or sometimes they visualized as ideal girlfriends, self-sacrificing mothers, sisters and daughters or they were immoral prostitutes, cabaret dancers, and strippers. In early Indian Cinematic context herself heroine had not the slightest importance, she was the one, or rather the love or fear she inspired in the hero.

In colonial era, at early phase of Indian cinema apparently women also reflected as 'ideal house wife.' In the films '**Sati Charitra**' (1920), ' **Sati Laxmi**' (1924), '**Dharmo Laxmi**' (1926), 'Ma' (1933), ' **Annapurna Mandir**' (1935), etc. In early Indian Cinematic context though the women represented as ideal wives those who were always proved themselves as good-pure-dedicating wives and self sacrificing- concern mothers but those 'ideal wives' projected as only suffering, self -sacrificing, devoting childbearing image and also incapable, helpless and controlled by patriarchal social structure.

Bhasin (1993) suggested that from a feminist view point it is observed that further patriarchy not only forces women to the mothers, it is also determined the conditions of their motherhood. This ideology of motherhood is one of the bases of women's oppression because it is created feminine and masculine character types which perpetuate patriarchy; it is created and strengthened the divide between private and public, it has restricted women's mobility and is reproduced male dominations.

Mazumdar (2010) explained that in the mid of **1930's** when Indian films were influenced by the Hollywood film patterns then the word "new women" had been introduced in Indian cinematic context. In the British colonial era, the term "new Woman" referred to modernize women of mixed Indian and Western parentage. The new women were figured on white and semi white bodies that either was suppressed as in the case of the cosmopolitan modern women played by Sulochona in her silent films or remained on the margins of high brow star discourse, as in the case of the stunt star fearless Nadia. It was highly notable that the westernized new women might be represented as protagonist but their self identity, enlightenment, jurisdiction; individuality could not be visualized on screen. In this context we discuss about Nadia who was famous as "**Fearless Nadia**". She was the actor of '**Haunterwalli**' (1935), **Miss Frontier Mail** (1936), Diamond Queen (1940) etc. It was really remarkable that the film 'Haunterwali' Nadia played the role's of brave Indian girls, who sacrificed royal luxuries for her people and her country. So from feminist dialect fearless Nadia was significant character who was not ideal wife or mother or not represented as epic character, seemingly she was fearless, stout-bodied and challenged to patriarchal dominancy (**Thomas, 2012).**

1930's to 1940's was the significant era of Indian National movement. With the emergence of nationalism and patriotism some social issues like untouchability, women education, demand of equal rights of women etc. were associated with Anti British movement. Women's India Association (**WIA**), The National Council of Indian Women (**NCIW**), All India Women's Conference (**AIWC**), was formed between the periods of 1920 to 1930. All these organizations concerned themselves with eradicating the social problems of women and educating them. At the same time the strong nationalist trend also ran through them. Women from all walks for live flocked to the national struggle in response to the Gandhi's call, in Civil Disobedience Movement and in symbolic gestures of protest just as **Salt Satyagraha**, **Harijan**

movement. **Gandhi** used several ideological prongs to mobilize people (many of them were women and dalit). There included a commitment of equal rights of women, untouchability, and as a corollary equal social responsibility which amalgamated with the National struggles. In that particular era Indian filmmakers were could not denied the national inspirations and the social movements and those were selected as the milieu of their creativity.

1936 was the significant era of Hindi cinema because Himanshu Rai's '**Acchutkanya**' generated social protest against untouchability. However, the idealistic core of the film centered on love affairs but the heroine represented to the untouchable lower cast and the hero represented to the Brahmin cast. Director visualized to heroine in different viewpoints, she not only criticized to the cast system but she condemned traditional forms of medicine, impersonal law of the state.

Kaul (1995) reported that after the screening of 'Acchutkanya' **Pandit Jawharlal Nehru,** wrote a letter to **Devika Rani**. He addressed "the film was highly acclaimed for it is serious theme of the problem of cast system and untouchability, especially as it was responding to contemporary discussions initiated by Gandhi and other reformist." It was true that 'Acchutkanya (1936)' created remarkable impact in Indian film Industry. After 1936 directors were excided from conventional methods of representation of women. The emphasis slowly shifted from the beautiful face to the body, from a mere shadow like chattel to nourished male fantasies to a person of flesh and blood. The seeds were sown by Shanta Apte. She was the first screen woman to rebel against marriage.

1950's to 1980's was the significant period of India's film industry. In the pre colonial era, especially in 1930's to 1940's while India's national and social movements made an enormous impact on Indian films, consequently in the beginning of 1950's contemporary socio- economic and political turmoil reflected in alternative films and in majority Indian alternatives film directors had been chosen to women as subjects of their films, where women highlighted as flesh-blood women those who were the integral part of contemporary socio-economic and political unrests. Might be women characters visualized as mothers, wives, daughters but they were not confined between the symbols of idealness and purity their human natures, struggles, subjugations, jealousy, desires, selfishness, portrayed with reality on screen. In between fifties to eighties directors brought out women as protagonists from margin to the centre of film scripts.

The golden era of Bollywood films was from the 1950s to the late 1970s. This was the time when, an India, which was rural but had rich and vibrant traditions, was portrayed. Films showcased the relationships, customs, norms and ethics of Indian society. The issue of poverty was addressed during this time. The audiences could easily identify themselves with the on-screen characters whose lives reminded them of their own. Some examples of films from this era include Kaagaz Ke Phool, Mother India, Pakeezah, Half Ticket, and Padosan. There are a few films from this golden era of Bollywood film-industry so popular that people from the later generation still remember them. This was also the time when the women were playing a very important role in the films holding a lot of responsibility on their shoulders to sell the films in the market. Women were given an equally dominant role in the Hindu films along with the male actors. A few examples include *Mother India* made in 1957 by **Mehboob**. The film was made ten years after India gained independence from the British rule. In this film the director, Mehboob, attempts to combine socialistic ideals with the traditional values.

The theme of marriage, being married, performing the roles and functions of the typical Indian wife, conforming to the rules of family, being the perfect mother, wife, daughter, daughter-in-law, etc. were all central to Indian film stories. Belonging to a patriarchal social structure and enacting the role of a woman in the confines of this structure and social order became the role of women in cinema as well. **Chakravarty** (1989), commenting on realism in Indian films says, "A woman's social and individual identities are therefore both conferred by marriage... while part of this has a dramatic function the overall traditional attitude to women remains in place."

The socio-cultural context imposes roles on women and these roles are carried onto cinema. This is where the persuasion theory of alter casting enters this discussion. According to **Terry and Hogg (**2000), this theory suggests, when a person accepts a certain social role, a number of social pressures are brought to bear to insure that the role is enacted. The social environment expects the person to behave in a manner that is consistent with the role; the role also provides the person with selective exposure to information consistent with the role. Alter-casting means that we 'force' an audience to accept a particular role that makes them behave in the way we want them to behave.

As opposed to the portrayal of women as ideal wives and mothers, the other popular portrayal is the exact opposite characterization, that of the vamp. "She flouts tradition, seeks to imitate Western women...drinks, smokes, visits nightclubs, is quick to fall out of love...portrayed as a morally degraded person...unacceptable for her behavior... punished for it" **(Gokulsing and Dissanayake, 2004)**. One of the most popular actresses to play vamp was an Anglo-Indian actress named **Helen Jairag Richardson**. She played the sexy stripper, the vamp, the cabaret dancer at the bar, etc. Helen was always considered best suited for the vamp role and never played a heroine or main female lead ever. So this stigma attached to the vamp seems to have an impact on the careers of actresses in the industry. Once a vamp, always a vamp! However, it is not clear if directors specifically chose to avoid asking Helen to play heroine because of the "vamp" stigma or because there may not have been as many good actresses (who also should be good dancers) around to play vamp.

Another popular portrayal is the anti-stereotype character of the courtesan dancer.

According to **Ganti (2004)**, courtesans were women who knew and performed songs and dances in the courts of kings, were well versed with poetry and literature and possessed tactful and engaging conversational skills; they were patronized by the ruling elite. Unlike prostitutes, they had a lot more control over their bodies and entered into monogamous physical relationships with their patrons. However, the British who were trying to displace this very ruling elite considered courtesans part of this elite and in an attempt to reduce their power and influence, started using them as prostitutes for British soldiers in India, stripping them off their socio-cultural status.

It appears that what happened to courtesan dancers in reality (stripped of their status, riches and emotions), happens to them in popular films as well—they are simply characters used by the male leads, and they have no more additional value.

Dwyer (2005), in her analysis of popular Indian film comments on the highest grossing film of the decade (1960-69), ***Mughal-E-Azam*** 1960, in which Anarkali, a courtesan dancer in the court of Mughal emperor Akbar, and Salim, son of King Akbar, fall in love. For the crime of love, the two of them are sentenced to death by the emperor. Salim is killed and Anarkali is buried alive although Akbar lets her escape through a secret tunnel. She says, "Film brings out themes that are popular in Hindi Film...struggle between public duty and private desire the self-sacrificing woman". The courtesan dancer is stripped off her status and emotions for having fallen in love with the prince who belongs to the ruling elite.

However, over the years women's roles in films have evolved and many blockbuster films have featured women in important roles. These roles give women ample screen time and performance time. But the important question is what these roles imply and how that might have an effect on viewers. As **Butalia (1984)** says, however a starting point may be that in spite of increased visibility, Indian women are not in general autonomous and self-defined in the films. This is not surprising given that 90 percent of the directors and producers are men. It is not an oversimplification to say that in popular Indian cinema women are seen very much in bad or good roles. The good ones are, more often than not (self-sacrificing) mothers, (dutiful) daughters, (loyal) sisters or (obedient and respectful) wives. They support, comfort and very seldom question their men. They are self-sacrificing and above all pure on the other side of the coin modernity often seems to be equated with being bad. Bad women, other than being modern, are often single, sometimes widowed. They may be westernized (synonymous with being fast and 'loose'), independent (a male preserve), aggressive (a male quality) and they may even smoke and drink. Often they will wear western clothes but the moment they suffer a change and reform their ways, they will clad themselves in a sari and cover their heads. There are, of course, exceptions to the above stereotypes, but they remain exceptions.

While courtesan dancers are one end of the spectrum, the vamps are on the other end. As discussed earlier, these are the women who would be cabaret dancers in bars and pubs, the cigarette-smoking, sexily clad, sensuous women who are open about their sexuality and easily flirt with and entertain either the male protagonist or the male antagonist in the film. Some of the most popular actresses who have played these roles in films were **Helen Jairag Richardson, Aruna Irani** and **Bindu Zaveri** from the 70s and 80s. While they have played vamp, two actresses, **Zeneth Aman** and **Parveen Babi** have played the relatively more unconventional female leads – relatively more westernized in their outlook as characters, more daring wardrobe and sensuous dance sequences.

According to **Das (2007)** - Parveen Babi (April 4, 1949 – January 20, 2005), was one of the most successful Bollywood actresses in the 1970s and was known for her portrayal of strong women who did not care about the conventional norms of society. She was the first Indian actress to have featured on **TIME** magazine's cover, in 1975.

In *Sholay* 1975, an all time blockbuster Hindi film, Helen makes only a special appearance as a gypsy dancer with a very sexy costume and dances as the male antagonist of the film watches her. One could compare that to the present day bar dancer, stripper, etc. only that it was done in the "gypsy" context at the time. The audience would look at **Helen**, her costumes and her moves as being justified by the theory that she is just a gypsy woman who is entertaining men out of her choice to do so. Many a time vamps become entertainers for the antagonist and at times even partner them and this further strengthens the idea of their being "bad" and "immoral". On the right is the heroine **Hemamalini,** sprawled out, with specific shots aimed at her hips during the entire sequence of the song, but this in the minds of the audience, is legitimised exposure because in the sequence she is dancing for the very desirous antagonist in order to be able to save the lives of the male heroes of the film. Although the shots used on Helen and Hemammalini, showing their hips and stomachs might seem to have similar effects on the viewer, the perceptions of these shots are very different because the contexts in which the heroine is objectified and the gysy woman/vamp is objectified vary greatly. Even in the film *Sholay,* there are two heroines with very opposing characteristics. One is the very talkative, boisterous but yet projected as homely and the hero's love interest, and the other is the widow, very quiet, introverted and portrayed as submissive and timid through the film. The role of the talkative woman is played by Hemamalini and the widow by **Jaya Bhadhuri**. Both the roles, though opposing in nature, clearly conform to the social norms of how a woman should behave and how a widow should behave. Dwyer (2005) comments on film *Sholay* 1975, the highest grossing film in Indian film history, "Hemamalini shines as the chatterbox 9tonga-driver who is forced to dance for Gabbar's sadistic enjoyment, while Jaya is silent apart from the flashback to the family's 10Holi party".

In the film *Tezaab* 1988, **Madhuri Dixit** is the heroine but her clothes are similar to the vamps of the 1970s. Such sensuous songs are usually referred to as "item numbers", item referring sometimes in a derogatory fashion and sometimes in a sexy and sensual fashion to the woman who is dancing. In the 1970s, these item numbers are mostly the work of the vamps and bar dancers. In the 80s, this demarcation becomes hazy and the heroines perform these item numbers themselves, but in a manner that conveniently bridges the dissonance in the perceptions of the Madonna and the whore. For instance, in the film *Khalnayak* 1993, Madhuri Dixit, is the main female lead. She is a police officer, who goes undercover as a prostitute, in order to clear the reputation of her Police officer boyfriend, Ram. She is not a prostitute but a police officer, under-cover, (which is not the main point here), trying to save her boyfriend. Since she is trying to save the male protagonist and the audience knows her mission, anything that she does becomes acceptable under those circumstances.

In recent times we have seen some remarkable films where the woman is not merely eye candy or a supporting character but the main hero that drives the story. For example: No One Killed Jessica, Dirty Picture, Kahani, English Winglish, Heroine etc.

In film "*No One Killed Jessica*" two female protagonists get together to fight for justice. The film solely rests on the two female leads that are fearless fighters and epitome of strength. Especially Vidya Balan as the sister of the slain model portrays courage to fight the system rather than give in and mourn the circumstances. The film was highly appreciated for its treatment and the characterization of the women which serves as encouragements to the women of entire nation.

In film "*Dirty Picture*" Vidya Balan play the lead role with much confidence and ease. She comfortably slips into the character of an actress who lives life on her terms and conditions, is unashamed and outspoken. As the film traces the rise and fall of the actress, her love affairs and heartbreaks, Vidya steals the show with her punchy dialogs, confidence about her sensuality and no-nonsense attitude. Dirty picture was a film which won her the national award and duly so and had men only as supporting character with the lady being the real hero.

Another remarkable film *Kahani* which showcases the inner strength of a woman and how that woman (she) is undeterred by situations. Kahani is the story of a pregnant woman out to find her missing husband and how she braves all odds to arrive at the bottom of it all. Once again **Vidya Balan** aces the role with a compelling performance that was received by one and all. On the one hand you pity the lady expecting a child but on the hand you cannot stop yourself from being awestruck at her determination and heroism. Truly it is an iconic film driven by its unique concept and leading actress.

A famous movie *English Winglish* is the story of an ordinary housewife whose confidence and self esteem get a boost owing to her own willingness and determination. **Sridevi** makes the character her very own and encourages every woman to command the respect she truly deserves.

Heroine the movie Directed by **Madhur Bhandarkar** throws light on the life of a film star which is often shielded away from the common man. But an actress too has her share of triumphs and despairs, affairs and heartbreaks like every normal woman, only that every move of hers is under scrutiny. Kareena Kapoor one gets to see the rise and fall of an actress and the story of her personal life. Though the film did not succeed commercially, it did achieve the purpose of showcasing the tough life behind the glamour through the eyes of a superstar herself.

There was a time when a female filmmaker's ability was questioned and there were not people ready to back her, but those were days of the past. Women today make the cinema they believe in and that too with the backing of not just top notch producers but the entire film fraternity. And these filmmakers have not restricted themselves to mere women-oriented themes but their gamut of cinema extends far and wide. From stalwarts like Sai Paranjpye, Kalpana Lajmi, Aparna Sen, Deepa Mehta, Mira Nair, Ashima Chibbar, Sonam Nair, Reema Kagti, Farah Khan, Zoya Akhtar, Kiran Rao, Gauri Shinde and some other famous directors who proved their self in Bollywood Cinema.

Conclusion

This paper can be criticized on a few counts such as there could have been other approaches to studying this subject. There is lots of literature available for Indian Cinema but lack of references. There are many ways to pick and choose from Indian cinema in order to analyze the roles given to women in cinema. The emphasis in this paper on very few films which highlights the woman characters in the Indian cinema. In conclusion this paper has found evidence in various forms, enough to say that women in Indian cinema have stereotyped roles. There was a time when a female filmmaker's ability was questioned and there were not people ready to back her, but those were days of the past. Women today make the cinema they believe in and that too with the backing of not just top notch producers but the entire film fraternity.

References

Bhasin (1993). What is patriarchy? Kali for Women: New Delhi, pp. 8.

Braudy and Cohen (2004). Film Theory and Criticism, Sixth Edition, Oxford University Press.

Brewer, M. B., and Brown, R. J. (1998). Intergroup relations. In D. T. Gillbert, S. T. Fiske, and G. Lindzey (Eds.), *The handbook of social psychology* (4th ed., Vol. 2, pp. 554-594). Boston: McGraw-Hill.

Butalia, U. (1984). Women in Indian Cinema. *Feminist Review*(17), 108-110.

Chakravarty. S, S. (1989). National Identity and the realist aesthetic: Indian cinema of the fifties. *Quarterly Review of film and video* (11), 31-48.

Das, J. (2007, July 13). A woman who was much ahead of the conventional norms of the society. *News India - Times*, 16.

Dwyer, R. (2005). *100 Bollywood Films*. London: British Film Institue.

Ellemers, N., Spears, R., Doosje, B. (2002). Self And social identity. *Annual Review of Psychology, 53,* 161-186.

Ganti, T. (2004). *Bollywood: Guidebook to popular Hindi Cinema.* London, New York: Routeledge.

Kaul (1995). Cinema and Indian Freedom struggle, pp. 40.

Mazumdar, N. (2010). "Spectatorial desires and the Hiearchies of stardom, in the book ' Wanted cultured ladies only; Female stardom and cinema in Indian, 1930s-1950s.' Oxford University Press, New Delhi, pp. 94.

Terry, J. D. (Ed.). (2000). *Attitudes, Behavior, and social context: The role of norms andgroup membership.* Mahwah, NJ: L. Earlbaum Associates.

Thomas, R. (2012). Fearless Nadia, Queen of the Stunts, in the book Women Contesting Cultures, Changing frames of Gender Politics India. Edited by Panjabi Kavita and Chakraborty Paromita. Stree publication, Kolkata, pp. 33.

Verkuyten, M. (2005). Ethnic group identification and group evaluation among minority and majority groups: Testing the multiculturalism hypothesis. *Journal of Personality and Social Psychology, 88,* 121-138.

Books

Ahmed, S. Akbar (1992). 'Bombay Films: The Cinema as Metaphor for Indian Society and Politics'. *Modern Asian Studies* 26, 2 (I992), pp. 289-320. Great Britain.

Burra, R. (ed.) (1981). 'Film India: Looking Back 1896-1960'. The Direc torate of Film Festivals, New Delhi.

Husain, S. (1989). 'Cinema', in Robinson.

Bagchi, Amitabha. (1996). Women in Indian Cinema. Retrieved from http://www.cs.jhu.edu/~bagchi/women.html

Laura Mulvey (1988). 'Visual Pleasure and Narrative Cinema'. In Con stance Penley (ed), *Feminism and Film Theory*, New York: Routledge.

Mahmood, S and Mitra, M (2011). Bollywood sets sights on wider market. BBC Asian Network, 24 June 2011. Retrieved from http://www.bbc. co.uk/news/business-13894702

Misra, Vijay (2006). 'Bollywood Cinema: A Critical Genealogy'. Asian Studies Institute, Victoria University of Wellington.

Monica Motwani (1996). *The Changing Face of the Hindi Film* Heroine, G Magazine Online.

Singh, Indubala (2007). Gender Relations and Cultural Ideology in Indian Cinema: A Study of Select Adaptations of Literary Texts, Deep and Deep Publications.

Spotlight on India's entertainment economy: Seizing new growth opportunities, Ernst and Young report, 2011.

Woke (2007). Bollywood vs Hollywood – The Complete Breakdown, Advertising and Marketing, Bollywood, Business and Industry. Retrived on 29 March 2009 from http://mutiny.wordpress. com/2007/02/01/bollywood-vs-hollywood-the-complete-break down.

'Update on Indian M and E industry.' *CRISIL Research*, December 2010.

Chapter 14

Contribution of Assamese Film Director Rupkonwar Jyoti Prasad Agarwala in Indian Cinema

*Bala Lakhendra**

The father of Assamese film and a great artist Rupkonwar Jyoti Prasad Agarwala will be remembered as the pioneer of Assamese Film who happened to be the first director, producer, and musician of the first film of Assam Joymati. A person whose ancestors has their original origin to Marwar of Rajasthan contributed so much to his birthplace Assam that there are hardly few other names in Assam which come closer to him. He is no other than Rupkonwar Jyoti Prasad Agarwala. He started writing since the age of 14 years only. At that time he wrote down the famous play 'Sonit-Konwari'. Some other plays written by him are Rupalim, KarengarLigiri, Lobhita, etc. He was a fantastic poet as well. He wrote more than 300 songs and gave music to most of them. These songs collection is known as Jyoti Sangeet. The most valuable gift of Jyoti Prasad Agarwala to Assamese world is 'Joymoti', the first cinema. He is the father of Assamese film and he has invested huge amount of time and his own money into it. In 1935 the movie was released. In 1939 he made the second Assamese movie 'Indramalati'. He also built a cinema hall 'Junaki' in

**Sr. Asstt. Professor*
Department of Journalism and Mass Communication,
Banaras Hindu University, Varanasi – 221 005
e-mail: lakhendra_bala@yahoo.com

tezpur in 1937. Along with 'Kalaguru' Bishnu Prasad Rabha, he produced the record play of 'Joymoti' and 'SonitKonwari'. His dramas, poems, short stories, journalistic writings, songs and music have inspired generations not only in Assam but also in the North-East region. His songs and music are popularly known as "Jyoti Sangeet".

Whenever we talk about the list of films produced in the decade of the 1930s. We find there are only two films released in this decade, the first Assamese Film Joymati in 1935, under the banner of Chitralekha Movietone. The second picture Indramalati filmed between 1937 and 1938 and released in 1939. He is believed to have been the first director to introduce playback singing in Indian cinema. Through Assamese film Rupkonwar Jyoti Prasad Agarwala gave a wider arena to the Indian Cinema which will be remembered for a long period.

Jyoti Prasad Agarwala and his Childhood

Jyoti Prasad Agarwala was born in 17 June, 1903 in Tamulbari Tea Estate ofDibrugarh. His father was ParamanadaAgarwala and mother was Kiranmayee. Rupkonwar's forefathers hailed from the village of Tai in the erstwhile princely state of Jaipur. They belonged to a wealthy merchant family whose substantial wealth invited the envy and wrath of the local zamindar who persecuted the family and forced them to flee to Churu in destitution. In 1828 Rupkonwar's great grandfather Naba-rangaram Agarwala, then a teenager, was the first from the family to come to Assam. When Naba-rangaram arrived in Assam he had nothing but a burning determination to recoup the lost fortunes of his forefathers.

Jyoti Prasad Agarwala and his Family

In 1830 NabarangaramAgarwala (1811-1865) started a small shop in Gomiri, a remote village located on the north bank of the river Brahmaputra in the eastern part of Assam. With his business acumen, enterprise and labour he prospered rapidly. But more significantly he chose to assimilate and integrate completely into the local Assamese community through marriage and adopted their language and culture, followed their customs and merged with the local way of life. However, unlike many who at that time had migrated to Assam for work or business, married local girls and adopted local titles, Nabarangaram decided to retain his original title "Agarwala". By the time he died in 1865 he had not only laid the foundation of a business empire, become a prominent personality of the then Assamese community but also spawned a lineage that would henceforth enrich the socio-cultural fabric of the State and contribute significantly to the building of modern Assam.

Nabarangaram's eldest son HaribilashAgarwala (1842-1916) continued his father's legacy of assimi-lation, enterprise, patriotism and social service. He was the doyen of the family and took the family fortunes to new heights. But he also made significant contributions to the development of trade and industry in Assam despite being discriminated against by the British administration, propagated Assamese literature and culture and actively involved himself in community development. He made an invaluable contribution to the Assamese language and literature when in 1899 he published for the first time ever the ancient hand-written manuscripts of Sri Sankardev and Sri Madhabdev. This exposed the rich literary and cultural heritage of Assam to the outside world and to the new generation of Assamese scholars and litterateurs. This singular effort gave a big boost to the movement for the revival and recognition of the Assamese language which till then was considered as an off-shoot of the Bengali language. By the turn of the century, because of British discrimination against native entrepreneurs, he was drawn to the Indian National Congress.

Later Haribilash's second eldest son Chandra Kumar Agarwala (1867-1938) and nephew Ananda Chandra Agarwala (1874-1939) influenced the growth of Assamese language and literature. Particularly Chandra Kumar Agarwala who, as an undergraduate student of Presidency College, Calcutta, spearheaded the movement for the revival and recognition of the Assamese language. A pioneer of Assamese journalism, he published in 1889 the first Assamese literary journal *Jonaki* and in 1918 launched the Assamese newspaper *Asomiya*. *Asomiya* successfully spread the awareness about the struggle for Indian independence in Assam.

Even though like other MarwarisJyoti Prasad Agarwala's forefather came to Assam seeking a fortune, unlike them NabarangaramAgarwala set a unique example of socio-cultural integration of two communities from two opposite corners of the country, the northwest and the northeast. This is an extraordinary case of patriotism, contributing towards a community's uplift and national integration which has few parallels in India.

Jyoti Prasad Agarwala and his Education

He started his education from Tezpur. He studied in Tezpur Government High School and completed his matriculation. During high school time itself he joined the freedom movement. After matriculation he joined National College of Calcutta and completed his I.A from there. For his graduation he went to Edinburgh University, Britain. He also joined his M.A. studybut before finishing it out of his interest in film he went to Germany for studying films.

Jyoti Prasad Agarwala and Freedom Struggle

During high school time itself he joined the freedom movement. Jyoti Prasad Agarwala's actual artistic and political journey begins after 1930. He dedicated himself fully in the freedom movement. He was even jailed for 15 months and fined Rupees 500 for his active involvement in the Independence movement. But he parallely kept on working on the art culture front and also for the upliftment of the Assamese society. He was a firebrand freedom fighter and revolutionary. A scion of one of the wealthiest and most illustrious families of Assam, he joined the freedom movement while still a student in his teens. However, from 1930 after returning from the Edinburgh University and Germany where he studied Economics and Film-making respectively, he plunged into the freedom movement with the blessings of Mahatma Gandhi when Gandhiji came to Tezpur and stayed at their ancestral home "Poki". He formed the "MrityuBahini" (Death Squad) on the principles of non-violence but with the motto *"KarengayyaMarengay"*. His patriotic songs were the inspiration behind the struggle for Indian independence in the region. During the 'Quit India' movement of 1942, under his fearless leadership people, particularly in north Assam, came out and courageously faced British bullets and many, like schoolgirl Kanaklata, MukundaKakoty etc., embraced martyrdom while trying to hoist the tricolour in places like Gohpur, Sootea, Tezpur and Dhekiajuli. He was also jailed and to escape imprisonment (so that he could continue guiding the independence movement) he had to frequently remain underground.

Jyoti Prasad Agarwala and his Writings

Jyoti Prasad Agarwalastarted hiswriting since the age of 14 years only. At that time he wrote down the famous play 'Sonit-Konwari'. For next few years during his student days he wrote many short stories. He was very good in studying children psychology. He wrote many stories for children. Some other plays written by him are Rupalim, KarengarLigiri, Lobhita, etc. His plays are acted on stage till date in Assam. Jyoti Prasad Agarwala was a fantastic poet as well. He wrote more than 300 songs and gave music to most of them. These songs collection is known as JyotiSangeet. It bacame a new genre of music itself in Assam in later days.Another contribution of Jyotiprasadagarwala is the publication of the newspaper 'Axomiya' in 1944. He also established an assamese music school in Tezpur.

Jyoti Prasad Agarwala and Assamese Film

Joymoti or *Joimoti* (Assamese), released on 10 March 1935, was the first Assamese film made. Based on LakshminathBezbaroa's play about the 17th-century Ahom princess SotiJoymoti, the film was produced and directed by the noted Assamese poet, author, and film-maker Jyoti Prasad Agarwala, and starred AideuHandique and acclaimed stage actor and playwright PhaniSarma. The film, shot between 1933 and 1935, was released by ChitralekhaMovietone in 1935 and marked the beginning of Assamese cinema.Set in 17th-century Assam, the film recounts the sacrifice of Joymoti, an Ahomprincess tortured and killed by the Ahom king Borphukan for refusing to betray her husband Gadapani by disclosing his whereabouts. The event is interpreted in contemporary patriotic terms, and calls for a greater harmony between the people of the hills and those of the plains. The hills are represented by the leader Dalimi, a Naga tribeswoman who shelters the fugitive Prince Gadapani.

On his way back from England, Jyoti Prasad Agarwala spent about six months at the UFA Studios in Berlin, learning film-making. Once back in Assam, he decided to make his first film. He established Chitraban Studios at the Bholaguri Tea Estate. Two camps were established: one near the Manager's Bungalow for the female artists, and the other near the tea factory for the male artists. Tea was manufactured by day, and by night actors performed at their rehearsals. Members of the cast were encouraged to keep up their physical exercises to stay fit.

A special property room was constructed, in which Jyoti Prasad Agarwala collected traditional costumes, ornaments, props, hats, etc. This grew into a museum. Technicians were brought in from Lahore; ice, transported from Calcutta.

The film was taken to Dhaka for editing, at which stage Agarwala discovered there was no sound for one half of the film. Unable to marshal the actors once again from their native places due to various constraints, he hired a sound studio and dubbed the voices of all male and female characters. On a single day, he recorded six thousand feet of film.

Joymoti was the wife of the Ahom prince Gadapani. During the Purge of the Princes from 1679 to 1681 under King Sulikphaa (LoraaRoja), instigated by LaluksolaBorphukan, Gadapani took flight. Over the next few years, he sought shelter at Sattras (Vaishnav monasteries) and the adjoining hills outside the Ahom kingdom. Failing to trace Prince Gadapani, Sulikphaa's soldiers brought his wife Joymoti to JerengaPathar where, despite brutal and inhuman torture, the princess refused to reveal the whereabouts of her husband. After continuous physical torture over 14 days, Joymoti breathed her last on 13 Choit of 1601 Saka, or 27 March, AD 1680.

Joymoti's self-sacrifice would bear fruit in time: Laluk was murdered in November 1680 by a disgruntled body of household retainers. The ministers, now roused to a sense of patriotism, sent out search parties for Gadapani who, gathering his strength, returned from his exile in the Garo Hills to oust Sulikphaa from the throne. Joymoti had known that her husband alone was capable of ending Sulikphaa-Laluk's reign of terror. For her love and her supreme sacrifice for husband and country, folk accounts refer to her as a *Soti*.

The film was released on 10 March 1935, at the Raonak Theatre, and was inaugurated by the Assamese writer Lakshminath Bezbarua. In Guwahati, it was screened at the Kumar Bhaskar Natya Mandir, the only cinema in Assam which then had sound. The film was not well received, consequently suffering a debilitating financial loss. It was able to collect only INR 24,000 from its screenings, less than half its budget of INR 50,000 (at the time), which today amounts to INR 75,00,000.

Joymoti, a study of the culture and history of Assam, carried with it the bright possibility of a film tradition. The significant similarities with the Russian montage reflect an element of influence. The film is noted for its constantly changing angles, unique sets (built from scratch on a tea plantation, with local materials), and other stylistics tactics employed by the imaginative Jyoti Prasad in this his film debut. By then a published poet and writer, his lyricism is clearly evident in this pioneering film.

For all indoor shooting, Jyoti Prasad set up a studio at Bholaguri Tea Estate, near Gohpur, which was owned by the Agarwala family. Named Chitraban, the studio was built using local materials such as wood, bamboo, and banana stumps. The set was artistically designed by Jyoti Prasad himself using bamboo mats, japis of different sizes, deer horns, buffalohorns, and Nâga spears. To furnish the royal court of the Ahoms, he used regal utensils such as maihang, hengdang, bhogjara, bata, sariya, and banbata. He imported a Faizi sound-recording system from Lahore, and the first camera into Assam from Mehta of Calcutta.The unit arrived at Bholaguri Tea Estate in December 1933 to commence filming, and camped in front of the garden factory. Jyoti Prasad arranged all accommodation arrangements personally, and set up a laboratory for developing film by the side of his 'Chitraban' studio.

According to NatasuryaPhaniSarma, who played a key role in the film, Chitraban was not merely a studio, but a film-training institute in itself. Apart from the acting, Jyoti Prasad also taught his actors certain film-making techniques—such as developing, processing, printing, and editing—and shared with them his knowledge of various film shots like mixed shot, fade out, zoom, dissolve, back projection, and model shooting. The 17th-century costumes used in the film were designed by Jyoti Prasad, and the make-up was done by the actors themselves, assisted by Sonitkowar Gajen Borua.

Although shooting at the Chitraban Studio started in April 1933, it faced an initial delay as Jyoti Prasad was unable to find a suitable young woman to play "Joymoti", as well as actors for a few other roles. He floated newspaper advertisements for actors and actresses, mentioning brief outlines of the film and descriptions of the characters. His idea was to get 'types' for his characters, not seasoned actors, even offering remunerations for successful candidates. One of his preconditions was that potential actors needed to be from 'respectable' families, as opposed to red-light areas, as had been the case during the 1930s in Calcutta. This was inspired by Jyoti Prasad's desire to liberate cinema from that "uncertain" reputation. After a prolonged search and detailed interviews, he discovered Aideu Handique in a remote village near Golaghat, for the role of Joymoti: she was to become the first actress of Assamese cinema. He then brought together the other chosen actors, of whom some had never seen a film, to acquaint them with his characters. He sought out a film-making trio, Bhupal Shankar Mehta and the Faizi Brothers from Lahore, as cameraman and sound-recordists.

During filming, the rainy season was to prove a challenge to developments in the technical process, with Jyoti Prasad having to suspend shooting for several days at a time, due to insufficient light in the absence of outdoor electricity. Shooting was carried out under sunlight by using reflectors. When the rain stopped, the banana stumps used to build the splendid Ahom court dried out under the sunlight, yet filming continued - japis ingeniously fastened over the dry patches. Filming was eventually completed in August 1934, and *Joymoti* released in early 1935 after Jyoti Prasad had completed his own editing.

The most valuable gift of Jyoti Prasad Agarwala to Assamese world is 'Joymoti', the first cinema. He is the father of Assamese film and he has invested huge amount of time and his own money into it. He first setup a studio 'Chitrban' in Bholaguri tea estate in Tezpur in 1934. he started making 'Joymati' from there. In 1935 the movie was released. In 1939 he made the second Assamese movie 'Indramalati'. He also built a cinema hall 'Junaki' in tezpur in 1937. Along with 'Kalaguru' Bishnu Prasad Rabha, he produced the record play of 'Joymoti' and 'SonitKonwari'.A list of films produced in the decade of the 1930s. There are only two movies were released in this decade. Rupkonwar Jyotiprasad Agarwala produced the first Assamese Film *Joymati* in 1935, under the banner of Chitralekha Movietone. The second picture *Indramalati* was filmed between 1937 and 1938 finally released in 1939.Just as Jyoti Prasad's Joymoti evokes great interest even today, similarly, it generated immense response from critics and enthusiasts alike right from the time of its inception. Curiosity about films as a medium of entertainment as well as a means of commercial venture arose when people came to know about the proposed attempt of Jyoti Prasad to make the first Assamese film. It is interesting to note how the people responded to Joymoti. Newspapers carried reports about Jyoti Prasad's initiative in trying to make the first Assamese film. They also published shooting reports from the sets itself.

That Jyoti Prasad himself nurtured similar intentions and hopes is evident from his public appeal prior to the release of the film, published in the *Teenidiniya Asamiya* dated March 5, 1935, where he wrote – 'The way Joymoti's illuminating visage has been able to shine through the dark annals of history with the help and co-operation of the people of Assam, in the same way, it is the wish of the writer of this appeal that Joymoti would be able to cross her provincial boundaries and shine all over the different provinces of India. With the help and co-operation of the Assamese people, the glory of the legend of Joymoti would spread all over India, in every household, among her teeming millions of men and women. Through Joymoti, Assam will be reflected in a new light in the whole of India.'

And when on March 10, 1935, Joymoti was premiered in Calcutta's Rownac Hall and consequently released in Guwahati at the Kumar Bhaskar Natya Mandir on March 20, 1935, Gopinath Bordoloi, the then Chairman of the Municipality in Guwahati and who later became the first Chief Minister of independent Assam, penned his comments after viewing Joymoti in the Assamese bi-weekly newspaper, Assamiya in the following words– "The artistic skill of the of the people of Assam in the past, the grandeur of the king's temples, etc. and the costumes of the king, the noblemen and the common people, the weapons used etc. have been so well displayed that anybody who does not see this film will be poorer in his knowledge and appreciation of the life and times of Assam of the bygone days.' He further wrote – 'Assam's lush green fields, Assam's bamboo groves, Assam's betel gardens, Assam's flora and fauna, Assam's hills and mountains, Assam's plains and streams, how wide and wonderful is Assam's Luit, how beautiful are its twinkling stars and its moonlight. The legend of Joymoti can exist only in a land as pure as this. Dalimi can sparkle like an angelic butterfly only in its undulating hills and streams. How can anybody remain at home and refrain oneself from visiting and experiencing this (Madhupuri) wonderland?"

But of course, along with praise came also critical analysis from literary personna like Rajanikanta Bordoloi who termed Joymoti as a *Buranjir Apalap* or a 'Historical Fallacy'. However, apart from a couple of such critical reviews, the overall response to Joymoti was positive. The film was perceived not only as a cultural statement of the Assamese people, which would elevate Assam's prestige in the eyes of the world, but also as an attempt to pave the way for establishing an industry that would involve and generate employment opportunities for men and women of Assam.

In a published article titled – *Asomot Chalachitra* - Films in Assam dated 30/12/33 in the *TeenidiniyaAsamiya*, a person named Nagendra Narayan Coudhury commented on the prospects of films in Assam and mentioned about the attempt undertaken by Jyoti Prasad in making the first ever Assamese film. He wrote - "Films are an exceptional discovery of the 20th century. It is the ultimate manifestation of shadow pictures. Presently, films are not only moving –but talking too. Today, through these talking pictures, we have had the opportunity to see and hear the songs and dances of the male and female singers of America, England or Europe etc, as well as view their realistic acting while sitting in a house in far off Assam. Deserts, seas, mountains, forests, cities, etc. can be presented in front of our eyes in an unprecedented manner. For this reason, in education, sermonising, forming public opinions and other related matters, films have become an indispensable thing. Whether in the myriad display of Nature, whether in the art of acting, whether in the technical dexterity, in every sphere the talking pictures have today overshadowed the bhaona, jatra, theatre and other dramatic presentations, acquiring the topmost position.``A nation is known by its theatre" (meaning through theatre a nation is known) is a quote which has been expressly proved by the bioscope. Admittedly, America's Hollywood has attained the highest position in this art of film-acting. It is followed by German, English and other European artistes. China has also accomplished much in film-acting. Many places in India like Calcutta, Bombay, Madras, Punjab etc. have also made great progress in films. Especially in Calcutta, some films like Puran Bhakat, Mourar Ei have made Bengal proud. However, in many such films, the actors and actresses are from different regions. Although a few Assamese actors have managed to get some opportunity in some outside production houses, Assam, for a long time, even though exposed to the variety of theatres, bioscope of the different regions, their national progress, culture, tradition, creativity and various arts and crafts had remained almost passive. However, such a state of affairs is not forever. Since the last few years, a few young men have had discussions on the possibilities of establishing a film company in Assam. Meanwhile, Kumar Shrijut Pramathesh Baruah from Gauripur had already established a company to shoot bioscope films. However, no Assamese got a chance to express his talents through that company. The said company also did not run for long.

Jyoti Prasad Agarwala and Assamese Film- Indramalti

In 1939 he made the second Assamese movie 'Indramalati'. ***Indramalati*** (Assamese) is the second Assamese language film, directed by Jyotiprasad Agarwala. It was released in 1939. Director Jyotiprasad faced a major financial crisis after his first film *Joymoti* (1935) failed commercially. He spent more than Rs 50,000 and was in debt in the late 1930s; he was fortunate to gather together just Rs 15,000 to make his dream of making a second film come true. Desperately seeking to compensate the loss he incurred in the making of *Joymoti*, he began shooting *Indramalati* in late 1937. This time, however, he did not use his Chitraban Studio for the outdoor shoot. Instead, he chose the 'Talbari' of his family, at Harigaon, two kilometres from Tezpur Mission Chariali. Within seven days, Jyotiprasad completed the outdoor shooting for the picture and often the camera was kept at a fixed point as the sets and artistes kept changing the angles. The film used over 15,000 feet of reel.On release in 1939 it was relatively successful, earning in excess of *Joymati*, aiding Jyotiprasad to go on to direct other films afterwards.

Jyotiprasad himself wrote the story of *Indramalati*, which was a tale of romance. The name of the hero was Indrajit while Malati was the name of the heroine. Significantly, Jyotiprasad was the first filmmaker to introduce the style of movie-making of using the names of the lead pair.

The role of the hero was played by Manoviram Baruah while Raseswari Baruah (Hazarika) was cast as Malati. Acclaimed theatre actor PhaniSarma was again drafted in to play one of the significant roles, that of Indrajit's friend. Even great Assamese musician Dr BhupenHazarika acted in the film and sang "Biswa Bijoyee Navajowan" at only age 13. Unlike casting for his first film, Jyotiprasad faced comparatively less trouble in finding actors for *Indramalati*. There were only nine major roles in *Indramalati*. Besides Manoviram Barua and RaseswariBaruah, the others were PhaniSarma, Thanuram Bora, Lalit Mohan Choudhury, KhargeswarAgarwalla, KashiSaikia, BedanandaSarma and BhupenHazarika. Other actors who were in the film included the Rupkonwar himself, JnanaviramBarua, Mani Lahiri, etc.

After the casting and seven-day outdoor shoot, the eight-member film unit left for Kolkata where they would shoot for the indoor locations. Sets were built in Arora Studio, Narkeldanga, where all the indoor shooting was done. An amazingly short three-day shooting schedule at Arora Studio was followed by the artistes, working hard round the clock. *Indramalati* was produced once again under the banner of 'Chitralekha Movietone and was very much a solo effort in that Jyotiprasad Agarwalla was the director, screenwriter, lyricist, music director, art director, costume designer and editor.

No artistes of *Indramalati*, like *Joymoti*, took remuneration. They even participated in the shooting wearing their own clothes. In some scenes, the costumes fail to maintain continuity.

Jyotiprasad also built a cinema hall 'Junaki' in tezpur in 1937. Along with 'Kalaguru' Bishnu Prasad Rabha, he produced the record play of 'Joymoti' and 'SonitKonwari'. Another contribution of Jyoti Prasad Agarwala is the publication of the newspaper 'Axomiya' in 1944. He also established an assamese music school in Tezpur. Jyoti Prasad Agarwala was a true Assamese in heart.

References

1. Tamuli, Babul (2002). "The making of Joymoti" at the Wayback Machine (archived October 27, 2009), *The Assam Tribune.*
2. The Telegraph - Calcutta (Kolkata) Northeast *Joymoti* goes Hollywood
3. Jyoti Prasad Agarwala and his films
4. Mazid, Altaf (2006). "Joymoti : The first radical film of India", *Himal Magazine*, March 2006.
5. Bora, Prafulla Prasad: "Film Making in Assam", *The Brahmaputra Beckons*, 1982.
6. "History of Assam: The Medieval Period". Govt. of Assam. Retrieved April 18, 2012.

Chapter 15

A Study of Female Portrayal in Satyajit Ray's Movies

*Sanjeeda Bano**

Any form of cultural production be it art, literature or cinema is the reflection of the society in which the creator lives. This reflection is incomplete without the depiction of women and their socio-cultural ethos because women constitute half of the population of any country. Even though the mainstream film focuses on male centered plots, yet the treatment of women have always been a favorite topic for great directors like Satyajit Ray, MrinalSen, AdoorGopalakrishnan and Rituparno Ghosh etc. The picturisation of women which took place from literary texts into films like Binodini in Choker Bali, Paro in Devdas and Rosy in Guide have beautifully put forwarded by their directors and accepted widely by audiences worldwide.

Satyajit Ray (1921-1992)one of the pioneering figures of Indian film industry is a genius who has created his own niche in the arena of world cinema through his films like *Pather Panchali* (1955), *Aparajito* (1956) and *Apur Sansar* (1959), *Devi, Charulata, Mahanagar* etc. The film world of Satyajit Ray would have been incomplete without the depiction of women and their socio economic condition in male dominated society. Having a "director's gaze", he nurtured respect for women and portrayed them as having more strength than men in various roles other than the stereotyped idea of a "woman belonging to the kitchen". Although on the surface level womenin Ray's films depict a society where they are silenced, and where their

**Research Scholar,*
Department of English,
Banaras Hindu University, Varanasi – 221 005
e-mail: sanjeeda999@gmail.com

experience and particular insights are undermined or dismissed. Yet, at deeper level they differ from those women who never revolt against such subjugation, their social backdrops, their positioning within the family and their financial status. His women protest against such marginalization and posit very strong argument for their socio-economic identity.

Born and brought up in Calcutta Ray was very much influenced by its socio-cultural scenario. Ray's portrayals of women are the products of his influences of Indian aesthetic as well as Indian social-historical perspectives. His conception of women is very much formed by the conception of Bengal renaissance. Bengal renaissance which took place in the wake of 19th century created new dimensions for the upliftment and enlightenment of women. Women who were brutally treated by patriarchal system, considered as second sex and being encircled with the prevalent superstitious conditions failed to tear the then-system now began to identify their position and role in the society. They tried to break the boundaries of four walls and showed their caliber and potential in each and every aspects of life. In the liberation of women the roles of Bengali social reformers like Raja Ram Mohan Roy (1772-1833)Ishwar Chandra Vidyasagar (26 September 1820 – 29 July 1891) and Rabindranath Tagore(1861-1941) are immense. Being a student at Shantiniketan and ardent follower of Rabindranath Tagore, Ray tried to expose the-then wretched conditions of women through his movies.Ray' approach to women has a wide variety of background and characterizations. Whether it was the upper middleclass woman in the 19th century Calcutta or the lower middleclass housewife in a 1960s home or a Dalit woman in rural Uttar Pradesh, the Ray women have a personality of their own.

As a director's gaze Ray nurtured respect for women and portrayed them as having more moral strength than men in various roles other than the stereotyped idea of "a woman belonging to the kitchen". In order to do this he does not projects his male characters as negative and hollow to show his women strong and powerful. He gives equal stress to men and women for the proliferation of their thoughts and expressions. The women of Ray belong to variety of backgrounds and characterizations. Be it the upper middleclass woman in the 19th century Calcutta or the lower middleclass housewife of 1960s or the Dalit woman of rural Uttar Pradesh The strongest characterizations came out when Ray started to work on Tagore's women who were coming from culturally rich and talented families.

The first important portrayal of women characterization emerges through the *Charulata* (The Lonely Wife) based on Rabindranath Tagore's story "Nastaneer". The protagonist Charu in *Charalata*is an excellent example of Bengali Renaissance woman. As an educated, skilled and extremely intelligent woman she is fond of music and has aesthetic sense towards creativity. Her confinement to the upper middleclass house in Calcutta by her husband Bhupatidoes not kill her aesthetic talents. In fact her separation from her husband who mostly remains busy in politics and social reforms in pre-independent days works as stimulus to proliferate her creativity. Bhupati, owner-editor of a liberal political weekly, vaguely aware of his wife's discontent, invites her brother Umapada and his wife, Mandakini, to stay. Umapada assumes the managership of the journal, but Mandakini a featherhead chatterbox, is poor company for the graceful, intelligent Charu. Bhupati's young cousin Amal (Soumitra Chatterjee) arrives for a visit; lively, enthusiastic, an aspiring writer, he establishes an immediate rapport with Charu that slides insensibly toward love. Umapada, meanwhile, plots to embezzle the journal's funds. Bhupati is shocked less by the financial loss than by the betrayal of his trust, and Amal, conscious that he too was contemplating a betrayal, hastily departs. Belatedly, from Charu's irrepressible grief,Bhupati realizes what has been happening and rushes from the house. He later returns and the film ends on a freeze: Bhupati and Charu's hands, extended but not meeting. Reconciliation may come, but only with time and difficulty.

Ray's next movie *Devi* is also an adaptation of Prabhat Kumar Mukherjee's short story of the same title, published in 1899. With its release in India in 1960 it was seen as an attack on Hinduism and their superstitious practice of imposing divinity on common man and woman. The film is set in Calcutta the city of goddess Kali during the latter part of 19th century. The central character is Doyamoi the wife of Umaprasad. Umas's father Kalinkar is a feudal landlord and the family is living in a luxurious estate. A turning point came into their life when KalinkarDoyamoi's father in-law sees in dream that Doya is actually an incarnation of goddess Kali and the bindi on her forehead is in fact the third eye of goddess Kali. From the very moment he began to find a parallel between the image of flesh and the image of stone. Like goddess Doya is put on the pedestal and worshipped by Kalinkar and the people around. Thus the sensual woman in flesh is converted overnight into an idol.

Doya is shocked by such kind of treatment of her and her reverence for the goddess leads to the oppression of her. From the vital young bride she is changed into a statue-like surrogate of the goddess. Due to the imposition of divinity she loses her feminine sensuality and daily activities of a woman in which she use to have interests. She is forced to live within the four walls of her room, unable to talk and play with her nephew Khoka who used to sleep with. She is always surrounded by male worshippers and her own wishes, time, and space are surrendered to them. Singh comments on the pathetic condition of Doya: "Surrounded by people, bonded in garlands, suffocated by incense fumes, and deafened by loud chants, Doya faints and collapses on the floor. Totally imbued in their devotion and fully absorbed in their rituals to the sacred object, nobody pays attention to the lifeless subject" (235).

The superstitious belief of the people is more endorsed when a sick child is cured from the sacred liquid of Doya's alter. Seeing this Doya herself is caught in dilemma whether she is the incarnation of goddess or not. Both Doya and Umaprasad decide to elope the city but their elopement is hindered by Doya's asking "what if I'm the Goddess?" This dilemma of Doya is shattered when she finds herself unable to save the life of her beloved nephew Khoka inspite of all her effort. After the untimely death of Khoka her condition becomes extremely pathetic and she acts like a mad woman and commits suicide.

Through the movie Ray seeks to suggest that both women in flesh and women in stone are two different entities and the amalgamation between the two is not possible. What the women of today demand is not the divinity but the treatment of women as women. The movie is also an attack on those feminist thinkers who are obsessed to embrace the goddess as the archetype for feminine consciousness. They reject the male images of divinity which have dominated our patriarchal world, and which have for centuries trivialized and debased womenin both the sacred and secular arenas. Instead of acknowledging god as Lord and Father, they try to discern such images where women are held as the goddess. But merely confronting the status and position of goddess is not going to bring the liberation of women. Such imposition will merely make their condition more pathetic and miserable."We are starved for images which recognize the complexity, richness, and nurturing power of the female energy. We hunger for images that recognize the sacredness of the feminine... We need images; we also need myths, for myths make concrete and particularize; they give us situations, plots, relationships. We need thegoddess and we need the goddesses..." says Christine Downing with a passion that touches every reader.

His another movie entitled as *Mahanagar* is based on Narendra Mitra's story ' Abataranika'(1943) with slight alternation by changing its end from pessimistic to optimistic. The theme of the movie is conceived as antithetical as portrayed in *Devi.Devi* is full of negativity and darkness as it has absence of gender equality, whereas *Mahanagar* has the concept of woman a new woman. The movie focuses on women's liberation from the shackles of four walls and seeks to find her own identity in the outside world. The novel opens with Subrata Mazumdar who is a bank employee, is returning home from his work. He has a joint family consisting his wife Arati (Madhabi Mukherjee), their young son, Subrata's unmarried sister Bani (Jaya Bhaduri), his father, a retired schoolmaster, and his mother. Subrata Mazumdar, a bank employee, with his meagre income finds it difficult to provide for his large joint family.

Arati is like an anchor holding the family together. Subrata talks about a couple where the woman too is going to work. Soon, Arati makes up her mind to take up a job to supplement the household income. With some help from Subrata, and much against established custom and opposition of the elders, she finds a job of selling sewing machines door-to-door.

Going out to work, Arati discovers a new life. She proves successful in her work and gains self-confidence. Subrata now feels insecure and resentful. His father too puts pressure on his son to force Arati to quit the job. Subrata asks Arati to quit as he plans to earn more by moonlighting.

The next morning, before Arati can give in her resignation, Subrata telephones her and asks her not to resign as he has lost his job. Now, Arati is the only earning member of the family. Subrata suffers as he watches his wife go out while he sits in bed and scans newspapers for jobs' columns. They begin to go apart.

Arati has found a new friend in a colleague - Edith, an Anglo-Indian woman. Her boss does not like Edith due to her being an offspring of 'our ex-rulers.' Blinded by his prejudice, he accuses Edith of loose character and fires her. Arati asks her boss to apologise to Edith. He refuses and warns her about her own job. Arati hands over her old resignation letter and walks away.Now neither Arati nor her husband has a job. On her way out, she meets Subrata. After the initial shock, they reconcile and are close to each other once again. Subrata understands her. Arati ponders that in such a big city at least one of them is sure to find a job. As they walk into the city crowd, the camera tilts up to a street lamp.

The movie reveals on the gender biases of Indian patriarchy system where a woman has to face the anger of every family member in order to stand herself as economically independent. They are not allowed to work outside the four walls of house even in adverse circumstances when their family undergoing through economic crisis. But through the character of Arati Ray tries to break this prejudiced notion towards women and shows that women are equally competent to earn money in this male dominated society. The character of Aratiis basically the character of a new woman who is ready to accept the challenges of new world. Her characterization reveals the blending of western influences as well as her own culture. she changes the concept of conventional ideal woman who silently tolerates physical and mental oppressions and replaces it by confident straightforward and educated women. She represents Ibsen's New Woman and stood for women's liberation.

Thus in short we can say that Ray's portrayal of women is not stereotyped and gender biased. His women characters are ready to fight with the adverse circumstance of their life and strive hard to establish their own identity in male dominated society. The women of his movies are basically the women of Bengal Renaissance who are culturally and traditionally rich. They have characteristic of both eastern and western women.They are educated, intellectual and modern in their thoughts and opinion. They are having the essence of true women along with the essence of new women. Both the characters of Doya and Aratipresents two aspects of women characters. Doya who is endowed with all the womanly quality of love, affection, respect and sympathy for each other and Arti educated, intellectual and modern in her thoughts tries to show that women are equally competent in outside society.

References

Blizek, William. *The Continuum Companion to Religion and Film,*vol. 36, Issue 3, 2007.

Chatterjee, Partha. *Colonialism, Nationalism and Colonized Women: The Quest in India,* American Ethnologists, 16(2), 1989.

Das, Santi.*: An Intimate Master,* Calcutta: Papyrus, 1998.

Ghosh, Bishnupriya. *Satyajit Ray' s Devi: Constructing a Third- World Feminist Critique,* Screen, 33(2), Summer 1992.

Houston, Penelope. *The Contemporary Cinema*, Harmondworth Pelican, 1968.

Monalisa, Bhattacherjee.*19th Century Bengali Women and the Films of Satyajit Ray: A Study,* IOSR Journal of Humanities and Social Sciences (JHSS), VOL. 3, Issue2, Sep-Oct 2012.

Nikky- Gunvinder Kaur Singh. "From Flesh to Stone: the Devine Metamorphosis in Satyajit Ray's *Devi*", *Journal of South Asian Literature,* vol.28, no. ½, pp.227-249, 1993.

Chapter 16

Haider: Textualizing Tragic Flaw in 20th Century Indian Cinema

*Nikhil Pratap Singh**

Postcolonial filmmaking, in so far as it seeks to make an intervention in dominant visual regimes tied to the economy of the contemporary world system, has tended to come to ruin on the shoals of a politics of liberation that seeks to realize itself through an aesthetic experience of transparence.

The major characters of Hamlet transformed as the King Hamlet takes from of Hilaal Meer, Gertrude becomes Ghazala, Prince Hamlet becomes Haider and the heroine of the play Ophelia becomes Arshia, while Claudius becomes Khurram. The movie Haider starts with Hilaal Meer, a doctor who agrees to perform an appendicitis operation of a pro-separatist group at Kashmir during the Kashmir conflict of 1995. To avoid any unwanted circumstances and obstacles, he performs the operation at his home. His wife Ghazala raises questions to his allegiance to see the operation. Hilaal Meer becomes accused during military raid on the next day of the operation. Ashootout ensues at Hilaal's home, during which the leader of the separatist group is killed and house is bombed subsequently in order to kill any other militant hiding there. Hilaal is taken away for questioning. After a long time, Haider, son of Hilaal returns from universality to seek facts and truth about his father's disappearance. He is shocked to see her mother singing and laughing along with her brother-in-law

**Research Scholar,*
Department of English,
Banaras Hindu University, Varanasi – 221 005

Khurram. With the help of her fiancee Arshia who is journalist, he starts to find his father at detention camps and in police stations.

As Prince Hamlet in the play Hamlet was contemplative and thoughtful by nature, he delays, entering into a deep melancholy and even apparent or feigned madness. When Polonius suggests that Hamlet may be mad with love for Ophelia, Claudius agrees to spy on Hamlet in conversation with the girl. But though Hamlet certainly seems mad, he does not seem to love Ophelia. He orders her to enter a nunnery and says derogatorily to her "Get thee to a nunnery or you will be breeder of sinners" and declares that he wishes to ban marriages. This brought about the suicide of Ophelia. In the movie Haider, depressed by the growing closeness and proximity between Ghazala and Khurram and unable to find any leads, Haider that he will be able to provide information about Hilaal, his father. Haider contacts Roohdar, who turns out to be part of a separatist group. Roohdar then narrates the story of how he met Hilaal in one of the detention centres, where they both were tortured. Roohdaar tells Haider that he wanted to pass on his father's message to him that is to take revenge for Khurram's betrayal. The same is done by the King Hamlet but in the form of a Ghost convey Prince Hamlet of the wrong done and invokes him to take the revenge for Claudius' betrayal, of his murdering the King and his debauched hasty incestuous marriage with his mother Gertrude. To avenge his father's death, Haider becomes mentally and emotionally scattered and starts to behave strangely. His uncle Khurram, after getting to know about the meeting of Haider and Roohdar, narrates to him that Roohdar has killed his father. He is in dual mind as to whose narration he should believe. This is much like Hamlet's strategy to confirm what the Ghost has proclaimed about the crime of Claudius where Hamlet plans' play within a play' to' catch the conscience of the King' as a mouse trap before he actually works upon the revenge. Hamlet is sensible in his insanity and in the sense that he feigns madness to be secret. But Ironically, a sort of double tragic flaw, Haider discloses his state of indecision to Arshia and also states that Roohdar has given him a gun to kill his uncle. Arshia unintentionally discloses to her father who informs Khurram about the gun. Khurram immediately orders to send Haider to a mental cure institution.

In the play Hamlet, Claudius is a corrupt politician whose main weapon is his ability to manipulate others through his skilful use of language. Claudius's speeches is compared to poison being poured in the ear and that is the method he used to murder Hamlet's father. Claudius's love for Gertrude may be sincere, but he married her as a strategic move, to help him win the throne away from Hamlet after the death of the King. In the movie, Khurram loves Ghazala but used her for the sake of power and tries to snatch the prestige in the society. He has the quality like Claudius to speak like sweet but poisonous. So both the characters of Claudius and Khurram in this way are similarly drawn and adapted.

Next morning Haider tries to kill his uncle but cannot accomplish his act of doing so due to his uncle is in prayers and then is captured by Arshia's father who orders to kill him but Haider manages to escape. He contacts Roohdaar, who suggests getting trained in Pakistan to avenge for his father's death and Haider agrees. He calls his mother on other side of border and informs her about it to which she asks him to meet her once before going. During the meet, Ghazala discloses that she had disclosed about terrorists hiding in their house out of fear to Khurram not knowing that he was an informer of the Indian army. Arshia's father traces them and is about to shoot Haider when Haider shoots him in the head and escapes. This is similar to when Hamlet avoids killing Polonius and indulges in soliloquy that his soul thereby would straight go to heaven if killed during prayers and later Polonius id killed in the process who was hiding behind arras.

Arshia is deeply hurt to listen to her father's death in the hands of Haider and later commits suicide. Haider goes to the graveyard where his father was buried. At the graveyard, Haider contemplates about the universal nature of mortality. Unaware of Arshia's death, on seeing her brother in the graveyard it hits his mind that the body is of Arshia. He runs towards her body where his brother sees him and informs Khurram. Afight ensues between Haider and Arshia's brother resulting in Arshia's brother's death. This is much similar of the Graveyard scene of the play Hamlet and his fight with Leartes, Khurram arrives with military and a gunfight ensues, meanwhile Roohdaar and Ghazala also arrive at the spot, where Roohdaar drops Ghazala. A fierce exchange of bullets and bombs leaves only Haider and few men on Khurram's side alive. Just when Khurram is about to kill Haider with a rocket launcher, Ghazala requests a chance to convince Haider to surrender. She confronts him but he says that he cannot die before avenging his father's death. Ghazala tells him that revenge only results in revenge and there is no ending to this vicious cycle, but he does not understand. In the fight somehow she pulls the pins of the hand grenade resulting in a big blast causing the death of the rest of the men and Khurram in order to shoot him in the eyes, his father's wish, but is remained of his mother's words "revenge only results in revenge" and thus decides to leave Khurram.

But in the play Hamlet, Claudius dies when the sword – fighting begins. In the film, there is no sword fighting but gun shooting used instead of it. Hamlet scores the first hit, but declines to drink from the king's by the poison. Laertes, Ophelia's brother, succeeds in wounding Hamlet, though Hamlet does not die of the poison immediately. In the movie Haider, Leartes is Liyaqot Lone. Claudius ids responsible for the queen's death, he dies from the blade's poison. Hamlet then stabs Claudius through with the poisoned sword and forces him to drink down the rest of the poisoned wine. Claudius dies, and Hamlet dies immediately after achieving his revenge.

So we can see that the movie Haider is a complete adaptation of Shakespeare's Hamlet in all respects and even the names of the characters bear similarity. The present contemporary political setting has been provided and themes superadded to make it relevant to the current scenario. It is true that human nature is the same irrespective of ages gone by and human psychology and instinct remain the same throughout. The greatness of Shakespeare lies in universality and we can see that Shakespeare is still a modern writer, poet and dramatist who continues to dominate the world cinema, his all plays, whether tragedies or comedies, history or romances, have widely influenced borrowings or adaptations into films and Cinema all over the world in all times and has been seen in post – modern framework in all its deconstructs and re-constructs. Tuntun Mukherjee opines :

Films responded to the realities of life in terms of the predominating anxieties regarding new – found liberties and persisting constraints; rural predicaments and indifferent urban space; changes in the familial domain and interpersonal relationships; divisions and widening gaps among the people and such other preoccupations. There was scope for melodrama to romance with modernity and realism in many ways. All the elements of melodrama – the binaries of theme and characterization (the 'heroes' representing the madness for revenge; the 'heroines' innocent and long suffering; the 'villains' metamorphosing from the corrupt politician into the capitalist or powerful) and narrative resolutions – mirrored the changing perceptions of the people, the specificities of Indian culture and society, the disappointments and pitfalls of the nation state. Evidently therefore, it is possible to describe 'Indian' cinema as a model for textualizing the 'nation' in many voices and pluralities which also convey the specificities of 'Indian-ness'.

References

1. Chan, Edward K. *Food and Cassettes: Encounters with Indian Filmsong. Global Bollywood ed. S. Gopal and Sujata Moorti. Spring. 2. 2001. Print.*

2. Kiarostami, Abbas. *Walking with the Wind. Voices and Visions in Film.* Harvard Film Archive. 28 February 2002. Print.

3. Mukherjee, Tuntun. *Bimal Roy: The Architect of Modern Indian Cinema. The Man Who Spoke in Pictures.* Ed. Rinki Roy Battacharya. New Delhi: Penguin. 34 – 46. 2009. Print.

4. http://en.wikipedia.org/wiki/Haider. per cent 28film per cent 29.

Chapter 17

Iron Man of India on Silver Screen: Contribution of Cinema in Remembering the Forgotten Hero "Sardar Vallabhbhai Patel"

*Hemlata Yadav**

True greatness cannot be hidden behind mere ordinariness.

Sardar Patel was an idolized Nationalist who put his country before everything. Without Patel's hard work, intelligence and leadership India's map would have been smaller. Acknowledging his leadership Gandhiji described him as "the Sardar". Sardar Vallabhbhai Patel was an important hero of freedom struggle but he was almost lost and forgotten by Modern India.

This paper seeks to discuss some aspects of Sardar vallabhbhai Patel's life as depicted on Silver screen. In this regard we find two main important movies – Richard Attenborough's "Gandhi" in 1982, Showing Vallabhbhai Patel and Gandhiji's friendly relationship and Vallabhbhai Patel as a great admirer of Gandhiji. Saeed Jaffrey played the role of Sardar Vallabhbhai Patel in "Gandhi". The second and most

**Research Scholar*
Indira Gandhi National Open University,
Maidan Garhi, New Delhi
e-mail: hemlatayadav2005@gmail.com

important film where we see Sardar Vallabhbhai Patel as a main character is Ketan Mehta's "Sardar" featuring Paresh Rawal as Patel in 1993. It is a biographical epic of Vallabhbhai Patel's political life. The movie tries to portray the strong political will of the great man, especially during the biggest crisis state of Indian history, the partition, and how he succeeds in it. Sardar Patel was responsible for shaping Unite India as we currently see in the map from Kashmir to Kanyakumari.

Films act as educators and persuaders, have image creating potential and can provide strong motivation to viewers. Films are a combination of story, mood and visual stimuli depicting their multidimensional and complex nature. If we see brief history of cinema we find that Lumiere Brother released two films named "Arrival of Train" and "Labors come out from the Factory" simultaneously on 28 December 1895 was the very first depiction of cinema. In the series to spread the cinema in other countries for profit Bombay became the first place for screening in India in 1897 at Watson hotel, than it is followed by Madras (Chennai), Calcutta (Kolkata) in India. Dada Saheb Phalke made the first silent Movie "Raja Harishchandra". The first talking movie of India "Alam Ara" was made in 1931 by Ardeshir Irani. In the span of more than 100 years of India cinema making film on a political issue or a political figure is the most controversial aspect. But according to the film Enquiry committed report (1949), Indian cinema was supposed to serve as an "effective instrument" for "national culture, education and healthy entertainment" to promote and further induce "a national character with its multifaceted aspects". In the regard of national character and unity we can put Ketan Mehta's 'Sardar'. National Award winning film Sardar was a tribute to Sardar Vallabhbhai Patel, a forgotten figure of India's independent struggle, same as Shyam Bengal's tribute to Subhash Chandra Bose in "The Forgotten Hero". 'Sardar' is an account of Vallabhbhai Patel's political life while India was taking shape as an independent country. "Sardar" movie concentrating on the last five crucial years of Sardar's life from 1945 to 1950 the time of Nation's freedom struggle at pre-independence, independence, partition and emerging problems of post independence period. Sardar Patel, with his intelligence, courage, and political efficiency solved problems one by one. Patel lives his political life with intelligence and with his intense love for unite India which overrides his mind in every situation. Ketan Mehta showed how Sardar with his quick decisiveness and ability to solved one problem after another monumental problem with intelligence and ease.

Ketan Mehta Dared to bring the life story of Iron Man of India to the silver screen in 1993. Making a film on any major Indian political figure is like throwing a spark into the flammable controversy. Indian film makers hesitate to take such political explosive and controversial subjects. Even a film based on Mahatma Gandhiji's life was made by Richard Attenborough. When Richard Attenborough was working his film, Gandhiji," Satyajit Ray spoke at the national film theatre at London's South Bank. He was asked whether he had ever considered making a film about Gandhi.

He neatly ducked the question; the impression that created was that he did not want to handle such a explosive subject". Shyam Benegal's film "the forgettable Hero" became the brand Ambassador and put an example to show political life on the silver screen which was formally forbidden in India's mainstream cinema. "Shyam Benegal breaks new grounds and deserves to be congratulated for becoming the first Indian Film director to have the courage to make a film about a major Indian political figure."

In movie "Sardar" Vallabhbhai Patel stands at the quiet center. Paresh Rawal's performance finds the right note and stays with it.. Movie shows the fine research by Vijay Tendulkar before writing script and screenplay. it covers almost all major political issues of Sardar initiative in shaping united India before and after Independence. This movie has it all whether it's hardcore reality, maturity, direction, historical feast, great acting, and researched screenplay. "Sardar" is not only an epic film but a film which takes a lot of intelligence, research, risk of controversial aspect and passion to make. The film begins with young Sardar Patel playing cards with his friends and ridiculing Gandhiji and his policies to achieve Independence. But his views changed with the motivated speech of Mahatma Gandhi in "Ahmadabad during 1915" Vallabhbhai decide to immerse himself in the freedom struggle. He started it with spreading awareness in the entire state of Gujarat. After Independence, Sardar Patel became home minister and deputy prime minister. He presided over the most difficult task facing the nascent nation-state namely the integration of over 500 princely states into the Indian Union. Patel desired nothing more than that the Indian Nation-State should preserve and flourish. His major concern was national unity. Patel worked shoulder- to shoulder in building a united and democratic nation.

Ketan Mehta has taken much liberty in describing the changing relationship of Sardar Vallabhbhai Patel and Jawaher Lal Nehru. Sometime Nehru and Patel seem to be rivals and at the other hand they were comrades and co-workers in nation building. They worked closely together in the congress from 1920s to 1947 and after that they shape the free Nation as prime minister and deputy prime minister in the first government of independent India when congress was choosing new president and first future India's prime minister, party considered Sardar as far more charismatic and appealing mass leader. But Sardar withdrew his name and supported Nehru's candidacy because of Gandhiji's wish. Sardar Patel also assured Gandhiji that they work together for greater cause of India's Independence'. He has truly depicted the transformation that undergoes in relationship between Patel and Nehru through the letter exchanges to each other. It also covers incidents regarding how Sardar opposed Nehru's decision to let UN intervene into Kashmir Issue, whether or not the U.N.O should monitor a plebiscite vote in Kashmir. Sharp differences arose between Vallabhbhai and Nehru which may well force Vallabhbhai to resign from his position as Home Minister. It was Gandhiji's Death which united them both. Ketan Mehta has made out Sardar Vallabhbhai Patel more political alert and efficient than Jawaharlal Nehru on the issue of Kashmir. Sardar Patel's stature and contribution to India were higher than Nehru but at that time huge injustice had been done by congress to Sardar Patel. He had never been given his due.

Historical Approach

Ketan Mehta wants to re-enact the actual Circumstances during the terms of Indian struggle for freedom through this movie. He has glorified Sardar Patel in his movie repeatedly and rightfully and as a part of Indian History he makes us realized that history cannot be changed and needs to be told as it was. Vijay Tendulkar' research script and screenplay is nothing but real history unfolds in front of our eyes. This movie gives the experience of historical as well as political journey during the period of 1946 to 1950. Based on deep research with historical proof, this movie became important for historical reenactment of a specific period. At the same time it is a film not a documentary so with the facts some drama is added by Ketan Mehta. This is something very obvious. Even Attenborough and Shyam Benegal had done this with 'Gandhi' and "the Unforgotten Hero". This movie is an historical account itself written on fact and research. But due to create continuity and interest scenes were dramatize. Real footage of Sardar Patel is the gloss of the movie and splendid historical experience. A big and effective portion of the movie depicted through real videos catalogs and newspapers and headlines. Ketan Mehta doesn't recreate actual bloody fights of Kashmir, Junagarh, Hyderabad and Punjab partition migration to deviate from movie's main theme of Sardar's biography. Instead it refers these historical events with actual B and W of newspaper front-page headlines and real B and W video images to make it more authentic. Ketan Mehta also used real video footage of independence eve in the movie. 'Sardar' movie is not only serves as a history lesson but at a time of disaster, it reminds us that we are after all, human, and thus capable of the most extraordinary and wonderful achievements, simply, through the use of our imagination, our will, and our sense of right.

Richard Attenborough's Oscar –winning 'Gandhi' was one of the most controversial biopic ever made. In 'Gandhi' we can see the Patel as an admirer of Gandhi and their friendly relationship with full of respect. The humbleness of Patel showed when he asked Gandhi not to call him Mr. Patel just Patel. In one scene of movie 'Gandhi'....

Gandhiji – "Sardar you have gained weight you must join me in the fast"

Patel replied with loving laugh –"if I fast, I die. If you fast people go to all sorts of trouble to keep you alive." .... This shows the respect of Gandhiji in Patel's heart. Sardar Patel was depicted one of the Gandhi's closets associates.

Both movies will bring Sardar Vallabhbhai Patel to the attention of a lot of people for the first time, not as a political leader, but as a self-searching, fallible human being with a sense of humor.

Vallabhbhai bowed out amidst intense debate on the creation of Pakistan by Mohammad Ali Jinnah of Muslim league. In a scene of hot debate on partition

Sardar Patel argued...... "Mr. Jinnah, same thing again. We are here to discuss India's Independence not partition, if there has to be partition it could be decided by the free citizens of the free country not by the British Government". This shows Sardar Patel's firm believes in unity and political brilliance during pre-post independence era. Mountbatten, the British Victory, along with Jawaharlal Nehru, Vallabhbhai Patel and others were in favor of partitioning India and allowing Jinnah to create two Pakistan, in order to prevent any bloodshed. Patel was against giving Pakistan the sum immediately after partition until the new Indian Nation is stable. Through argues and conversations Ketan Mehta shows the unavoidable acceptance of partition by Sardar Patel and Gandhiji. The real video footage of partition are also connect the movie with the historical aspects. Political created circumstances of partition are shown pretty well, Circumstances are tried to be proved truthful with the help of newspaper's clippings one by one. This movie is the picturisation of political consequences which led to the partition of India and the bloodshed. The British viceroy, along with Jawaharlal, Vallabhbhai, and others were in favor of partitioning India and allowing Jinnah to create two Pakistan, one each on the borders of Rajasthan and Bengal respectively in order to prevent tragic bloodshed. Riots broke out to in Rawalpindi, and Amritsar, Vallabhbhai instructed the administration to make all efforts to look after the Hindus in refugee camps, as well as assured protection for Muslims, who chose to stay in India. In a scene Sardar Patel himself visited tensed area of Nizzamuddin in Delhi and assured them that they will be provided with necessary police protection while Delhi was placed under a 24 hour curfew.

Ketan Mehta delves initiative of Sardar Patel in two peasant movements – Kheda struggle, his first major participation in freedom struggle that leads British government to grant tax relief for peasants, second in Bardoli Satyagarha-Sardar Patel's successful non-cooperation movements, on the path of Gandhiji. Because of sincerity and devotion in nationhood Sardar Patel became one of Gandhiji's closets associates. In 'Sardar' movie Ketan Mehta doesn't make Gandhi and Nehru as weak figures to make Sardar more powerful figure.

Conclusion

Sardar Patel was known for his staunch Vision of Integrating many kingdoms in India. His firm belief in rural and agricultural development and his vision in building a socially powerful and economically progressive India beautifully narrated in the movie. The point of the film is not that Sardar Vallabhbhai Patel strengthens the nation politically and geographically, but rather the way he makes this difficult journey. This journey is so masterfully and artistically directed by Ketan Mehta. It is a real historical stuff unfolding against your eyes. It takes a lot of intelligence and passion to make and appreciate a film like 'Sardar'. Very well researched and Ketan Mehta handled it very well. Realistically treated subject, heavy political talks with documentary like approach, this is one of the best films made on struggle of independence and it's after math historical masterpiece. Ketan Mehta also refers and tackles by unsung heroes of freedom struggle like H.M. Patel V.P. Menon and Moraraji Desai. In the time of high pressure Sardar Vallabhbhai Patel made decision what they thought its best for future generation. Sardar Patel's dilemma about some of his sharp decisions sometimes make him restless "sometimes I ask myself why I am here and what I am doing and whatever it is that I am doing is correct or not if it is the coming generation will bless us and if it is wrong they will abuse us. No one will think about how honestly we serve the nation no one will understand in the given circumstances it is the best option. They will certainly say to hell with your honesty and your circumstances what did we gain who were you to decide us and then sleep deserts sleep 'do you sleep easy?' Hari Bhai" (H.M.Patel). How successfully Ketan Mehta depicted these circumstances and situation on silver screen. It's our privilege to nourish the efforts of our national heroes who can raise India from servitude and apathy. Make India proud of herself. These kinds of historical rich movies cannot be neglected, and be critically examined. Researchers will look into this field of study cinema in historical perspectives, which is in need of further investigations. I must quote Jyotika Virdi, "Expanding the archive source and the historiographical method to include popular film text could an extension of the subaltern History project."

References

Burk, Peter. New Perspectives on Historical Writing, Polity Press Cambridge, 1991.

Carr, E.H., What is History, Macmillan. London, 1962

Chandra, Bipan., India's struggle for Independence, Penguin Books, New Delhi, 1989.

Gandhi, Mahatma., The Story of My Experiments with Truth, translated by Mahadev Desai, Lexicon Books, New Delhi 2011.

Kumar, Kapil., Congress and Classes, Manohar, Delhi, 1988.

Schulze, Brigittee "the Cinematic 'Discovery of India' : Mehboob's Re-Invention of the Nation in Mother India", social Scientist Vol.30, NO 9\10 (Sep-Oct 2002).

Tehelka, 4 June 2005.

Vasudev Aruna., Liberty and License in Indian Cinema, Vikas Publishing House,Delhi, 1978.

Vasudev, Aruna., Frames of Mind Reflections on Indian Cinema, UBS Publishers, Bombay, 1995.

Virdi, Jyotika,. The Cinematic Imagination: Indian Popular Films as Social History, permanent Blake, Ranikhet, 2003.

Chapter 18

Indian Cinema and its Globalization: A Filmy Twist

*Sunita Arya**

Lights! Camera! Action! Three words that transport us into a world of dreams, hopes, joys and sorrow, and allow us to be touched by the magic of movies! The Indian film industry is celebrating 100 years of cinema. In today's context, the Indian cinema is not just defined by regions or nations, but have become transnational. Bollywood gives Indians an identity and a means to define themselves; almost it gives Indians access to a wider world. In other words, diasporic Indians, though they live in countries which are often far away from India, also inhabit a greater India of feelings and emotions, an India of the heart and head, one of whose primary sources is Bollywood. Bollywood has been the second cinema of the world, but it is only now that this fact has gained recognition and acceptance. As early as the 1930's, Indian cinema circulated in the Far East and since the 1950's it has been popular. In what used to be known as the "second", and "third worlds". Indeed Bollywood has been one of the defining markers of Indian or south Asian identity abroad. Indian cinema has become global. The first International Film Festival Awards (IIFA) function was staged in London's prestigious Millennium Dome. This was an unambiguous proclamation that Indian cinema had arrived on the international stage. Acceptance of Indian films abroad is due to the qualitative change that has come about in Indian films. Their quality is now of international standards and the market for them has

**Assistant Professor, Department of English,
Vasanta College for Women, Rajghat
Banaras Hindu University, Varanasi – 221 001
e-mail: sunitaarya.bhu@gmail.com*

registered a phenomenal growth. Popular Hindi cinema has, since the first film was made in India in 1913, played a central role in the formulation of the national identity and in the promotion of normative behaviour.

Themes and images of globalization in Bollywood are not a recent emergence. For decades, Hindi films have alluded to transnational identities to keep up to certain preconceived and fixed notions of 'Indianness'. But notions began to change and a very popular song from Raj Kapoor's Shree *420*(1955) comes up perhaps as the earliest example. The first lines of the song, hugely successful in India and the Soviet Union, are:

> *"My shoes are Japanese*
>
> *My trousers English*
>
> *The red hat on my head is Russian*
>
> *But my heart remains Indian."*

(Kaur, R. and Sinha, A.J. – *Bollyworld: Popular Indian Cinema through a Transnational Lens*)

Lip-synced by Raj Kapoor merrily strolling down the road with a backpack, became a symbol for classic Bollywood; *i.e.* "assert[ing] an Indian identity in the face of global consumerism." Even in times of Raj Kapoor, Indian cinema had quite a bit of international following. 'Mera Joota Hai Japani' would be on the lips of many a Middle Easterner who did not even understand the Hindi language. Russia as well as the far away Africa too had legions of fans of what is now popularly known as Bollywood, the Indian film industry. By foreshadowing the widespread economic shifts to come in later decades, the song became a "narrative about the production of nationalism through its intricate entanglement with the global that though the Indian nation is swamped with all kinds of foreign influences on products, this does not need to undermine the strength of patriotism.

Yet, despite the far-reaching pockets of fans, Indian cinema was by no means a global enterprise. What has made it so popular in the recent years is the burgeoning global Indian Diaspora that now stands at about 20 million worldwide and still growing on. The direct impact of such clout has had a far reaching effect on globalization of Indian cinema. Increasing interest in, and influence of Bollywood productions. Films such as *Taal, Lagaan*, and *Devdas* have competed with Hollywood releases at box offices in the U.S. and England. Conversely, Hollywood releases such as *Moulin Rouge* have known to be inspired by the dazzling sets and the song-and-dance routines of the standard Bollywood fare.The catering of Bollywood to global Indian audiences. This is evident not only in NRI story-lines of films such as *Pardes* on to *Kabhi Khushi Kabhi Gham*, but also in the Westernized settings and styles of many recent releases. Case in point is the multi-starrer *Kaante,* which is not only styled like a Hollywood thriller, but is also based on one –*Reservoir*

Dogs. But regardless of the theme, setting, or style, global Indian audiences now play a critical role in the success or failure of Bollywood productions. Both *Lagaan* and *Devdas*, based on highly traditional themes, have had a considerable chunk of their revenues come from overseas audiences. Interest in India-centric themes is crossing over to mainstream, as is evident in films such as *Monsoon Wedding* and the Universal Studios film *The Guru*. In England, it has been *CottonMary, East is East*, and the recent hit, *Bend it Like Beckham*.Increase in numbers and visibility of NRI filmmakers such as Mira Nair, Deepa Mehta, Nagesh Kuku Noor, Gurinder Chada, and many others. Such a trend further encourages aspiring novices such as Piyush Dinker Pandya (*American Desi*), Anurag Mehta (*American Chai*) and many others.

Globalization has four aspects, namely, movement of goods, capital, technology and people across borders. In terms of movement of goods (*i.e.*, movies) Indian movie industry has a long history of presence in the international market. *Awara* sent the Soviet Union and other Communist bloc countries crazy in the 1950s. Mehboob's *Aan* had a French release after its premiere in London. Long before that Himansu Rai made visually stunning films in cooperation with the Germans in the early 1930s, like *The Light of Asia* and *A Throw of Dice,* and many more which were shown in Europe as Indian films with Indian stories. By then the Bombay film industry had been around for 35 years. The industry is as old as the cinema itself and certainly older than Hollywood, which has its beginnings in thelate 1900s (Desai, 2007).

In the 1990s, the rise of Hindu nationalism, the liberalization of the Indian economy and the renewed affection of the Indian middle class for cinema halls, previously deserted in favour of home entertainment, generated more production and more revenue. This period coincided with a new academic interest in Bollywood (Gopal and Moorthy 2008, Silva 2004, Virdi 2003: 210, Prasad 2003).Reputed writers specializing in the theory of globalization and cultural studies like Arjun Appadurai and Carol Breckenridge, although their analysis of cultural consumption and Indian modernity is not based on cinema, nonetheless started to take into account the importance of the big screen in the national imagination. To quote the words of D. Bhoopaty, 'cinema is widely considered a microcosm of the social, political, economic, and cultural life of a nation. It is the contested site where meanings are negotiated, traditions made and remade, identities affirmed or rejected' (Bhoopaty 2003: 505). Indeed popular Indian cinema in Hindi constitutes a particularly interesting area of study as much because of its history as because of its key role in the creation of the national identity and its place in the collective imagination. Directors, producers, distributors, financiers, officials in the Central Board of Film Certification (Censor Board) all seek to ensure the projection of lucrative, aesthetically pleasant and acceptable contents. This results in a prescriptive and normative body of works that have, over the years, reflected and mostly shaped ideas of national identity, gendered behaviour, and acceptability. As Ashis Nandy noted, 'the popular film *is* low-brow, modernizing India in all its complexity, sophistry, naiveté and vulgarity. Studying popular film *is* studying Indian modernity at its rawest, its crudities laid bare by the fate of traditions in contemporary life and arts. Above all, it is studying caricatures of ourselves' (Nandy 1998: 7). These distorted reflections, one might add, not only exaggerate features but also paradoxically dictate patterns of normality. In this sense, they shape and impose exemplarity by broadcasting role models, figures of idealization and identification at once. Popular cinema is thus a major actor of social engineering.

In 1997, the *Financial Times* wondered somewhat cynically, 'Which of us in London or Los Angeles has ever seen a Hindi popular movie?' (Andrews, 1997). This type of remark would be more unlikely today since most of the major international capitals have hosted Bollywood festivals and films been broadcasted on mainstream TV channels. The Government of India set up the Export Promotion Council as early as in 1958 to promote the export of Indian films mainly to the United States and United Kingdom and, in the early 1980s, Indian films were being distributed in over a hundred countries (Bhoopaty 2003: 159), in addition to being present wherever the Indian diaspora settled since the days of silent films. Successive Indian governments as well as distributors have always tried to exploit a captive expatriate market by providing the Indian diaspora with a common national cultural identity through the audio-visual media. This strategy, although focused primarily on the expatriate Indians, now aims to reach a broader non-ethnic audience (although in 2009, the cinema industry's growth has decreased and was mainly based on domestic theatrical collections, Federation of Indian Chambers of Commerce and Industry; KPMG: 17-18), along with the Indian high income, urban and young audience. The NRI role models on screen aim at pleasing these audiences, already familiar with international migrations and capitalism.Indian movie industry, notably Bollywood, has come a long way inthe last two centuries.

The character of the expatriate Indian perfectly illustrates this phenomenon. A few films like *Dilwale Dulhania Le Jayenge (DDLJ*, Aditya Chopra 1995*)*, *Pardes*(Subhash Ghai 1997), *Kuch Kuch Hota Hai* (Karan Johar 1998), *Kabhi Khushi Kabhi Gham* (*K3G*, Karan Johar 2001)*, and Kitne Door... Kitne Paas* (Mehul Kumar 2002) and *Namaste London* (Vipul Amrutlal Shah 2007) have given the Indian Diaspora pride of place and have generated new practices or rejuvenated old ones (like the rekindled observance of the *Karva Chauth* festival in Northern India). The elites of the popular Hindi film industry, like producer-director Yash Chopra, are very conscious of their role. He for instance declared, during his address at the first Pravasi Bharatiya Divas (PBD), a government-sponsored conclave for the Indian diaspora, that 'our moral responsibility is to depict India at its best. We're the historians of India [...]. The Indian Diaspora must maintain its identity, its roots' (Chopra 2003). The late 70s and early 80s continued to reassert the negation of the West in the form of angry heroes fighting against government and societal corruption, and trying to adjust India's role in the changing dynamics of global politics. Bollywood in the '90s saw a string of big budget melodramas aimed both at the burgeoning Indian middle class and the diasporic Indian audiences, as producers quickly recognized its potential to make the film industry bigger than it already was. This new breed of films termed urban stories, diaspora cinema, or NRI films, were glossy, consumerist fantasies featuring middle-class worlds and transnational lifestyles that captured the imagination of audiences within India and abroad. Soon, the biggest producers began financing films focused to some extent on the NRI.

The air and the ambience was simmering just beneath, waiting for a concrete shape to create a beautiful and happy marriage between Indian values and Western lifestyles of the resident Indian and the Indian diaspora, where tradition wins even in the West, and running away like the ill-fated lovers of *Qayamat Se Qayamat Tak* did not remain audience-savvy for long. Filmmakers were looking out for this new brand of "Indianness" in terms of plot, story, theme, music and cast. In 1995, Aditya Chopra, son of veteran filmmaker Yash Chopra, made his debut with *Dilwale Dulhaniya Le Jayenge*, where he showed that despite the male protagonist being a NRI, he respects Indian family values and shuns the idea of eloping with the woman he loves. With this 'reformed' image of Bollywood lovers, NRIs to boot, Chopra created a film that was young and universal in its appeal, rooted in traditional customs and values. The film released to unprecedented hype, and became one of the biggest grossing and the longest running films in the history of Indian cinema. As of April 13, 2007, *DDLJ* entered its 600th week of continuous running in theatres, a record perhaps unmatched anywhere in the world. For many film historians and sociologists, *DDLJ* essentially marked the beginning of diasporic Bollywood films, and has since been the subject of many a film analysis.

"At this dynamic moment in history, when the first and third worlds are involved in major confrontation of cultures, the third world with its multi-culturalism is engaged in an attempt to reframe their cultural identities to save the threat of cultural genocide through the effects of a rampant globalization."(*Datta, Pulkit: Bollywoodizing Diasporas – Reconnecting to the NRI Through Popular Hindi Cinema*, 2008). He goes on to add that the notion of diaspora is no longer confined within a population sharing common national and/or ethnic identity that is geographically distant from their 'original' or 'native' place. Rather, paradoxically, a community which has not been 'relocated' or 'displaced' in the geographic/historic sense can also receive such films with similar diasporic disposition. As a powerful socializing agent, cinema an important tool as well as site of struggle for Bollywood filmmakers to find a way out through subject explorations that would fit into the constantly changing parameters of phrases like "Bollywood", "Indianness" and "Globalization".

On the other hand, the widening parameters of these concepts and ideologies also open up new windows of exploration that spread out the borders of these phrases to invite, welcome, acknowledge and affirm multiple areas, subjects, budgets and genres of cinema. The possibilities are infinite, pervasive and ever-changing. In addition, fewer films in the past few years have continued this trend of showing NRI heroes as champions of ethnic nationalism and unabashed liberalism. This change reflects the evolution of the entertainment market and of the political discourse, mostly after the Congress party's return to power in New Delhi in 2004. Ethnic nationalism has lost currency, and speeches about 'inclusive growth' have replaced those about 'India shining'. Moreover, the cinema industry is becoming more regional thanks to new corporate investments in a previously untapped market while the audience is increasingly segmented into niches, and the 'aspirational middle class' genre of the 1990s 'targeting metro and NRI audiences' has given way to other more diverse and, to borrow the Federation of Indian Chambers of Commerce and Industry's terminology, 'Indianized' contents (Federation of Indian Chambers of Commerce and Industry; KPMG: 32, 34, 170, 171). However, some films like *Hum Tum*(Kunal Kohli 2004), *Salaam Namaste* (Siddharth Anand 2005), *Kabhi Alvida Naa Kehna* (Karan Johar 2006), and *Love Aaj Kal* (Imtiaz Ali 2009) still revolve around NRIs, but they do not directly address the issue of migration, which merely provides the excuse for exotic foreign locations. The NRI, not so much of a role model anymore, has become one of the normalized figures of Indian society on the big screen, not as much because of the world economic crisis or because of return migrations as because he has been fully integrated into the mainstream imagination of Indianness. At the same time, while films can show NRI characters without emphasizing their status or migration, NRI actors known for their weak Hindi, like Katrina Kaif, have become over the past few years new role models and trigger the desire for a reconciled modernity that could transcend territorial and linguistic barriers.

Bollywood consists not only of films but of the range of products intrinsically linked to every Bollywood film: music, dances and DVDs, which connect India and the diaspora in a loop that is, on the whole—and along with IT and outsourcing—emblematic of India. In reality, the Indian film industry produces more films than any other country in the world, averaging over 1000 features a year, a quarter of which are Bollywood films.Thanks to the information highway and the opening up of technological gizmos where films can be downloaded on cell phones and exported through DVDs across the globe, regional films, mainstream and off-mainstream, have reached many countries of the world almost simultaneously with their home premieres. Rajnikant and Kamal Hassan's films are a great rage across the Middle-East, in the US and so on. The native citizens of Greece and Romania are great fans of Amitabh Bachchan's films, while France, Italy and other European nations swoon equally over the films of Satyajit Ray, Mani Ratnam and Adoor Gopala Krishnan.

The word Bollywood has been extensively analyzed and criticized. Here I will only mention Madhava Prasad's article "This thing called Bollywood", which raises important questions about the relation between Bollywood and the media, and points out that Bollywood is a signifier for social and cultural transformations that extend well beyond cinema itself.As he explains: "They [Bollywood films] have figured prominently in the emerging new culture of India. They have produced another variation of nationalist ideology of tradition and modernity, and most interestingly, they have relocated what we might call the seismic center of Indian national identity somewhere in Anglo-America" (Prasad, 2003).The importance of Bollywood cinema in the context of the large South Asian diaspora is recognized as an important cultural subject for diaspora scholars, as cinema has played a prominent role in the expansion of an Indian diasporic culture. Cinema is therefore the most popular and significant cultural form and commodity in the transnational Indian cultural and political economy. As Desai explains:

South Asian diasporic identities are centrally configured and contested through cinema, its production and consumption. While South Asian media are consumed by many parts of the South Asian diaspora, the production of South Asian diasporic media is centred in the West, specifically in the United States, Canada and Britain [...] South Asian diasporic cinema is a developing cinema that negotiates the dominant discourses, politics and economies of multiple locations (Desai, 2005: 373).

Let us now consider the following facts: Amitabh Bachchan, who was voted the greatest star of stage and screen in a BBC online poll and has been immortalized in wax at Madame Tussaud's Museum in London ; his daughter-in-law, Aishwarya Rai made the cover of *Time* magazine, and even taught Oprah Winfrey and her viewers how to put on a sari; The Simpsons ended their trip to India with a dance set to a Hindi film song; Bollywood films sold more tickets in the United Kingdom than English-language films; Bollywood stars advertise trendy Western food and fashion bands; these stars also campaign on behalf of international humanitarian foundations; in the *Pravasi Bharatiya Divas*("Overseas Indian Meeting") celebrated annually for the Diaspora, Bollywood stars have replaced Indian diplomats and politicians, and have been much more successful at attracting enthusiastic audiences of NRIs, PIOs and Westerners (Kavoori and Punathambekar, 2008).

To this we could add more data from Europe: in 2001-2002 the big-budget musical *Bombay Dreams* opened in London; the department store Selfridges transformed its basement into a Bollywood set; the Victoria and Albert Museum curated a special exhibition dedicated to Hindi Cinema's visual culture focusing on advertising and song picturisation, and the British Film Institute toured a series of films through various regions of the UK under the title "Imagine Asia". As Kavoori and Punathambekar have put it, facts such as these are interesting not only because they serve as useful starting points for considering Bollywood's interactions with the rest of the world over the past decade, but more importantly, they signal that as Bollywood emergences as a space for cultural production and for the expression of what is now decidedly global, this entails categories such as *nation, public, culture, modernity, identity and politics*, and challenges our assumptions and our understanding of the relationships between these categories (Kavoori and Punathambekar, 2008).

It is worth mentioning that Bollywood is putting India on the world map, as art-cinema did much earlier starting with Satyajit Ray, and more recently thanks to Bengali director Aparna Sen, Buddhadeb Dasgupta (whose *Uttara* earned him the Special Director's Award in Venice), Jabbar Patel, Shyam Benegal, Adoor Gopalakrishna, who have received recognition at A-list festivals (such as Cannes, Berlin, Venice, Rotterdam). Not to mention internationally known NRI directors such as Mira Nair *(Salaam Bombay, Monsoon Wedding)* or Deepa Mehta *(Fire, Earth and Water, Midnight's Children).*This further highlights the potential for Indian cinema to reach a global audience, and reinforces changing perceptions of India—a fact that Academy Awarded-winning director Shekhar Kapur (director of *Bandit Queen, Elizabeth* and *The Golden Age*) aptly summed up in his now-famous statement that Bollywood will determine global entertainment in the 21st century. Bollywood, which refers to the Indian filmmaking industry known for its insanely long and melodramatic musicals, makes an interesting little case-study in cultural globalization.And the most famous actor in the world isn't named Tom, Brad, or Ben. It's Amitabh Bachchan, according to a recent worldwide BBC survey. No matter that even the smallest Hollywood films have budgets that dwarf the biggest that Bollywood has to offer. Brad Pitt's take for 'Troy,' for example, was alone almost double the entire budget of the most expensive Bollywood production of all time. In fact, the exorbitant salaries of Hollywood stars may be one of the factors that will bring Indian movies home. While Hollywood is dragged down with exorbitant production costs, Bollywood is free to make and distribute as many movies as they please. And people watch them. Lots of people. Over half the world's population finds their primary source of entertainment in Indian celluloid.

Shekhar Kapur, a very prominent Bollywood filmmaker, is quite enthusiastic about the cultural force inherent in Bollywood. "Indian cinema," he says, is "explosive, because of the way it's catching on. Indian and Asian cultures are going to be recognized as the new pop cultureglobally. Everything and anything that's Indian - yoga, fashion, music - has suddenly now become more popular and mainstream in the west. Indian movies can also make the crossover."

Kapur sees a cultural invasion just around the corner. "The sheer size of the market potential would lead to a process of reverse cultural colonization." Mira Nair, another prominent Indian filmmaker, is on the same page with Kapur. "I came from India to Harvard in 1976," she says, "and I was one of only three Indians in the undergraduate class. Five years ago, when I went back, Harvard had 1,500 South Asian students. Which means in five more years, America will be run by people who look like us. We bear no illusions about the elite anymore. We are the elite." Nair directed the critically acclaimed Bollywood - cum - London films '*Salaam Bombay*' and '*Monsoon Wedding.*' Another Indian cross - cultural import is the Andrew Lloyd Webber - Shekhar Kapur produced '*Bombay Dreams,*' a Broadway show that tells the somewhat worn out story (albeit in a new locale) of a destitute young man who finds fame and fortune. The young man is an Untouchable, the lowest Indian caste, and he finds his fortune in Bollywood. Never mind that '*Bombay Dreams*' has been called everything from 'mind - numbing' to 'insane' by critics. What really matters is that it is there, co-produced and co-written in an equal collaborative effort by Indian and Western artists.

Already on the aim facility of the London Stock Exchange Indian film companies – Eros, Adlabs, India Film Company, and UTV –have raised hundreds of millions of pounds from hungry institutional investors.Western film companies are taking a significant equity share in these companies. (Desai 2007.) On 24 January 2005, Percept Picture Company joined hands withMichael Douglas' production company Further Films and Sahara One to co-produce the $50-million *Racing the Monsoon*. On 1 September Sahara announced another tie-up, this time with Hollywood producer Donald Rosenfeld for *Tree of Life* starring Colin Farrell. These are two among a total of six Hollywood co-productions. (Kohli- Khandekar 2006.)Elsewhere too, such references of the globalization of Indian cinema are on the rise. An event unimaginable just a decade ago.Indian movie exports have grown for around 60 per cent recently. The USA and Canada are two major export destinations accounting for 30 percent followed by the UK with 25 per cent and Mauritius and Dubai with 10 per cent each. Other major markets include South Africa, Russia,Fiji, New Zealand and Australia where there is numerous Indian diaspora present. Making a film for the diaspora market is a sure moneymaking venture if compared to filming for the Indian domestic market (Desai 2007). With the international audience, there is notable acceptance of Indian movie themes combined with some of the cross-over movies made by international movie production houses. The earnings of these movies can be compared to some of the Hollywood box office hits. Some Bollywood movies have made more than 50 per cent of their overall gross profit margin from international box office collection. This is a welcome trend which needs to be kept. One of the critical success factors for these movies is to identify ideas from within the Indian themes which appeal to the audience. The other critical success factor is to tie up with a leading international distributor; movies made by people of Indian origin have had up to 2–3 times higher international revenues in comparison to the national bestsellers (cii- A.T. Kearney 2007).India has announced ambitious plans to double its share in the global film industry by the end of this year. This signals the country's determination to establish itself as a cultural as well as economic powerhouse. There are numerous reasons why we should believe that. Firstly, the government, which intends on using Bollywood to build up India as a 'soft power', believes the Indian film industry is capable of capturing five percent of the global market this year. The share is now at two percent (Johnson, 2007).

In terms of technology, the Indian Hindi movie industryhas therefore started with the import of technology from abroad. For the past few years numerous Indian producers have been using special effects technology and training from abroad, particularly from Hollywood.

Last but not least, India has made significant progress in terms of cast as well. Hindi movies have now more and more Hindi movie stars and other people working on international movies, particularly in Hollywood, whereas more and more artists from aboard work for the Indian movie industry.Bollywood is facing a number of challenges in the process of globalization. Small and fragmented market is a big issue. To unlock Bollywood's potential and crack open global markets, production, distribution and retail need to function in unison with the market. If we contrast India with China, the latter does not even have a potential. Despite continuing loses, box office revenues that are one-fifth of India's and quotas on imports, Hollywood is full of enthusiasm for China. In 2005 it invested another USD150m into the film business inChina. The money mostly went into film making and building film retail infrastructure in China. This is because the Chinese film market remains, in spite of all its problems, an easier, more organized market if compared to India. Only by increasing local market share Indian companies will be able to make their market attractive, report profit gain to investors and gain the heft needed to enter global markets (Kohli-Khandekar, 2006).

Domestic and diaspora markets are too large for Indian cinema to adapt themselves to Western tastes. There are also the Third World markets, however, the real money lies in rich OECDcountries. Bollywood hasmade a lot of progress in the recent years, particularly after having been given the Industry status. The first International film festival Awards (IIFA) function was staged in London's prestigious Millennium Dome, instituted in 2000, the ceremony is held in different countries around the world every year with the most recent onebeing held in Kuala Lumpur, Malaysia. This was an unambiguous proclamation that Indian cinema had arrived on the international stage. Acceptance of Indian films abroad is due to the qualitative change that has come about in Indian films. Their quality is now of international standards and the market for them has registered a phenomenal growth.There is a huge Indian diaspora in countries like the UK, Canada, the Middle East, and South Africa which all represent a big market for Indian films. This is also the time when Indian economy is booming and as in consequence India is viewed in a positive way by other countries. Brand India is gradually gaining share in the global market. However, Bollywood's share in the global movie market is still relatively insignificant. All in all, it has been a long story of nearly nine decades, with the early shaky screen images having been turned into a multi-pronged and vast economic empire. Today it is the biggest movie industry in the world in terms of number of films. The industry has produced approximately 27,000 feature films and thousands of documented short films. Having established itself as an industry and being duly recognized as one, the Indian popular cinema has over its course made a lot of progress in almost all areas, such as retail infrastructure, financing, marketing and distribution. With a huge spread of Indian diaspora and the growth of Brand India, it has made inroads in the international market. In fact, in the recent past, the export sales of many Indian movies were higher than the domestic sales. The industry has made progress in all four aspects of globalization, (*i.e.* goods/services, capital, technology and people). In the future in order to get a big market share and give Hollywood a run for its money, however, the industry needs to put in a lot of money and effort, particularly in the international marketing and distribution.

References

Appadurai, Arjun; Breckenridge, Carol A. 'Public Modernity in India', in Carol A. Breckenridge (ed.), *Consuming Modernity: Public Culture in Contemporary India*, New Delhi: Oxford University Press, pp. 1-20. 1996. Print.

Bhabha, Homi. *The Location of Culture*, London: Routledge. 1994. Web.

Bhagwati, Jagdish; Dellafar, William. 'The Brain Drain and Income Taxation', *World Development*, 1 (1-2), pp. 94-101.1973. Print.

Bhoopaty, D. 'Cinema and Politics in India', in Kiran Prasad (ed.), *Political Communication: The Indian Experience*, Delhi: B. R. Publishing Corporation, pp. 507-17.2003. Web.

Blom, Hansen Thomas. 'In Search of the Diasporic Self: Bollywood in South Africa', in Raminder Kaur and Ajay J. Sinha (eds.), *Bollyworld: Popular Indian Cinema through a Transnational Lens*, New Delhi: Sage Publications, pp. 239-60. 2005. Print.

Breckenridge, Carol A.ed.*Consuming Modernity: Public Culture in ContemporaryIndia*, New Delhi: Oxford University Press.1996. Web.

Cii-A. T. Kearney. 2007. Cii-A. T. Kearney study on transforming for Growth: Future of the Indian media and entertainment landscape.

Http://cii.in/documents/executivesummarycii_atkearneyup.pdf.

Chopra, Yash (2002). Interview by author, 26 December, Bombay.

Chopra, Yash (2003) 'Address', Pravasi Bharatiya Divas, 10 January.

Deshpande, Sudhanva. 'The Consumable Hero of Globalized India', in Raminder Kaur and Ajay J. Sinha (eds.), *Bollyworld: Popular Indian Cinema through a Transnational Lens*, New Delhi: Sage Publications, pp. 186-203. 2005. Web.

Desai, M. 2007. Bollywood needs to change its act. *The Hindu,* November 25. Http://www.hinduonnet.com/thehindu/mag/2007/11/25/stories/2007112550030100. Htm.

Dwyer.100 Bollywood Films – BFI Screen Guides. London, UK: British FilmInstitute, pp-76-79

Dwyer, Rachel; Pinney, Christopher (eds.) (2001) *Pleasure and the Nation: the History, Politics and Consumption of Public Culture in India*, New Delhi: Oxford University Press.

FICCI-PricewaterhouseCoopers. 2006. The India entertainment and media Industry: Unravelling the potential. Http://www.pwc.com/extweb/pwcpublications.nsf/docid/be7e56c3ff8e90a6ca2571850 06a3275/$file/Frames.pdf.

Federation of Indian Chambers of Commerce and Industry; KPMG (2010) *Back in the Spotlight. FICCI-KPMG India Media and Entertainment Industry Report*, New Delhi: FICCI.

Johnson, J. 2007. India seeks to double share of world film industry. *Financial Times,* January 15.

Kaur, Raminder. 'Cruising on the Vilayeti Bandwagon: Diasporic Representations and Reception of Popular Indian Movies', in Raminder Kaur and Ajay J. Sinha (eds.), *Bollyworld: Popular Indian Cinema through a Transnational Lens*, New Delhi: Sage Publications, pp. 309-29. 2005. Web.

Kaur, Raminder; Sinha, Ajay J. (eds.) *Bollyworld: Popular Indian Cinema through a Transnational Lens*, New Delhi: Sage Publications.2005. Print.

Kohli-Khandekar, V. Action Stations! *Businessworld Online*. Http://www.businessworldindia.com/Jan0906/coverstory01.asp. 2006. Web.

Nandy, Ashis.*The Secret Politics of Our Desires. Innocence, Culpability and Indian Popular Cinema*, New Delhi, Oxford University Press. 1998. Web.

Prasad, M. Madhava (2003) 'This Thing Called Bollywood', *Seminar*, 525, May, URL: http://www.india-seminar.com/2003/525/525 per cent 20madhava per cent 20prasad.htm

Punathambekar, Ashwin. 'Bollywood in the Indian-American diaspora: Mediating a Transitive Logic of Cultural Citizenship', *International Journal of Cultural Studies,* 8 (2), pp. 151-73.DOI:10.1177/1367877905052415. 2005. Web.

Pulkit, Datta.*Bollywoodizing Diasporas: Reconnecting to the NRI through Popular Hindi Cinema*, B. A. Dissertation,Ohio: Miami University.2008.

Ramdya, Kavita.*Bollywood Weddings: Dating, Engagement and Marriage in Hindu America*, Lanham: Lexington Books. 2009.

Rao, Shakuntala.'The Globalization of Bollywood: An Ethnography of Non-Elite Audiences in India', *The Communication Review*, 10, pp. 57-76. 2007.

Ravindran, Visa.'Values in Transition: Media, Technology and Communication', in Kiran Prasad (ed.), *Political Communication: The Indian Experience*, Delhi: B. R. Publishing Corporation, 2003. pp. 149-65.

Therwath,Ingrid. « 'Shining Indians': Diaspora and Exemplarity in Bollywood », *South Asia Multidisciplinary Academic Journal* [Online], 4 | 2010, Online since 17 December 2010, connection on 11 May 2016. URL: http://samaj.revues.org/3000

Virdi, Jyotika.*The Cinematic Imagination: Indian Popular Films as Social History*, New Brunswick and New Jersey: Rutgers University Press.2003.

Chapter 19

Feminine Cinematic Constructs and Re (Thinking) Women in the Indian Cinema

*Manjari Shukla**

For knowing and analyzing India's culture in this century, Indian cinema has been a major point of reference. It has fashioned and articulated the changing scenarios of modern India to an extent that no preceding art form could ever achieve. Often we have observed that men in most societies are seen as breadwinners while role of women is restricted to being a good homemaker. As societies entered the world of modernization and globalization, the role of women changed drastically and dramati-cally. The role of Media is important in the modernization of societies and it has greatly affected the image of women in today's modern world. A number of researches have been done on the role of women in different societies. However little has been said about the importance of films in portraying women in their shifting roles over different decades and the impact it has on societies in general. Over past decades, Indian cinema has witnessed a significant transformation in the way women are portrayed through films. It can be observed that contemporary films portray women as more independent, confident, and career oriented.

The present paper will take up few films of Bollywood and will try commenting on the fast changing role(s) of women portrayed in Indian cinema and its influence on the patriarchal nature of Indian society. The issues which these films raise and

**Assistant Professor, Department of English,*
Vasanta College for Women, Rajghat
Banaras Hindu University, Varanasi – 221 001

address are extensive and varied. The aim is to link the changing character played by women in films with the emerging status of women in India, as films are a reflection of changes in the social structure.

It is already a known fact that cinema has always been a reflection of the ethos and ideology of any society at a given point of time. The medium(s) to accentuate this reflection varied from costumes to music to items of luxury; but the most crucial medium became the characters. The mind-set, thinking, apprehensions or the prejudices of the various characters in one way or the other were the same as those of the general public.

In the initial years of Indian cinema, pertaining to the norms of the conservative society, the ideal woman was depicted to be 'submissive and shy', 'dependent and fragile', usually 'clad in a sari', whereas the famous vamps of Bollywood donned bold outfits. Women who dressed in a style more influenced by the West were usually considered to be morally degraded. If we look at the 1970s or '80s, the favorite vamps of that era like Bindu, Helen or Aruna Irani were some of the first women to smoke, drink or engage in pre-marital sex onscreen, unlike other actresses. Such activities were a sign that the women characters had questionable morals, though when a male actor did the same onscreen he was seen as being macho. The actresses on the other hand would not even dare to do so as they were expected to be 'docile', 'shy' and 'dependent' women because these were the virtues of a so called 'well-cultured' Indian woman.

Progressing in the '80s, women portrayal in Indian cinema gradually shifted its paradigm and they were taken to be little more serious. This was reflected in a few women-centric movies like *Umrao Jaan* and *Paakizah*. Drastic change were seen in the role of women in 90's, when their roles became more substantial. The definition as well as execution of being an actress became much more, than just playing eye candy and dancing around trees. One of the best examples of this was actress Seema Biswas's role in the movie *Bandit Queen* in 1994. She portrayed the character of a woman who was far more than the docile and fragile figures of the 80s. She was strong, courageous. All this was happening simultaneously with the changing roles of women in the Indian society. Women were getting liberated and independent. They were better educated and had innumerable working opportunities and this was reflected in Indian cinema.

It was in the first decade of the 21st century that the role of Indian woman was (re)defined with utmost vigor and vitality in the world of cinema. From movies like *Astitva*, *Lajja*, *Chandani Bar* and *Page3* in the early years to *Dor*, *Turning 30*, *Fashion* and *No One Killed Jessica* in the latter half of the Nineties, their characters were as strong as that of the male protagonists, but more profound. She could be anything from a perceptive politician to a bold journalist to a prostitute or a super-successful industrialist. The role of the Indian female was revolutionized in cinema–just like in real life. She became this fierce, successful, dominating, independent and ultramodern woman of today.

For a long time, women mainly played as decorative objects in Hindi cinema. Each decade has offered its own brand of women in Hindi cinema. The ordinary woman has hardly been visible in Hindi cinema. During the time of Meena Kumari, Madhubala and their peers, the camera was seen paying attention more on the face of the leading lady in contrast to her body. This thought process also changed radically from the 1990s, when the body (figure) of the heroine became more important than the face. The *sati-savitri* image underwent a radical make-over probably with Nutan, who, without showing skin, made a powerful presentation in strong roles such as *Seema* and *Bandini*. There was a positive deviation from the *sati-savitri* image, when Geeta Bali promoted the image of a mischievous tomboy.

Women in Indian cinema are portrayed with certain assumptions ranging from cult movies to celluloid blockbusters like *Sholay* to more recent *Fashion* that employ themselves as in severe gender roles and issues. They are portrayed either as damsels in distress or demented feminists. The discussion in the paper is now carried to the movies, which to some extent reflect the cinematic imagination and transformation of Indian women.

A woman carrying a plough on her shoulder, her face twisting in agony – this is the first look of *Mother India*'s poster. This distressed woman is Nargis, playing the role of a rural Indian girl named Radha. The story is about Radha and her family's struggle to make ends meet during days of abject poverty and their suffering at the hands of Sukhilala, a cunning moneylender. With an interesting climax, the film makes up for its lack of a happy ending. The audience is then able to understand the significance of the movie's title and how a woman, with strongly held values and beliefs, sacrifices her own happiness for the sake of justice.

The movie is regarded as one of the finest classics of Indian cinema. The female figure emerges here as the epitome of justice and as a mother god like figure in her village. The movie depicts her powerful persona in such a way, that towards the end, in order to maintain justice, she even kills her son.

Bandit Queen: The true story of Phoolan Devi, an Indian woman arrested in the state of Uttar Pradesh in January 1983 for kidnapping and murder, provides the plot for this gripping Indian-British Film, directed by Shekhar Kapur. The maximum part of the story is taken from Devi's prison diaries. Played by Seema Biswas, the character in the film shows an independent thinking girl, who was dissatisfied with the rigid caste regulations and the dull rural life she is expected to lead.

As a young woman, she is captivated by Vikram (Nirmal Pandey), a dashing young member of a bandit gang. His gang kidnaps her and she is raped by the leader. Vikram kills the leader, assumes that position, and makes Devi an official member. Vikram is eventually shot during a leadership dispute after a former member, SriRam (Govind Namdeo), returns from prison. Devi becomes more involved in the violence after she kills her former husband with a rifle butt. The film's bloody climax comes after she is gang-raped by SriRam and his gang in her own village. Devi gets her revenge in what became known as the Behmai Massacre of February 1981. The movie follows the story of a commoner, who eventually takes the path of crime, in order to do justice to herself as well as others, giving them a message to raise their voice and weapons, whenever there is a danger to their self.

Zubeidaa, directed by Shyam Benegal, is a tale of a young man's (Rajit Kapur) quest to uncover the life and times of his mother, Zubeidaa (Karisma Kapoor), who has been more of a mysterious stranger to him.

The story of the film is set in the early 1950s. Zubeidaa is the only daughter of filmmaker Suleman Seth (Amrish Puri). Unknown to her father, Zubeidaa acts in a film 'Banjaran'. When her father learns of this, he forbids her from pursuing a film career and hastily arranges for her to marry Mehboob Alam, the son of his childhood friend, without consulting Zubeidaa. Soon after they are wedded, Zubeidaa and Mehboob have a son, Riyaz. Tragedy strikes when due to a misunderstanding between the two families, Mehboob is forced to divorce Zubeidaa and the shocked girl retreats into a shell. The film is a saga of the trials and tribulations faced by a ravishing beauty, Zubeidaa, who dares to lead life on her own terms. *Fashion* released in 2008 is a film that sadly reconfirms moralistic misconceptions most people hold against the fashion industry. And against an ambitious woman who wants to make it big in the glamour world. Meghna, played by Priyanka Chopra is a small town beauty queen who dreams of walking the ramp as a supermodel. When Parents don't support her, she packs her suitcase and moves to Mumbai.

From then on, her story of struggle is a laugh. She makes friends with an assistant designer who puts her on to a casting agent, who supplies models to parties for the glamour quotient. She meets the right people who are immediately impressed by her spunk and confidence and sooner than later, she is crowned the new face of Panache, a coveted company that rules the fashion business. The trajectory Meghna traces is smooth but at the same time challenging. Her determination and the spirit to never give up is the boosting force that keeps her going. In contrast to her character is the character of Kangana. The treatment given to these two characters is marvelous by Bhandarkar, as he portrays them with verve and dynamism and shows how the same fashion industry could be friendly as well as cruel, depending on the people and how they take it. The movie again captures the attention of the audience depicting a different shade of the Modern Indian Woman.

The next movie in cue is *Kahaani* which commences on a chaotic, breathless note with the arrival of a heavily pregnant Vidya Venkatesan Bagchi (Vidya Balan) in the frantic pace of Kolkata (also playing the only protagonist that has more scenes than its brilliant leading lady). While journeying with Vidya through her frustrations and anguish in this deftly written script by Ghosh and Advaita Kala, *Kahaani* often pauses for light interactions to offer a glimpse into the everyday activities of Kolkata which is soaked in Rahul Dev Burman's timeless tunes. Vidya Balan has the potential to excel in a role that requires her to be sensible, adamant, sharp, vulnerable and pregnant. Like she's done with every subsequent release, Balan replaces the memory of her last performance (*The Dirty Picture*) with a sparkling new one. The movie beautifully traverses the amazing journey of Vidya, who is here in Kolkata to find answers to unanswered questions. The concept behind a jigsaw puzzle is most fascinating. The three-step model of the movie involves drawing an intricate picture laden with buried details and fine clues, cutting it into several unrecognizable segments and assembling a jumble that carries a seemingly simple challenge — to fall in place, to make sense. Even though Vidya is the central character, still all the other characters of the movie around her are impressive in all accord.

This movie again projects the image of a self-dependent woman, who manages her way to get through all the tricky mazes of life, just to reach the destination she is bound to triumph over. *Dirty Picture* showcases a film producer, desperately seeking a hit. He finds a 'starlet' in the smalltime but sexy and extremely ambitious girl Reshma. He immediately rechristens her as Silk. This is the rise and fall story of a non-entity who turns the biggest sex-symbol in cinema, loosely modeled on the lines of real-life temptresses of the 80s Silk Smitha. But the same people, who make a star out of her, pull her down subsequently. Superstar Suryakant (Naseeruddin Shah) sees this woman as a potential threat to his stardom and decides to clip her wings. Even Ramakant (Tusshar Kapoor), who loves her, ditches her for her indulgence in substance abuse. On the contrary, filmmaker Abraham (Emraan Hashmi), the man who hated her the most, gets attracted towards her. The barefaced demeanour of the film candidly highlights the exploits of the industry and the unapologetic attitude of its female protagonist. The film is more a behind-the-scene account of Silk than her onscreen antics, and hence it touches the audience on a whole new different level. The continuing frustration and pain received at the hands of people Silk, badly trusted, forces her to take the decision to end her life. The girl who reached the zenith of stardom is brutally thrown from the heights, just because she was a threat to the patriarchal movie industry. The movie makes us think on various levels and poses question on the industry, which differentiates between actors just on the basis of their genders. It can be very well said that the portrayal of women in Hindi cinema through these constructs, theories and perspectives can neither be directly applied to nor superimposed on Indian mainstream cinema's treatment and portrayal of women. One has to develop a mode of analysis that is culture-specific and situation-specific. Feminist film theories mainly are drawn upon psycho-analysis, semiology and structuralism. Against the backdrop of the Indian socio-economic backdrop, there is a need to develop a new theory, within which the real woman lives and works. The theory will study the intersections of these standpoints with celluloid women in Indian cinema. The question now arises how much the real women are distanced from the women of celluloid? Does distancing help nurture better images of the celluloid women or does it hinder the image more, thereby distancing the audience from these films? Globalization has changed it all and there is a need to look at the woman portrayals in Hindi cinema in today's era with new eyes and through a new pair of glasses which are tinted with the 'razzmatazz' of Western packaging, and sophisticated marketing strategies.

References

Bandit Queen. Dir. Shekhar Kapoor. IMDb Distributors, 1994. Film.

Dirty Picture. Dir. Milan Luthria. Alt Entertainment, 2011. Film.

Fashion. Dir. Madhur Bhandarkar. UTV Motion Pictures, 2008. Film.

Ganti, Tejaswini. Bollywood: a guidebook to popular Hindi cinema. UK :Routledge, 2004. Print.

Kahaani. Dir. Sujoy Ghosh. Viacom 18 Motion Pictures, 2012. Film.

Mehta, Rini Bhattacharya and Rajeshwari Pandharipande. Bollywood and Globalization: Indian Popular Cinema, Nation and Diaspora. UK :Anthem Press, 2010. Print.

Mother India. Dir. Mehboob Khan.IMDb distributors, 1957. Film.

Ram, Anjali. "Framing the Feminine: Diasporic Readings of Gender in Popular Indian Cinema".

Women's Studies in Communication, Vol. 25, No. 1, (Spring 2002):25-52. Print.

Zubeidaa. Dir. Shyam Benegal. Yash Raj Films, 2001. Film.

Chapter 20

The Inter-relation of Cinema and Literature

*Garima Singh**

"Literature always anticipates life. It does not copy it, but moulds it to its purpose. The nineteenth century, as we know it, is largely an invention of Balzac."

Oscar Wild

Literature has had a major impact on the development of society. It has shaped civilizations, changed political systems and exposed injustice. Literature gives us a detailed preview of human experiences, allowing us to connect on basic levels of desire and emotion. **Literature affects people by teaching them, entertaining them and inspiring them to take action in life.** According to Gulf News, literature has "shaped civilizations, changed political systems and exposed injustice." Literature also helps people understand other walks of life. Narratives, in particular, inspire empathy and give people a new perspective on their lives and the lives of others. Society has great effects on literature, philosophy, and cinemaor on any genres of art. Literature is born of social beliefs, thoughts, ideologies, and society is a great river and literature is a rivulet, a tributary and literature gets lots of materials, resources from society. With that said, society improves at times through its greatest minds and of course Gorky, Tolstoy, Dickens and then like had great impacts on their societies on the other hand Cinema is a universal teacher. It educates

**M.Ed. Student*
NCERT, R.I.E, Ajmer, Rajasthan
e-mail: garima.bhu86@gmail.com

the people in different branches of learning. Cinema like literature a reflection of society, as it reflects both present and past. Cinema is a form of communication as it communicates the untold pain and overlooked issues of society. It is a powerful vehicle for culture, education, leisure and propaganda. The function of cinema is "to delight and instruct". The prior function of any movie is to delight the audience and then to instruct, for movies are also taken as a form of literature.

In the words of - Amitabh Bachhan

"Indian cinema has virtually become a parallel culture. Talk of India with a foreigner and debate virtually centresaround Indian films."

In a 1963 report for the United Nations Educational Scientific and Cultural Organization looking at Indian Cinema and Culture, the author (BaldoonDhingra) quoted a speech by Prime Minister Nehru who stated, "...the influence in India of films is greater than newspapers and books combined." Movies have the power to leave an indelible impact on the minds of the viewers. They not only make us think, but also play an instrumental role in changing the way we think. At a time when the cinema is the biggest media culture and that literature has an audience so small, "the cinema should not be seen only as a cinematic phenomenon, not even as an artistic phenomenon, but as the possibility of acquiring the balance, freedom, the possibility of becoming human "(Bernardet, 1985: 34). Statistics show that the search for the source text significantly increases with the adaptations of novels (in the recent case of The Da Vinci Code, The Lord of the Rings and Harry Potter). Not only in Hollywood but in Bollywood and other genres of Indian cinema is not coming up with wonderful adaptation of classic literature and contemporary too.

Prominent Literature in Indian Cinema

For a long time, there has existed an interrelationship and mutual influence between literature and other forms of artistic expressions. This has resulted in painting and music based on works of fiction, drama and poetry, as well as literary works emulating pictorial styles and musical structures. The creative exchange between literature and film was initiated in the last decade of the 19th Century. Initially, film was most related to photography and painting. Popular film developed with the emergence of the 18th Century novel. Both the 18th Century novel and film relied heavily upon realism as a technique. Early films were concerned, just like with realism in literature, daily lives of ordinary people. The subject matter and audiences were people of low social standing.

An analogy stands out for film and literature. The basic structural units of the novel were replicated in film. In the novel we have: the word, sentence, paragraph, chapter and the entire novel. In film we have the frame, shot scene and sequence. The word in literature and the image in film were similar in so far as they are visual phenomena, both perceived with the eye.

Despite different degrees of explication, both writers and filmmakers use language or languages. Some differences may exist however. For instance, whereas the film is multi-sensory communal experience emphasizing immediacy, literature is a monosensory private experience that is more conductive to reflection. A film is usually viewed in others' presence who become a larger part of the film's experience. Each audience member acknowledges the presence of the others. Audience response can also affect perception of a film. A novel is typically a private experience in which the relationship between the author and the reader is relatively direct and immediate. Others' responses do not impinge on the novel, thus making it conducive to reflection as the reader can pause and mull over or re-read. Movies based on popular novels are a tradition believed to be first implemented in Hollywood.

But the Indian industry has its own collection of adaptations which we are unaware of, at least in most cases. Everybody talks about ChetanBhagat's works being made into films. What about the other ones which deserve an equal recognition? Let's take a look at some worthy novels that served as an inspiration for some interesting Indian Movies.

THE NAMESAKE (2004- NOVEL) THE NAMESAKE (2006 MOVIE)

Originally published as a novella, The Namesake was one of the first novels written by JhumpaLahiri, the famous Indian American author. Imagine the struggles of an Indian family who have to leave behind their culture and ideals to survive in a contrasting environment in the United States. Mira Nair directed the film based on the Bengali family, which had Irrfan Khan and Tabu in the lead roles. The film was well received and obtained positive reviews from the critics. It was completely based on the novel with very minor variations. Being born and brought up in a country like the US, the emotions, troubles and apprehensions that an Indian kid undergoes trying to understand his culture and adapt to it, is beautifully narrated by the author. A reflection of events that are common and prevalent in various families, the novel and the film are most enjoyable.

PINJAR (1950 – NOVEL) | PINJAR (2003 – MOVIE)

Set during India's partition, Pinjar is one of the most acclaimed works of the Indian poet and author, Amrita Pritam. It describes the hardships faced by the rural Indian women, who were bound by the strict laws of the society during those times. It also gives a detailed account on the partition and the effects it had on the people of both nations – India and Pakistan. Adapted into a movie of the same name, Pinjar won the National Award for Best Feature Film apart from several other acclaims. Directed by Chandra Prakash Dwivedi and starring alongside ManojBajpai and Sanjay Suri, UrmilaMatondkar has done justice to her role as Puro, the young Hindu woman who is kidnapped by a Muslim and later forsaken by her family. Amrita Pritam's extensive experience has helped her give life to a strong, resilient character that stands as a personification for women who need an inspiration to resist violence against them and fight for their rights.

CRACKING INDIA (1991 – NOVEL) | EARTH (1998 – MOVIE)

Written by the Pakistani author, BapsiSidhwa, Cracking India is another one of those novels based on the Partition of India and its repercussions. But here we get a glimpse of the events from the viewpoint of Lenny, a girl from a rich Parsi family who witnesses the hostility between the various religions in our country. Inspired by the novel, Deepa Mehta decided to make a film based on it entitled '1947: Earth', which was India's official entry for the Academy Award for Best Foreign Language Film. The story also delves into the love triangle between Lenny's (played by Maia Sethna) caretaker, a Hindu, portrayed by Nandita Das and two Muslim men played by Aamir Khan and Rahul Khanna.

THE BLUE UMBRELLA (1980 – NOVEL) | THE BLUE UMBRELLA (2005 – MOVIE)

One of the most famous Indian authors of British origin, Ruskin Bond is known for his fascinating novels for children. Set in the backdrop of a small imaginary village in Himachal Pradesh, this story is literally about a beautiful blue umbrella that a small girl named Binya gets, in exchange for her lucky leopard claw necklace. The umbrella grabs the attention of the village folk, including the local shopkeeper who tries to acquire the umbrella from the girl in vain. But when a plot to steal the blue umbrella with the help of his shop boy goes wrong, the villagers despise the shopkeeper, earning him a bad reputation. Binnya feels guilty that her flaunting of the umbrella has caused all these problems and seeing him realize his folly, she gives the blue umbrella back to him to make him happy. Though it's a simple story, Bond plays with the subtle feelings which was good enough to adapt this story into a film of the same name, directed by Vishal Bharadwaj. With the lead roles played by Pankaj Kapoor and Shreya Sharma, the film earned the National Award for Best Children's film.

CHOKHER BALI (NOVEL) | CHOKHER BALI (2003 – MOVIE)

To what extent would people go to experience love? Or maybe lust? Rabindranath Tagore illustrates some of the consequences when you let your hormones get the better of you in this Bengali novel. We are well aware of the restrictions posed on widows in those days and the kind of life they were forced to lead. But they have their desires to lead a complete life like any other woman and their yearning for love is totally justified.

OTHELLO (1603 – NOVEL) | OMKARA (MOVIE)

Based on one of the famous works of Shakespere, Omkara was directed by Vishal Bharadwaj with Ajay Devgan, Saif Ali Khan and Kareena Kapoor in the lead. Dealing with a number of factors like love, mistrust, infidelity, and retribution etc, Othello is quite famous and is still performed at theaters in many parts of the world.

SUSANNA'S SEVEN HUSBANDS (NOVEL) | 7 KHOON MAAF (2011 - MOVIE)

Yet another famous adaptation from Ruskin Bond, Vishal Bharadwaj completed the script with the help of Bond to make this film with Priyanka Chopra in the lead, who murders her seven husbands in her never-ending pursuit for love.

DEVDAS (1917 – NOVEL) | DEVDAS (1955 and 2002 – MOVIE) and DEV.D (2009 – MOVIE)

One of the most famous love stories of our country, Devdas is a Romantic Novel written in Bengali by Sarat Chandra Chattopadhyay. The characters of Devdas and Paro had become so famous that they were adapted into movies of various languages, including Hindi, where it was remade thrice.

PARINEETA (1914 – NOVEL) | PARINEETA (2005 – MOVIE)

Another Bengali novel set in the early 20th century by Sarat Chandra Chattopadhyay, this story of the love between Lalita and Shekhar, two childhood friends, enters troubled waters when another man ente.

Junoon (1978)

This ShyamBenegal classic about the crazy infatuation of a Pathan (Shashi Kapoor) for his young Anglo-Indian captive (Nafisa Ali) amidst the chaos of the Sepoy mutiny of 1857, was based on the short story "A Flight of Pigeons" by Ruskin Bond. Bond is a well known Indian writer (of British descent) who writes in English and most of his stories are based in the Himalayan regions of Uttarakhand.

SHATRANJ KE KHILADI (1977)

Legendary director Satyajit Ray's only foray into Hindi cinema is a sumptuous historical drama set in the turbulent last days (1856) of the reign of NawabWajed Ali Shah of Avadh (or*Oudh* as it is known in the *Raj* literature). The movie is based on a story by renowned Hindi writer MunshiPremchand, and stars Amjad Khan, Sanjeev Kumar, Saeed Jaffrey and Sir Richard Attenborough. Premchand's writing was characterised by his realistic depiction of mostly rural protagonists and the use of vernacular Hindi as opposed to the more Sanskritised version preferred by other writers.

HAIDER (MOVIE 2015) HAMLET(PLAY)

No other state evokes patriotism among Indians in quite the same way that Kashmir does. So when it comes making movies on a strife-torn region, Bollywood filmmakers have always chosen to view the issue through nationalistic goggles.

That may perhaps explain a widely held opinion among the people in Kashmir that Bollywood has failed to present a realistic picture of political and societal tensions in this 24-year-old conflict.

Movies in the past two decades have either talked about the sacrifices made by the soldiers in Kashmir or present the people in a stereotypical fashion.

There is no doubt that no movie can perfectly portray the sense of injustice and alienation that the people of Kashmir feel today. But Vishal Bharadwaj's *Haider*, an adaptation of William Shakespeare's play *Hamlet*, has not just come close to portraying that uncomfortable picture but for the first time many Kashmiris are feeling an association with this movie.

Contribution of Literature in Indian Cinema

The world cinema is replete with movies based on literary works. There is no beginning and end of the amalgamation of literature and cinema, still this journey can be traced roughly from the BBC series on complete works of Shakespeare we to the latest Lee film Life of Pi based on YANN Martel's novel of the same name. This journey is not only interesting but also thought provoking. Even Indian Film Industry is not untouched by this fast emerging genre. I this segment Satyajit Ray's PatherPanchali and DevAnand's Guide are the milestones of yesterday while Bhardwaj's Omkara, Haider and Amir's Three Idiots are one of the blockbusters of contemporary cinema. One of the many thought provoking dialogues from the movieHaider :

Shaq pehaiyaqeento,yaqeenpehaishaqmujhe

Kiska jhootjhoothai, kiskesachmeinsachnahi

Haikihainahi, bas yahi hi sawaalhai

Aursawaalkajawaabbhisawaalhai

Dilki gar sunu to hai, dimaagki to hainahi

Jaan loon kijaandoon, main rahoonki main nahi

If I am certain about my suspicion, I am also suspicious about the certainty

Whose lies are absolute lies, whose truth has no truth

Does it exist or does it not, that is the only question

And the answer to that is just another question

My heart says it exists, my mind says it does not

Should I take a life or should I take my life,

Should I continue to live or should I just die

These lines sum up Haider's reflection on life, his confusion as he is faced with betrayal and the pain of losing a loved one and with trust and the joy of having a loved one in his arms. Is it better to kill someone and live a life full of pain and troubles or is it easier to just die and relieve oneself of all the miseries. This all gives a new life to a plain and simple dialogue and makes it immortal in the list of timeless movies. People who have never read Hamlet read this play for the sake of understanding the theme of the play.

Classic Collections

1. THE GUIDE (1958 – NOVEL) | GUIDE (1965 – MOVIE).
2. THE CITADEL (1937 – NOVEL) | TERE MERE SAPNE (1971 – MOVIE).
3. SAHEB, BIBI GOLAM (NOVEL) | SAHIB, BIWI AUR GHULAM (1962 – MOVIE).
4. A FLIGHT OF PIGEONS (NOVEL) | JUNOON (1978 – MOVIE).
5. SHATRANJ KE KHILADI (1924 – NOVEL) | SHATRANJ KE KHILADI (1977 – MOVIE).

As it is well known India produces a massive number of feature films in many different languages, including several dialects. In 1999, the total number of films produced, in as many as 35 official languages and dialects, was 601 - up to October but one could add about 30 - 40 feature films to this number up to end December,1999. Since its beginning with the film 'Raja Harish Chandra' (1913), the cinema has remained the most powerful media for mass communication in India. Since its beginning with the film '*Raja Harish Chandra*' (1913), the cinema has remained the most powerful media for mass communication in India. Cinema has the ability to combine entertainment with communication of ideas. It has the potential appeal for its audience. It certainly leaves other media far behind in making such an appeal. As in literature, cinema has produced much which touches the innermost layers of the man. It mirrors the episodes in such a manner that leaves an impact on the coming generations. Cinema presents an image of the society in which it is born and the hopes, aspirations, frustration and contradictions present in any given social order.

Collaboration of literature with cinema increases its far reaching appeal which now encompasses various socio-economic issues which were marginalized so far. Cinema couldhave never reached to the height of present if literature based movies were not there into the existence. The movies like Pinjar and Chokher Bali give substance to the stature of the women while Chithariyavar, a Malayalam gives a voice to Dalit's. The gender issues and identity crisis are beautifully brought to the fore by Rituparno Ghosh in his Bengali movie, Chitrangada: The Crowning Wish. Though both literature and cinema are arts of narration, their ways of representation are completely different. Our texts reach out to local audiences only when they are modified in order to make them relevant to the cultural and ideological concerns of the new audiences that were far moved from the writer's vision. On one hand it provides a larger audience to literary texts, while on the other, we observes an acute decline in the readership of these texts in the presence of their audio- visuals counterparts. Thus we can say that literature contributes a lot in making of cinema, in other words we can say that literature is the soul of many timeless movies which are said to be the milestones of Indian cinema.

Effect of Literary Cinema on Society

Movies can, but do not necessarily, have a great impact on society. Mostly, they do so by showing people different ways of life and different values that may go on to affect the values that people hold. Indian movie culture has definitely influenced us badly. Movies are a part of Art, learn to recognizance. Which also indicates Indian modern societies have a less medium of communication. Usually, films are mirror of our culture and society as well. We can gain lots of Creative ideas, we can know various hidden facts about our country, we can know more about various hidden heroes of our country who have sacrificed for us, we can know more about our different culture. And positive aspects are endless.

Man has instincts, different thoughts flow which leave an effect on the minds. The person laughs with the films and tears with them. Scenes of 'Shaheed Bhagat Singh', a film by Raj Kumar Santoshi and Manoj Goswami makes people national-minded and sentimentally involved in the film show. The fim dialogues are occupying places in our real life. Dialogues of MugleAzam found place in the normal interaction of people for a long time. People talked and walked like Prithvi Raj, the great king Akbar. In the same way, plays by Agha Hashat and Devdas by Sharat Chandra left a deep impact on the masses. In the same way, film 'Sholey' created an imending effect on so many. It is powerful vehicle for culture, education, leisure and propoaganda. It is hard to decide if films have a larger impact on the Indian Society or the latter has on the former. But as the question takes one side I will try to answer only the first part.

The female who was often neglected in major socio-economic aspects took the central theme in Satyajit Ray's classics. In a traditional Indian society where arranged marriages was a strict norm the movies somehow gave a complete different outlook to Man-woman's relationship. Even though sometimes exaggerated, the role of films in "teaching romance" can not be completely ignored. The most important contribution has of course been the entertainment. The emotional dramas with some great screenplays has been blockbusters. Many a times Indian cinema has remained a place where, as Manmohan Desai said, "people would forget their misery,a dream where there is no poverty and where the fate is kind.." For a society which is largely poor it remained a place where people could visit places from Kashmir or Ooty to US and Switzerland. Also for long, guests to a family were treated with a movie in a nearby theater which remain a common place today where friends want to hang out.

Conclusion

Cinema, on the whole, is a powerful means of recreation as well as of education. It is not itself bad. The film producers should select good stories classical mythology, historical subjects and Indian literary master-pieces. Documentary films on scientific, historical and literary subjects should be shown to students. The producers are misusing cinema for making huge profits. It should be moral duty of producers to produce noble and inspiring films. The Government should take care of this. If cinema industry produces noble and inspiring films, the cinema would be a true friend, philosopher and guide of the masses. Today, most of the people are busy with their daily routines and schedules. There is hardly any time for them to relax from their busy schedules. Entertainment was not easily available previously. But now-a-days there are many option available for entertainment sources like malls, restaurant, theaters, amusement parks, pubs and discotheque, etc. which have helped them to take time from their busy schedules to relax and entertainment. With increasing employment, the purchasing power of the people has increased and most of them are ready to pay more to get the best quality. Theaters, these days provide many facilities like shopping, entertainment and movie experiences. Taking these aspects into consideration, research is being done to reach to a conclusion.

Literature is the means of creating the most powerful cinema. Because of literaturecinema is getting immense exposure. It highly contribute in making cinema. Literature plays an important role in bringing about social reforms in our society. Social films showthe evils of dowry, child marriage, unsociability, drinking, smoking, drug addiction etc.Cinema also highlights against communalism. It portrays how communalism poses agreat danger to the unity of the country. The cinema promotes national integration, communal harmony and awareness to many untouched issues, may it be dyslexia or any piece of classic literature which was forgotten by the people can be revived through cinema.

REFERENCES

Joseph, A., and Sharma, K. (1994). Whose News? The Media and Womens Issues (pp. 21). New Delhi, Sage Publications.

Gokulsing, K.M., and Dissanayake, W. (1998). Indian Popular Cinema: A narrative of cultural change. (pp. 88). U.K., Trentham Books Limited.

Jain, J., and Rai, S. (2009). Films and Feminism: Essays in Indian Cinema. (pp. 10). Jaipur, Rawat Publications.

Cinema and the Mirror. Retrieved March 14, 2012 from http://www.filmreference.com/encyclopedia/Independent-Film-Road-Movies/Psychoanalysis-CINEMA-AND-THE-MIRROR.html

Bollywood's 'homely' heroines. Retrieved March 3, 2012 from http://www.indiatogether.org/2003/sep/wom-heroines.htm

Role of Women in Indian Cinema. Retrieved March 5, 2012 from http://oorvazifilmeducation.wordpress.com/2010/10/08/interview-with-shoma-chatterji-role-of-women-in-indian-cinema/vii Chakravorty, M. (2002). Cinema and Society: Reflection of Patriarchal Values in selected Hindi Blockbusters. Unpublished Masters Dissertation of the Faculty of Journalism and Communication, TheM.S.University of Baroda.

Datta, S. (2000). Globalization and Representations of Women in Indian Cinema. Social Scientist, Vol. 28, No. 3/4, (March. – Apr., 2000), pp 71-82 Retrieved March 5, 2012 from www.jstor.org/stable/3518191?origin=JSTOR-pdf

Bagchi, A. (1996). Women in Indian Cinema. Retrieved March 5, 2012 from http://www.cs.jhu.edu/~bagchi/women.html

Basu, S. (2008). Feminist Film Review: „Fashion and other Bhandarkar Flicks. Retrieved March 3, 2012 from http://sanjukta.wordpress.com/2008/11/02/fashion-movie-review/**Author:** Ms. NidhiShendurnikarTere is a Junior Research Fellow at the Department of Political Science, M.S.University of Baroda (Gujarat). She is currently pursuing Ph.D in *„Mediation of Conflict between India-Pakistan and the Role of the Press and New Media*. She cleared

bollyviewer-oldisgold.blogspot.com/.../indian-literature-in-bollywood.ht..

Cinematizing Shakespeare: A Study of Shakespearean...

Ijellh.com/cinematizing-shakespeare-study-shakespearean-presence-india...

Cinematizing Shakespeare: A Study of Shakespearean...

DOMESTICATING SHAKESPEARE: A STUDY OF INDIAN

...www.eajournals.org/.../Domesticating-Shakespeare-A-study-of-Indian-ad

Impact of Literature on Cinema: A Study | DipakWayal...Gender Relations and Cultural Ideology in Indian Cinema: A...

How the Arts Impact Communities - Princeton University

https://www.princeton.edu/~artspol/.../WP20 per cent 20- per cent 20Guetzkow.pdf

pandolin.com/adapting-literature-into-indian-cinema/

http://www.online-literature.com/forums/forum.php?s=0fdb04bb9b667d09134eb0fbaa

www.academia.edu/.../Impact_of_Literature_on_Cinema_A_Study

www.matrizes.usp.br/index.php/matrizes/article/viewFile/149/2

The literature-cinema connect - The Hindu

www.thehindu.com/features/friday.../film...literature.../article6886556.ec...

Literature and cinema: link and confrontation - MATRIZes

How the Arts Impact Communities - Princeton University

https://www.princeton.edu/~artspol/.../WP20 per cent 20- per cent 20Guetzkow.pdf

www.academia.edu/.../Impact_of_Literature_on_Cinema_A_Study

Literature in Indian Cinema - Movies List on MUBIhttps://mubi.com/lists/literature-in-indian-cinema

Shakespeare in Bollywood | bollywood | Hindustan Times

www.hindustantimes.com/bollywood/shakespeare...bollywood/story-g3D.

Satyajit Ray filmography - Wikipedia, the free encyclopedia

https://en.wikipedia.org/wiki/Satyajit_Ray_filmograph

Satyajit Ray | Indian film director | Britannica.com

www.britannica.com/biography/Satyajit-Ray

https://books.google.co.in/books?isbn=81762998

Chapter 21

Analysing Historical Element in Indian Cinema

*Nairanjana Srivastava**

Making a historical movie is the best way to make people understand their past. Dramatization of history has great cultural values and responsibilities as well. Studies show that movies on historical plots easily and effectively create impression on the minds of its viewers of a particular period or characters. So much so that sometimes if not adequately researched or projected properly this impression leads to even corrupt understanding of historical events. Still, dramatizing history is a tool in the hands of creative minds who want to make education entertaining.

In Indian context special mention is to be made to those alter-stories of Vedic times which were performed at Yajnanic occasions. Ancient Indian history is greatly indebted to these stories and we must believe that they bear similar values as that of modern dramas. Vedic Gatha, Narashansi or Danastuti, Akhyaan, Akhyayika are the places where information related to contemporary society was kept hidden in the form of performing arts. Gradually history writing boldly came out of the veil and from here started a serious affair of data collection and directive accounts-writing, under the banner of 'Purans'. But history could never be kept aloof of the performing side as a big part of historical accounts was documented by court poets who used to perform eulogies in the courts of kings with full drama.

But a valid apprehension strikes here whether dramatizing history compromises on the true historical values of events or not? Is it possible to maintain the neutrality of characters or any plot in spite of mixing drama into it? Gary Gutting maintains in

**Assistant Professor, A.I.H.C. and Arch.,*
Vasant Kanya Mahavidyalaya, Kamachha, Varanasi – 221 010

his observation that "a film drama can present historical events, vividly and movingly perhaps, but it has no place for evidence supporting the truth of the presentation. As a result, simply looking at the movie, we have no way of knowing to what extent the presentation is accurate." Indeed a correct assumption as films unlike historians' book cannot provide sources and discussions in detail. Further being a dramatized version it is likely that at some point the filmmakers exercise their rights to override historical accuracy for the sake of better theatre.

The present paper tries to interrogate both the sides of the problem. It is the responsibility of a history student to stop malignancy in history in the name of popular entertainment and at the same time it is the right of any creative person to enjoy a period drama, with full creative freedom.

History in itself is enough calculative, neutral and objective in nature. As a lesson from the past, when the requirement arises of educating people via history, it becomes a dry task to follow history without interpreting past incidents. Interestingly, the subjective part of history, at no point of time was devoid of interpretations. In Indian context, these interpreting narrations were considered body for the soul called 'Itihaas'. The oldest historical sequences were represented as stories or Gathas, which were sung at the time of sacrifices. Similarly,Narashansi, Akhyaan and Akhyaayikas were other places in the Vedic literature, where the oldest political history of Indian subcontinent could be preserved. This peculiar nature of Indian history writing continued further with the composition of Puraans and Mahakavyas, and the political as well as traditional history could thus be guarded in the form of interesting moral stories. Thus history, Specially Indian history, is deeply indebted to drama or Interesting narrations for its longevity and vibrant continuation.

But in spite of adhering to the abovesaid fact, we often face difficulty in accepting whatever is served in the name of historical drama. Does dramatization of history educate people with a logical insight of real past incident? Although historians dealing with the history of India, are in a habit of filtering evidences from imagination, still Indian history, so hard earned, cannot appreciate efforts of absurd imagination. Period films like Razia Sultan, Gandhi, Netaji Subhash Chandra Bose, Ghandhi: My Father, Dr, Babasaheb Ambedkar, Vikramaditya, Jodha Akbar, Bhopal: A Prayer For Rain, Bajirao Mastani and alike show a long tradition of well researched film making. But unfortunately few others made mockery of great personalities of yester years like Mangal Pandey, Bhagat Singh, Asoka etc. From imagining every detail of day to day life to creating exciting romantic angles, absurd drama harm history more than spreading education about it.

Another relevant question is, upto what extent historical dramas burden themselves with a sense of social responsibility....! Apprehension is, the camera is often rolled to gain popularity and earn money. This contradiction does surely affect research and money invested into period films and the outcome is worthless historical dramas. It may be a kind gesture of cinema if it tries to value authenticity over entertainment, because imagination has no limits, but at the same time it will be rated as a crime if a culture loses its history, deshaped by popular entertainment and mis-communicated by ill researched dramas.

To meet the shortcomings of a period drama statutory warnings often maintain that all the characters shown in the film/drama are imaginary and that the picturization has nothing to do with real history. These warnings, although, try to amend the harm, still call for a rethink into the matter. The authenticity of the characters borrowed from history should not be compromised at any cost or with any such warning. Researches show that the cinematic effect on its viewers often surpasses the true history or the original writings. Audience can be easily misguided by impressive imaginary portrayal of historical characters/scenes. Butler, whose research focuses on how cognitive psychology can be applied to enhance educational practice, notes that "The misleading effect occurred even when people were reminded of the potentially inaccurate nature of popular films right before viewing the film. However, the effect was completely negated when a specific warning about the particular inaccuracy was provided before the film." These warnings, to a limited extent, can supplement this factual lacking of dramatization of history. But still the question of distorted information exists there. Movies based on historical plots cannot stand with the original texts in their supplying analytical insight into the issues.

The characters in a period drama are also highly demanding, especially if we take ancient Indian history into account. The body-language, pains, warmth of a character is nowhere mentioned in the available texts and literature. So the biggest constraint to make a movie on an Asoka or Akbar will be finding unregistered parts of their lives, their intentions, politico-social inclinations and between-the-line emotions. In such a condition if a movie maker comes up with a dry script, devoid of popular entertaining factors, there will be no viewing of that film and without viewership a film cannot spread information about a subject. Hence actors have a very tough task in period dramas of portraying almost unknown and that too with maximum possible perfection. In the times of Banabhatta,Kalidas, Bhaasa,Bharavi, Dandi etc. it was the writer or the poet who used to perform their compositions in the courts of the kings, therefore the portrayal of legendary kings Raghu, Parikshit and likewise was only a pleasure-something and history had a minimal role in the conception of the theme. It was not expected from actors to perform characters with high definition accuracy. Whereas in cinema this freedom becomes a matter of subjugated skill. Actors are challenged by the lack of evidences every time they play a period drama.

History is a branch of knowledge which has a subtle approach towards past. It doesn't pass judgements but only compiles past incidents. Therefore period drama should be made with utmost sensitivity. Recent examples of successful authentic period drama are Jodha Akbar and Bajirao Mastani. These movies succeeded in following the middle path between selfish commercialization and insipid knowledge.

Based on true incidents these movies enveloped love lives of the two protagonists under well researched historical sequences. Although Jodha Bai is a controversial character in history, the way she has been put into the authentic set-up is admirable. The characters of Mastani Bai and Kashi Bai in the movie Bajirao Mastani are in maximum coherence with the available sources on the subject. Another beautiful example of a historical movie is 'Amrapali', based on a true character, this movie brings out contemporary feel of spiritual quest, imperial grandeur and gender distinctions beautifully and authentically. Others like Bose: The forgotten Hero and Baba Saheb Ambedkar are movies which are very well researched and presented with utmost sense of historical accuracy.

Summing up, history and drama are two ways of entertaining and educating sensible stock. Mixing both these mediums together we can develop a separate branch of knowledge wherein historical dramas will effectively enhance the historical understanding of people both intellectual, as well as it also leaves certain impact upon rustics. Undoubtedly it will also help researches coming on a desk for popular use.

References

1. Gary Gutting is a professor of philosophy at the University of Notre Dame, and an editor of Notre Dame Philosophical Reviews. He is the author of, most recently, "Thinking the Impossible: French Philosophy since 1960," and writes regularly for The Stone.
2. inaccuracies (Devi was actually Asoka's first wife; he married Kaurwaki later). The criticism is unfair to some degree given that it's necessary to take liberties with true stories in order to create a narrative arc, but since the film's explanation of Asoka's profound change doesn't jibe with the facts, his confounding transformation remains, unsatisfyingly, a mystery.
3. Ashutosh Gowarikar, Jodha Akbar, 2008, source: You Tube.
4. Lekh Tandon, Amrapali, 1966, source: You Tube.
5. Sanjay Leela Bhansali, Bajirao Mastani, 2016, source: You Tube.
6. Santosh Sivan, Asoka, 2001, source: You Tube.

Chapter 22

Women and the Indian Cinema

*Amrita Katyayni**

Cinema is the reflection of ethos of any society. Commercial Indian cinema is the single most powerful medium of communication in Indian society. The social issues taken up by Indian cinema, its methods of dealing with these, reinforcing certain values, all these go deep. The study on representation of women in Indian cinema is of paramount importance in understanding the status of women in our society. It is therefore an important question that what are the sorts of roles women play in Indian cinema? How are they projected? Do women film stars serve as models for Indian women?

It is not an oversimplification to say that in popular Indian cinema women are seen very much in bad or good roles. The good ones are are portrayed more often as (self sacrificing) mothers, (dutiful) daughters, (loyal) sisters or (obedient and respectful) wives. Bad women, other than being modern, are often single. They may be westernized (synonymous with being fast and 'loose'), independent (a male preserve), aggressive (a male quality) and they may even smoke and drink. Often they will wear western clothes. The good women characters are mostly depicted as submissive, shy and dependent.

Movies on Women Characters

One of the earliest movie based on Indian Woman was *Mother India*: The film projects the female character radha as, an extraordinarily powerful woman and as a

**Assistant Professor, Department of Education,*
Vasanta College for Women, Rajghat
Banaras Hindu University, Varanasi – 221 001

mother whose life is made up of self-denial and sacrifice for the sake of her two sons and who, till the end, remains fiercely loyal to her absent husband. She kills her own son when he becomes an outlaw. She is a perfect example showcasing a woman's strength, willpower and sense of righteousness. movie left a mark on everyone who saw the powerful film.Contrary to this, the character of *Rosie* in 1965 classic : Guide showed women in a different light. At a time women were expected to be dutiful and follow their husbands even when unhappy, character Rosie left her cheating and unsupportive husband and decided to choose her passion for dancing and someone who valued her as a person. Later, she again followed her heart and drifted apart from her lover when he did not turn out to be what she had expected. Rosie was one of the rare characters in Hindi cinema who stood for what she believed in and made her own choices.

During these times, featured movie *Pakeezah* which centred around a female character. It is the story of a pure-hearted singer-dancer who is raised in a brothel and who falls in love and elopes with a noble man, her unforgiving past keeps haunting her, forcing her to return to her brothel.

Later in 70's, the movie *Umrao Jaan* too portrayed a female character who is sold to a brothel by a corrupt cop after her father testifies against him. Many years later, she grows up to be an accomplished poetess and a renowned courtesan, Umrao Jaan. The character canvases the strength, emotions and feelings of a woman.

The movie *Manthan* is worth mentioning, the character of Bindu in the movie is a strong, independent woman who stands up for her and her community's rights. She goes against higher authorities to set up a local milk cooperative that could help villagers earn a better livelihood. She is not afraid of raising her voice against wrong and stands up to influential personalities with confidence. Another movie during these times was *Khoon Bhari Maang* which portrayed a widowed Aarti who falls prey to vicious plans of a conspiring man, who marries her, then drowns her with help of her best friend, and gains her wealth. But Aarti survives and returns in a to take revenge of her injustices.

The movie *Bazaar* set in Hyderabad, India, highlights the issue of bride buying in India, through the depiction of the tragedy of a young girl being sold by needy parents to affluent expatriate Indians in the Gulf. In the 2000's the character of Janki in *Lajja* portrays one of the most powerful identifies of a woman. It portrays that apart from women being loving and caring, they can also be fierce and stand up for what is right. Janki represents a free and fearless attitude which does not care about others' opinions. Movie also raises important questions on the sensitive issue of Indian mythology and religious beliefs in the perspectives of women.

In the recent list of movies *Black*, portrays Michelle as the visually and hearing impaired character. It is one of the most powerful portrayals of a physically handicapped person in Indian cinema. The relationship of Michelle with her aging teacher and how she helps him to rediscover life is very liberating, inspiring and shows the true strength of a woman.

The movie *Fashion* features an aspiring fashion model and her transformation from small-town girl to supermodel. It tries to portray the life of women in fashion industry and their problems. Fashion also explores feminism and female power in Indian fashion. Rani Mukherjee's portrayal of a fierce cop in *Mardaani* perfectly showcases the true strength of a woman. The character is based on a real life cop who solved several child trafficking cases. Shivani Shivaji Roy single-handedly beat up some of the worst criminals. The perfect mix of strength and respect, Roy is an inspiration.

The simple character of Gita from *Swades* is a highly educated village girl who gave up lucrative offers in the city and chose to stay in the village to teach kids and reform the village. In todays times, when most of the youth in villages are interested in migrating to urban cities for better jobs and opportunities, the movie sets an example of an empowered woman who is dedicated towards the betterment of her village. Her unconditional love for the villagers and her selfless acts made her a strong character which many women would aspire to. Similarly in the movie *Chak De,* Preeti Sabrawal portrays the character of an independent, self-respecting and dignified hockey player who refuses to give up her career for her celebrity boyfriend. She not only stands up for herself but is a role model to all the ladies who sacrifice their dreams at one point or another because of their partners' different priorities. Another movie *English Vinglish* is the story of a housewife who wants to learn English to make herself more presentable and acceptable to her children and husband, touched a chord in the hearts of Indian audiences with its simplicity. It once again establishes the fact that a woman can do what she wants.

The powerful portrayal of boxer *Mary Kom* by Priyanka Chopra is also one of the strongest female roles in Indian Cinema. Mary Kom went against her family and chased her dream to become a boxer. It is very inspirational foe many aspiring career women. In a country where sports is not taken seriously as a career, especially for girls who are supposed to get married and look after their family, character in the movie sets an example for all of us. Yet another movie "*No One killed Jessica*" portrays the character of a journalist who stands for the truth and brings an influential culprit to justice in spite of all the odds. She not only single-handedly reopened the case but also got the public involved and finally gave the much needed justice to the family of aggrieved girl. The character is the perfect example of a modern, empowered woman who can bring a larger change.

To the recent list of women centered movie is "*Queen*" played by Kangna Ranaut. The character Rani's transformation from a once shy and timid girl to a confident and liberated lady was amazing. Rani depicts a real life simple character and has the ability to inspire many girls to come out of the shadows and feel confident about themselves. Movie "*Margaritta with a Straw*" portrays a rebellious young woman with cerebral palsy who leaves her home in India to study in New York, unexpectedly falls in love, and embarks on an exhilarating journey of self-discovery. Other movies like *Piku, Angry Indian Goddesses, Gulaabi Gang* are also based on independent women characters.

Conclusion

Our society is a patriarchal one and the ideal woman is expected to be an ideal wife, mother daughter etc. The same ideology is applied to portrayal of female characters in Indian cinema. The women in earlier movies were depicted as submissive, shy, dependent and in traditional roles of a mother, wife etc. Mostly commercial movies centered on male characters with actresses playing just the eye candy and dancing around trees. In spite of some apparent concern with 'women's issues', commercial cinema projects woman as a sex object on the one hand, and as an unequal partner on the other. There are perhaps few films: perhaps one film in every 100 that attempts to look at a woman as a human being in her own right. The Indian society has seen upsurge in women education and employment with liberalization and globalization, the implication of the same could be seen in different movies which are made in recent times portraying women other than their traditional roles as in movies like *Manthan, Fashion, Swades* etc.

The hypocrisy in projection of female characters is the result of our patriarchal mindset. Indian cinema remains male dominated and thus lesser movies centering on women issues. The number of women representation in cinema industry too remains low. It is only when more and more women choose to join the film industry; there can be a paradigm shift. This can further help in addressing women issues and the portrayal of women as an independent human being apart from the traditional roles.

Chapter 23

Impact of Corporatisation in Indian Movie Industry: An Overview

*Ranjan Kumar Bhattacharya**

Indian Movie industry has done great progress since the Motion pictures first came to India in 1896 when the Lumiere brothers unveiled six silent shorts films in Mumbai. India's first feature film "King Harishchandra" (a silent movie) was released in 1913. The first 'talkie' movie released in India was 'Alam Ara' in 1931. India is the biggest producer of feature films in the world. The industry has produced approximately twenty eight thousands feature films and more than thousands of documentary films. Indian movie industry was an unorganised sector till the long period of time, but there was wind of change when the Govt. of India granted 'Industry' status to the Indian film Industry in 2001. Before that during initial year the 'studio system' and 'star system' prevailed. It has opened the path for producers to get bank credits on lower interest rates rather than relying on black money. A lot of things which are informally were formalized. RBI formulated guidelines for the banks for funding the film industry. This facilitated the much needed institutional financing, which was earlier unavailable. The production, distribution and exhibition were integrated giving greater control to the corporate over the functioning and

**Assistant Professor,*
Department of Commerce,
Vasanta College for Women, Rajghat
Banaras Hindu University, Varanasi – 221 001
e-mail: ranjanmgs@rediffmail.com

accountability. Now the Indian movie industry has completed 100 years of film production and exhibition as an industry in 2013.

Status before Corporatisation

The industry was dominated by producers and studios of Mumbai and Chennai. Since 1950s, it has spread across several regions of the country, with movies being produced in Hindi Bengali, Tamil, Telugu, Marathi Malayalam and several other regional languages it can be shown through this figure:

Table 23.1: Language-wise Distribution of Films Released in India

Tamil	14 per cent	Marathi	8 per cent
Telugu	15 per cent	Malayalam	7 per cent
Kannada	11 per cent	Hindi	16 per cent
Bengali	10 per cent	Others	19 per cent

Source: Central Board of Film Certification, India, 2011.

Before corporatisation there was a monopoly of big producers and stars in the industry. Production of film was unorganised, which usually led to production delays and further increased the total cost of production. Securing finance to complete the film was tough, because film producers would usually get finance in parts. Disbursement of the next instalment of money was dependent on saleability of the film to financers. The time taken to secure money for completing the next part of the film industry led to delays in producing films. As a means of finance institutional funding were not available.

Indian Hindi movie production worked on informal basis before corporatisation. There was no documentation of contracts. Mostly it was done by verbal agreement and mutual relationship. The method of working of Hindi film production was not systematic. Another problem before corporatisation was underworld involvement in Mumbai cinema. The Mumbai Underworld have been known to be involved in the production of several films. On occasion they have been known to use money and muscle power to get their way in cinematic deals. This was result of failure to attain legitimate source of finance. In 1990s many such links came to force like-Sanjay Dutt, Divya Bharti, Gulshan Kumar (T–series) Rakesh Roshan, Preity Zinta and so many. Many times, the mafia pressurized actors or actress to do particular film because they had invested money in it. In this way before corporatisation this was the dark period of Bollywood industry in our country.

Status after Corporatisation

Before corporatisation the status of Indian film industry was not good. After corporatisation the film industry has adopted market driven practices, which have resulted in greater efficiency in film production. It also prompted international studios to enter into collaborations with Indian production houses to produces and distribute movies. In 2001, corporate sector has changed the path of Indian movie industry. Now the movies are made, marketed and distributed globally. Professional service providers have replaced improvisers and developed offerings in areas such as editing, digitisation, archiving, animation and film making. Many production houses are listed on stock exchanges.

Bollywood has made a lot of progress in the recent years, particularly after having been given the industry status. The Govt. has established National Film Development Corporation Limited (NFDC) in 1975 to produce and co-produce films. Institutional funding for the films increased after grant of "industry" status in 2001, when the RBI formulated guidelines for the banks for funding the film industry. This facilitated the much needed institutional financing which was earlier unavailable. In order to get the funding, the industry had to adapt new corporate governance requirements such as adherence to standard accounting practices, business plans, targets and time schedules and insurance as mandated by banks and financial institutions. Profitability and commercial success became essential which required professionalism, efficiency in film making and adoption of market driven practices. It resulted in the entry of corporate entities in all section of the film industry. Deregulation of film screens also helped in the corporatisation of the Indian movie industry. With better corporate governance practices, many international studios such as Walt Disney, Warner brothers, and Sony entered into collaborations with local production houses to produce and distribute movies. These collaborations have proved to be win-win situation for the collaborators, because international studious have gained distribution reach and domestic companies have utilised the latter's experience in project management. Corporation of the film industry has also encouraged film producers to float new companies on stock markets.,

There is no limit of FDI which means foreign studious can produce films in India without any local partnership –after corporatisation, the resources have been streamlined,more control on the supply chain made the process of making film faster. Now films are made within 6 month time.this definitely generates more revenues. The producers helped in effective execution of the shooting, when the corporate financed as well as look after into other aspect of the film.

Marketing of Film with Corporatisation

Marketing of films has also transformed with corporatisation.where only 3 per cent to 5 per cent of the total film budget was used for marketing a film in the earlier days, it is now as high as 45 per cent. The focus of marketing a film is to maximise the revenue earned by a film in the first week. Increasing use of technology has also helped and corporate have adapted to the latest channels of marketing. Corporate participation in the Indian movie industry has increased in production, distribution and ownership of film screens. Corporatisation introduced several new measures to reduce uncertainty in revenues earned by a film corporate pre-license cable and satellite rights and distribution rights across geographies, which helps them to recover about 40 per cent to 80 per cent of film production costs even before the film is released. Cost of the film production has also been reduced by adopting measures such as revenue sharing with leading film actors. Producers have developed new sources of revenue, including the sale of merchandise and partnering with companies to advertise their products in the film. Now net revenues of corporate involved in film production have increased at a rate of about 16 per cent P.A. form US $ 68 billion in 2008 to US $ 1.05 billion in 2011. Whereas net revenues of corporate involved in film distribution have also increased at a rate of about 19 per cent P.A form US $ 3.31 billion in 2008 US $ 5.57 billion in 2011. It can be shown through this table-

Table 23.2: Total Net Revenues of Listed Companies (US $ billions)

Particulars		*2008*	*2009*	*2010*	*2011*	*2012*
Film Production	*No. of Companies	85	73	78	82	57
	Net Revenue	0.68	0.69	0.90	1.05	0.90
Film distribution	*No. of Companies	66	72	72	69	45
	Net Re\venue	3.31	3.99	6.60	5.57	4.44

Source: IMaCS Resources.

* Number of Companies for which financial results are available.

Impact of Corporatisation and Challenges

The major and the biggest impact of corporatisation is that finance is procured with legitimate means which put an end to underworld era. In fact, after the film **chori chori chupke chupke** case, there was no news of underworld hand in film production. Earlier actors sought for special protection, but now it has changed after corporatisation. Now films are made within 6 months time which generates more revenues. There is more professionalism shown by the actors as well as the rest of the crew. Now, actors shoot for only one film at a time and sign a film only after getting a bound script. Bank credit is easily available and finances could be raised through other instruments. Independent producers formed a group and made corporations. A new business model came into play. Corporations who had no film making experience would collaborate with independent producers to make films. The producers helped in effective execution of the shooting, while the corporate would finance as well as took after into other aspect of the film. At this time, when costs have gone high, there are hardly any independent producers. Most have formed their companies or work with other corporates.

There are many challenges that the corporation have to face in the film industry to survive in the long run. Like uncertainty in film making business, piracy and revenue sharing etc. The biggest challenge for a corporate that enters in Indian Hindi movie industry is uncertainty in film making business. Apparently providing finance does not ensure making a hit film. Hence a lot of corporations have shut offices and have gone back to their main business. Piracy is a burning issue at this moment.

Due to piracy, bollywood losses hundreds of crores every year piracy happens on two levels – Music and Movies. The worst hit of the two is the music industry. This is one challenge that the industry has to seriously tackle. Another challenge is the revenue sharing model, which is not uniform for all films. During the first half of last year, there was dispute between distributers and multiplex owners who generate around 60-70 per cent of theatrical revenue in India.

Conclusion

From the above discussion we can say that corporatisation was slow for a long time, but in recent times it has been picking up at a good pace. Now we are over the hump. Everything is aligned with big business, and the corporate sector can get in and start funding movies. It is more like a regular business than some kind of street business model. Going forward it will only increase. It will become more and more like Hollywood. Corporatisation has encouraged new and talented film makers to produce films and original ideas.. International reach of Indian film is another offshoot of corporatisation and a new approach towards marketing strategies.

References

1. Desai, M. "Bollywood needs to change its act", *The Hindu*, New Delhi November, 25, 2007.
2. Johnson, J. "India seeks to double share of world film industry", Financial Times, January 15, 2007.
3. FICCI-PricewaterhouseCoopers, "The India entertainment and media industry: Unravelling the potential by Rattin Dutta and Deepak Kapoor, March, 2006/Http://www.pwc.com/extweb/pwcpublication.nsf/docid
4. "Financing for Hindi films shifting industry Dynamics" by Sunil Khetrapal, April 13, 2010.
5. "How Corporatisation is changing the face of the film industry" by Rajesh Naidu, Economics Times, New Delhi, October 24, 2011
6. "A Report on the progress of the Indian film industry and the impact of corporatisation" November,2013/www.ibef.org.
7. "Corporatisation of Hindi film industry" by B.Islam, March 19, 2010.

Chapter 24

100 Years of Indian Cinema: The Dream Continues

*Vibha Singh**

Indian films are unquestionably the most seen movies in the world. Not just talking about the billion strong audiences in India itself where 12 million people are said to go to the cinema every day, but of large audiences well beyond the Indian subcontinent and the diaspora, in such unlikely places as Russia, China, the Middle East, Turkey and Africa. People from very different cultural and social worlds have a great love for Indian popular cinema, and many have been Hindi Films fans for over fifty years. Indian cinema is world famous for the staggering amount of films it produces. The number is constantly on the increase and recent sources estimate that a total output of some 800 films a year are made in different cities including Madras, Bangalore, Kolkatta and Hyderabad. Of this astonishing number, those films made in Mumbai, in a seamless blend of Hindi and Urdu, have the widest distribution within India and Internationally.

Era's of Indian Film Industry

Silent Era

The cinematographe (from where we have the name cinema) invented by the Lumiere brothers functioned better the Kinetoscope of Edison and Dickson. The Lumiere brothers who invented the cinematographe started projection of short

**Assistant Professor,*
Department of Sociology,
Vasanta College for Women, Rajghat
Banaras Hindu University, Varanasi – 221 001

(very short, one to two minutes long) films for the Parsian public on November 28, 1895. Cinema was shown for the first time in India by the Lumiere brothers on July 17, 1896 at the Watson Hotel in Mumbai. This was just six months after their first show in Paris. Indian cinema thus has more than a hundred years of history, like the European or American film industry. That first show was just a show of a series of visuals, moving scenes and nothing more, but it inaugurated a long line of movies made by talented Indians. Today India has the distinction of being the country that produces the highest number of feature films every year. The earliest show of moving pictures in India was done in 1896. But for the next fifteen years there was no indigenous production of movies. N.G. Chitre and R.G. Torney of Bombay were the first to make a film based on a story. It was Pundalik, a film based on the life of a Holy man in Maharashtra, it came out in 1912. When Dadasaheb Phalke the father of Indian Cinema, released his epochal feature film Raja Harishchandra on 3rd May 1913, it is unlikely that either the exhibitors or the pioneer film maker realized they were unleashing a mass entertainment medium that would hold millions in sway for the next hundred years. The French might have introduced the concept of moving images but little did anyone know that India would one day become the largest film industry in the world. It's a miracle that Indian cinema has withstood the test of time despite the vast cultural differences in the past 100 years. Dadasaheb Phalke is acclaimed as the father of the Indian cinema because he laid the foundation for the future of the Indian film industry and because he trained several young film makers in his studio in Nasik. The Phalke award perpetuates the memory of this pioneering film maker and it goes to the person who enriches Indian cinema through remarkable contributions to it. Phalke will always be remembered for his contributions to the development of the Indian film industry. Other silent movies started coming out from Calcutta Studios were 'Satyavadi Raja Harishchandra'(1917) and 'Keechaka vadham' (1918). But Phalke's Nasik studio was the first regular studio where he could also train many promising young people as film technicians. It was still the era of silent movies all over the world. During the Silent Era (1896 – 1930) over a thousand films were made in India however, only ten of them have survived and now restored and preserved in the Pune archives. Meanwhile American and European films continued to grow in popularity, though a major source of worry for the imperial Government was that they would 'corrupt' Indian minds. In 1917 the European Association warned the Government against a film called 'The Surpentine Dance', which was certainly calculated to bring the white men and women into low esteem in the Indian mind.

The Talking Era

The silent era came to an end when Ardeshir Irani produced his first talkie 'Alam Ara' in 1931. If Phalke was the father of Indian cinema, Irani was the father of the talkie. The talkies changed the face of Indian cinema. Apart from looks, the actors not only needed a commanding voice but also singing skills as music became a defining element in Indian cinema. The year also marked the beginning of the Talkie era in South Indian films. The first talkie films in Bengali was 'Jumai Shasthi', Telugu 'Bhakta Prahlad' and Tamil 'Kalidas' were released in the same year. The courtly love stories of the Urdu Pars Theatre are probably the reason behind Indian cinema's dependence on romantic themes and the way they link love, obstacles and tragedy. Another popular genre of this period was the historical film based on stories of real characters or legendary hero's.The importance of the historical film lay in its patriotic undertones. The grandeur of Pre – Raj India, the splendid costumes, the etiquette of the nobility and high drama were a direct invitation for national self esteem and the will to be independent. Of course India did not need to be independent to produce films, thousands of miles of celluloid had run through the projector gate before the British finally packed their bags in 1947. Despite having first blossomed under a political power so alien to its own conventions, Indian cinema's thematic and aesthetic development seems to have remained largely free of direct concern with colonial rule. Individual film directors were deeply concerned by the independence movement led by the Congress party and demonstrated their allegiance to the concept of a free India in films such as 'Sikandar' (1941) and 'Shaheed' (1948).

The forties was a tumultuous decade of the film industry. The first half was ravaged by war and the second saw drastic political changes all over the world. In the middle of the Second World War in 1943 came 'Kismet' starring Ashok Kumar which became one of the biggest hits in the history of Indian cinema. It had some bold themes, first anti-hero and an unmarried pregnancy. It clearly showed that the filmmakers of the era were bolder than the times in which they were living in. A close relationship between epic consciousness and the art of cinema was established. It was against this backdrop that filmmakers like V.Shantaram, Bimal Roy, Raj Kapoor and Mehboob Khan made their films. In the meantime, the film industry had made rapid strides in the South where Tamil, Telugu and Kannada films were taking South India by storm. By the late 1940s, films were being made in various Indian languages with religion being the dominant theme. 1940s to late 1950s was also the golden era of music. Shankar Jaikishan, O.P. Nayyar, Madan Mohan, C. Ramchandra, Salil Chaudhury, Naushad and S.D. Burman all had their distinctive style. Each vied with the other to produce some of the most unforgettable melodies India has ever known.

When talkies came an unexpected criticism from art lovers was that sound destroyed the aesthetic quality of the movies. Moreover, the universal language of the cinema was adversely affected. People speaking different languages could watch the silent movie and derive meanings from the acting, expressions and the visual effectiveness of the whole movie. Cinema is a visual medium and it has its own language. An Englishman must be able to appreciate a Hindi or Tamil movie as much as a Hindi or Tamil speaking Indian should be able to enjoy an English movie even if the movies are silent ones. But can we imagine how a silent movie would appeal to us now? We have become so used to sound movies. And in India, we cannot easily appreciate a movie without songs and dance. The silent movies are now in the archives and they are taken out for research or for satisfying someone's historical curiosity. Though colour movies started to come out of American studios from 1935 onwards, it took more decades for color to come to Indian screens.

Golden Era

The decade of 50s and 60s are considered as the Golden Age of Indian cinema. Film makers created authored and individual works while sticking strictly within the set conventions of the films. The example of Mahatma Gandhi and Prime Minister Nehru's vision of the newly independent nation was also highly influential throughout the decade, and many excellent Urdu poets and writers worked with film makers in the hope of creating a cinema that would be socially meaningful. It is no surprise that the 1950s is regarded today as the finest period in Indian cinema, and the era has profoundly influenced generations of Indian film makers in a way that no other decade has done since. Filmmakers like Satyajit Ray, Ritwik Ghatak, Guru Dutt, Bimal Roy, Mehboob Khan, K. Asif, Raj Kapoor, K.V. Reddy, L. V. Prasad and Ramu Kariat made waves in their respective film industries and they went on to make classics like Awara (1951), Do Bigha Zamin (1953), Pather Panchali (1955), Shree 420 (1955), Mayabazar (1957), Pyaasa (1957), Mother India (1957), Madhumati (1958), Mughal-e-Azam (1960), and Chemmeen (1965)among many other films. In the south, N.T. Rama Rao, M. G. Ramachandran, Sivaji Ganesan, Rajkumar, Prem Nazir dominated the film industry for more than three decades before making way for the next generation of actors like Rajinikanth, Kamal Haasan, Mammootty, Mohanlal, Chiranjeevi and Nandamuri Balakrishna. These films show a complex and sophisticated mix of characters, plots, ideas and morals. The important film makers of this period not only made commercially successful works but also mastered the language of cinema. They understood how performance, photography, editing and above all music could be used to create a new aesthetic. It was around this time that Indian films started to receive regular worldwide appreciation and films such as 'Awaara' made Raj Kapoor and his costar Nargis major celebrities in places as far afield as Russia and China. Mehboob Khan's 'Aan' (1952) and 'Mother India' (1957) also won large audiences beyond the Indian sub continent. The average Indian film does not pretend to offer a unique storyline. A new twist to a familiar storyline helps a film to succeed, if the audience is looking for originality, they know it is principally to be found in the score. Film music is of such primary importance in today's Indian cinema that it more or less determines the box office fate of most movies.

Masala and Art Movie Era

The 70s completely changed the way films were made especially in Hindi film industry. Changing social norms and changing economies influenced movies and the companies that made them. The narrative style changed. The story structure changed. Characters changed. Content changed. Masala films were the demand of the time. The genre promised instant attraction and had great entertainment value. It was the age of the angry young man and Amitabh Bachchan rose to prominence.The sucess of 'Zanjeer' (1973), 'Sholay' (1975) and 'Deewar' (1975) had great contribution in the life of Amitabh Bachchan. While Dev Anand, Rajesh Khanna, Jitendra and Dharmendra continued to bask in the glory of back to back hits, the actresses were not far behind. Right from the time of Savitri, Vyjayanthi Mala, Nargis, Waheeda Rahman and Sharmila Tagore to Sridevi, Rekha, Smita Patil, Hema Malini, several actresses became heartthrobs of the nation. Cinema dominated in the 1970's by the Sippy's. Hrishikesh Mukherjee, B.R. Ishara and Vijay Anand were jolted out of their wits when Shyam Benegal assisted by Blaze enterprises, shot into prominence with 'Ankur'(1974), and later with 'Nishant'(1975), 'Manthan'(1976), 'Bhumika'(1977) and 'Junoon' (1978). Benegal turned his back on the standard 'Kalyug'(1981) and 'Aradhana' (1981) genre, injecting a dose of caste – politics into his first three films. He was closely associated with the making of Govind Nihalani's 'Akrosh' (1980), a political film about the exploitation of illiterate Adivasis. 'Ardh Satya' (1983), 'Party'(1984) and his TV serial on the partition of India, 'Tamas'(1987) have been significant success.

While the films of Mrinal Sen, Mani Kaul and Kumar Shahani did not fare very well at the box office, those of the 'middle cinema' reaped a good harvest. Saeed Mirza's 'Albert Pinto Ko Gussa Kyoon Aata Hai'(1980) and 'Salim Langde Pe Mat Ro'(1989), Rabindra Dharmaraj's 'Chakra' (1989) and Ketan Mehta's ' Bhavni Bhavai'(1980) both in Gujarati and Hindi, ' Mirch Masala'(1987), and later ' Maya Memsahib' (1993), ' Sardar'(1993) started a trend in the making of socially conscious and political films which were entertaining as well. Both the New Wave and the Middle Cinema wilted under the impact of multichannel television, ' Commercial cinema', the commercialization of the National Film Development Corporation (NFDC), and above all the abysmal lack of exhibition outlets. The gradual decline of the Film Society movement too had a role in the fading away of 'Parallel cinema'. While Indian commercial cinema enjoyed popularity among movie goers, Indian art cinema did not go unnoticed. Adoor Gopalakrishnan, Ritwik Ghatak, Aravindan, Satyajit Ray, Shyam Benegal, Shaji Karun and several other art film directors were making movies that gave India international fame and glory.

As the century drew to a close, there was a revival of the New Wave spirit with some assistance from the NFDC, Doordarshan, overseas TV companies such as channel four of Britain and private financiers. Some termed this revival the 'Second New Wave', even though most of the film makers involved in the revival was also part of the first New Wave and others in different regional languages of the country helped keep the spark of 'alternative' cinema alive. The establishment of the National Centre for Children and Young People (NCYP) provided an impetus to the making of films targeted at Indian Youth.

The eighties saw the advent of women film makers such as Vijaya Mehta's 'Rao Saheb' (1985), Aparna Sen's '36 Chowringhee Lane'(1981) and 'Parama' (1984), Sai Pranjpye's 'Sparsh' (1980), 'Chashme Baddoor' (1981) and 'Katha' (1983), Kalpana

Lajmi's 'Ek Pal' (1986), and Chingaari (2006) and Mira Nair's' 'Salaam Bombay' (1988). It was also the decade when sultry siren Rekha wooed audiences with her stunning performance in 'Umrao Jaan' in 1981.

And then in 90's, it was a mixed genre of romantic, thrillers, action and comedy films. A stark upgrade can be seen on the canvas as technology gifted the industry dolby digital sound effects, advanced special effects, choreography and international appeal. The development brought about investments from the corporate sector along with finer scripts and performances. It was time to shift focus to aesthetic appeal. And stars like Shah Rukh Khan, Rajinikanth, Madhuri Dixit, Salman Khan, Aamir Khan, Chiranjeevi, Juhi Chawla and Hrithik Roshan began to explore ways to use new techniques to enrich Indian cinema with their performances.

In recent years, Hindi cinema has undergone a massive change due to the emergence of new age filmmakers like Anurag Kashyap, Rajkumar Hirani, Dibakar Banerjee and Vishal Bhardwaj. Of late, Tamil and Marathi cinema has witnessed similar changes with several new filmmakers coming forth to cater to a niche audience.

Cinema–An Industry

As the world has become a global village, the Indian film industry has reached out further to international audiences. Apart from regular screenings at major international film festivals, the overseas market contributes a sizeable chunk to Bollywood's box office collections. Regular foreign investments made by major global studios such as 20th Century Fox, Sony Pictures, and Warner Bros put a stamp of confirmation that Bollywood has etched itself on the global podium. The early years of the 21st century witnessed several dramatic developments in Indian cinema. Cinema was at last declared an 'Industry' in 2001 by the Indian Government and no sooner did this happen than the gradual 'corporatisation' of the entertainment and media industry took off. Banks, insurance companies and the Federation of Indian Chambers of Commerce and Industry (FICCI) were persuaded to support the industry. The decline of the active dependence on funding from the 'underworld' of Bombay also had its beginnings around this time. But perhaps the greatest impetus to the shake up of the industry was the rapid proliferation of ' multiplexes' (multiscreen theatres) and digital cinema theatres, first it started in metros and later in the big cities such as Bangalore, Hyderabad, Ahmedabad and Pune. Multiplexes offer a different experience to cinema goers, for in most cases they are part of a shopping malls and comprise theatres of different sizes. Thus small budget films could be released in multiplexes and digital cinema theatres. Ticket rates are much higher in such multiplexes than in single screen theatres and therefore attract upper middle class families.

Audience are also showing interests in small budget experimental films which are rarely touched on in mainstream cinema. Young directors like Nagesh Kukunoor's 'Hyderabad Blues' (1998), 'Bollywood Calling' (2001) and 'Iqbal' (2005), Sudhir Mishra's

' Hazaaron Khwaishein Aisi'(2003) and Anurag Kashyap's 'Black Friday'(2004) have been able to make a mark thanks to the multiplex phenomenon. Small low budget films like 'Joggers Park' (2003), ' Being Cyrus' (2005), ' Mixed Doubles' (2006) and other feature films were released in such theatres. At the end of the first decade of the 21st Century, there were at least 300 screens in around a hundred multiplexes across urban India. The potential of low budget films at the box office has led to the introduction of new and bold themes by young directors both in the mainstream and parallel traditions. Patriotism 'Lagaan' (2001), rural development 'Swadesh' (2004) Homosexuality, old age 'Being Cyrus' (2005), HIV Aids 'My Brother Nikhil' (2005), live in relationships 'Salam Namaste' (2005), communication with the physically and mentally challenged 'Black' (2005), 'Iqbal' (2005), nationalist history 'Mangal Pandey :The Rising' (2005), have been some of the issues taken up for analysis in feature films and documentaries over the last decade.

Major Studios of the Film Industry

The creation of the major studios in Madras, Calcutta, Lahore, Bombay and Pune in the 1930s was a crucial move in the development of a proficient Indian film industry. Studio owners including Himanshu Rai, Devika Rani, V. Shantaram, V. Damle and S. Fatehlal set the tune of film production, playing an essential role in promoting national integration. People of all castes, religious, regions, sects and social classes worked together in the various studios. Film production has always prided itself in the way it has been inclusive and continues to be a shining example of communal harmony and tolerance. Hindus and Muslims work together and promoting and national integration and communal harmony has always been a favourite theme of the Indian film. The studios including Bombay Talkies, the New Theatres in Calcutta, Prabhat Film Company and Gemini and Vauhini in Madras were also responsible for broadening the choice of screen – subjects with music as a primary ingredient. Like the great Hollywood studios, they experimented with different stories and themes while each developing their own brand of film making. The key films of this period show the origins of themes and subjects that have recurred over subsequent decades of film making. For example, the New Theatres films, particularly the 1935 classic 'Devdas' by actor/director Pramathesh Barua made the film in both Hindi and Bengali versions.He gave Indian cinema its most recurrent theme - the love triangle. Devdas is an adaptation of Sarat Chandra Chatterjee's Bengali novel of the same name. This film also gave its most enduring male character - The tragic romantic hero. Devdas is a high caste Brahmin who cannot marry the love of his life Parvati, his neighbour's daughter, because she is of a lower caste. He later befriends Chandramukhi, a prostitute who gives up her profession and turns to spirituality. In a downward spiral of self – destruction, the Hamlet like Devdas becomes an alcoholic and ultimately dies at the gate of Parvati's marital home. The story of Devdas touched millions of Indians in the 1930s who felt that his anguish would become their own if they dared marry against parental authority. This theme returns regularly every decade either in a direct remake e.g. Bimal Roy's 'Devdas' (1955) and director Sanjay Leela Bhansali's new version released in 2002, or as an important theme, as in Guru Dutt's ' Pyaasa' (1957) or Prakash Mehra's 'Muqaddar ka Sikandar' (1978). V.Shantaram was a co – founder along with V. Damle, S. Fatehlal and Dhaiber of the Prabhat Film Company based in Kohlapur and later Pune. He made many stunts and action films early in his career favoured socially progressive subjects and dealt with themes considered taboo. Shantaram's best work includes a period drama about the vengeance of women 'Amar jyoti' (1936) was the first Indian film to be shown at an International Film Festival, in Venice. Some important films which raised questions on certain social issues were - the rehabilitation of a prostitute 'Aadmi' (1937), and the promotion of Hindu – Muslim friendship 'Padosi'(1941). In 1942, V. Shantaram left Prabhat studio to start his own production company and studio, Rajkamal Kalamandir, in Bombay. There, he continued to make internationally acclaimed films based on social concerns, including 'Dr Kotnis ki Amar Kahani' (1946) and 'Do Aankhen Barah Haath' (1957). Bombay Talkies also made social films, the most celebrated example of which is Franz Osten's 'Achhut kannya' (1936) starring Devika Rani and Ashok Kumar. It was one of the first films to deal with the evils of untouchability. Bombay Talkies made many popular movies, including Gyan Mukherji's ' Kismet'(1943) a film that introduced another favourite theme in Hindi cinema – the lost and found. Though the lost and found theme can be traced back to mythology in the story of Shakuntala, 'Kismet' made it popular in cinema. An interesting twist on this popular theme occurs in Manmohan Desai's 'Amar Akbar Anthony' (1977) in which the director depicts three brothers separated as young children and brought up by members of the three main Indian religions : Hinduism, Islam and Christianity (hence the names Amar, Akbar and Anthony). The film was a massive success and Desai himself made several other films combining the importance of communal harmony with the theme of loss and recovery. In his ' Naseeb' (1981) Amitabh Bacchan hero is called 'John, Jaani, Janardan' and is proud to be seen as Christian, Muslim and Hindu. As long as the separated family members are played by well – known stars, the audience never seems to tire of the repetitions of themes.

End of Studios

Financers who made money during the war years found film making an easy way of gaining quick returns, and this new method of financing movies ultimately brought about the end of the studio era. The studio owners could not afford to pay high fees for their staff and stars, and so freelancing made a return a system whereby all film practitioners were employed on a contract – by – contract basis. The studio system was over by the late 1940s, and widespread freelancing, established by the 1950s, set the pattern for film production thereafter.

Indian cinema has grown quite big during the past century, especially during the past six decades. This period saw the growth of the cinema into a mass medium. Despite thematic peculiarities drawbacks, social conditioning and cultural inhibitions it has proved its merit in technical perfection, artistic evalution and directorial innovations. Indian cinema, by and large has remained on the path of clean popular entertainment. In the coming decades it can give more attention to the social dimension of the medium, particularly its use in mobilizing the masses through effective messages on serious issues such as social justice, environmental safety and a more rational and scientific approach to human problems. Indian cinema despite all its peculiarities has been a reflection of the socio-economic, political and cultural changes that took place in the country. Here's hoping that Indian movies continue to entertain us the way they've been doing since 10 decades.

References

https://en.wikipedia.org/wiki/Cinema_of_India

http://www.mbaskool.com/infographics/11568-100-years-of-indian-cinema.html

http://blogs.widescreenjournal.org/?p=2563

http://www.wipo.int/wipo_magazine/en/2013/01/article_0001.html

http://www.oxfordreference.com/page/filmindian/celebrating-100-years-of-indian-film

http://sarai.net/the-many-lives-of-indian-cinema-report/

www.toolexpressnz.co.nz/case-study-on-100-years-of-indian-cinema-in-english.pdf

www.artensuite.com/index.php/thesis-on-indian-cinema

www.newsonair.com/100-YEARS-OF-INDIAN-CINEMA.asp

www.mpoki.wmwikis.net/file/view/100-years-of-indian-cinema-essay-in-hindi.pdf

www.crl.du.ac.in/ical09/papers/index_files/ical-19_109_244_1_RV.pdf

www.shodhganga.inflibnet.ac.in:8080/jspui/bitstream/10603/20681/8/08_chapter.2.pdf

Chapter 25

Impact of Indian Cinema on Women: A Content Analysis

*Punita Pathak**

Bollywood aka Hindi movies industry with the various regional cinemas has a major influence in daily life and culture in India for decades. In fact Indian considers *maa* and *cinema* as the two most important part of their life. Over the century, movies have acquired the highest position for the entertainment and almost a religion in the nation. Movies sway the Indian society in different ways, and impact individual's personal lives. It is hard to decide if films have a larger impact on the Indian Society or the latter has on the former. Indian cinema has for long exerted a deep influence on every section of the society. Among them the impact of Indian cinema on the role of women in the society has taken a great leap.

Somewhat around 1950 the technology and story content along with the presentation of the movie changed a lot in Indian cinema. This was the time when India, which was rural but had rich and vibrant traditions and the relationships, customs, norms and ethics of Indian society was portrayed. Women were given an equally dominant role in the Hindu films along with the male actors. A few examples include *Mother India* made in 1957 by Mehboob. The film was made ten years after India gained independence from the British rule. In this film the director, Mehboob, attempts to combine socialistic ideals with the traditional values. The audiences could easily identify themselves with the on-screen characters whose lives reminded them

**Assistant Professor,*
Department of Political Science,
Vasanta College for Women, Rajghat
Banaras Hindu University, Varanasi – 221 001

of their own. Some other films in which women played a major role were Pakeezah and Padosan. Gradually Indian cinema infiltrated the life style of Indian women along with the clothing, working, independence, and outlook has been portrayed in the movies and it gradually influenced to all the women beings. Discussing about the clothing, one of the earliest movie influences on Indian fashion was *Mughal-e-Azam* in 1960. The sense of change in fashion is still continuing with movies such as *Hum Aapke Hain Koun and Bunty Aur Babli*. The Indian cinema has infiltrated so much into the Indian women daily life that basically be it the clothes they wear, the way in which they speak, their social behaviour, is all affected by commercial movies directly or indirectly. But apart from the life style, Indian cinema has also been a medium to propagate the eradication or overcoming some deep rooted evil of the society for the uplifting of Indian women. For example, the film *Baabul* raised the issue of widow remarriage, *Queen* about the journey of a young woman in her honeymoon who was ditched by her fiancée, *Bandit Queen* about a rebellious woman against the upper caste zamindars. In recent years the portrayal of women as politicians, social activists, professionals, sportswoman in movies is also inspiring a major part of women population especially in the young urban sector. Few examples in the context are *Rajneeti, Mardani, Corporate, Mary kom, Ki and Ka*. The list is endless and we are fortunate to be part of that era of Indian society when women are really considered to be equal to man in each and every aspect of life.

But there is a darker side of the Indian Cinema too, which is the unrealistic and stereotyped portrayal of women. More or less women are portrayed in much the same way in all Indian media *i.e.*; dumb, dependable, weak human being with only sexual gratification to offer. Most commonly women are shown as the love interest and have little else to do in the movie except please the hero with her beauty and romance. It is a rare thing that heroine is portrayed as an individual with intellect, her ideas and thoughts pertaining to anything other than romance or family. Another characteristic of this stereotype is which is strictly followed is virginity. The heroine's virginity is placed on a pedestal and her chastity is considered to be a pre-requisite to get respect. On the other hand the unchaste and bold women, who are shown to be sexually active, are generally characterized as negative characters, a degradation to women's sexuality. This degradation of women is further escalated by the infamous *'Item Songs'* of Bollywood, which is another very common women's stereotype. It is observed that characterization of women as sexual objects of desire is the objective in these songs: *Munni badnaam hui, Sheila ki jawani, chikni chameli*. Further in Dhoom 3, Katrina Kaif only had a 15-minute run-time where she had to strip down to impress Aamir Khan and dance in skimpy clothes to songs. Gradually it is observed that skimpily clad actresses dancing to the tune of vulgar and anti-feminist lyrics seems to be the norm in any popular Bollywood movie. Perhaps the most worrying aspect to this objectification of women by the Indian film industry is that women are playing a major role in degrading their own feminine spirit, by agreeing to be classified as 'item girls' and consciously playing such roles in movies which require them to act as mere objects of sexual desire and not as intellectual individuals.

On the contrary Indian cinema has also produced various mainstream women centric films that have featured women's social issues and their social and sexual abuse. *Fashion, Heroine, PAGE 3, Corporate* or *Dirty Picture* have been very successful commercially and feature women as the main protagonists in the movie. However, a common theme runs throughout these movies which show successful women: women are almost always portrayed to be prone to failure and fall prey to social evils like alcohol, drugs, when they earn success in life. It can be inferred that such movies portray women as weak characters who get ruined by the freedom that is accompanied by success. Even in critically acclaimed movies that portray women as victims of social or sexual abuse like *Water* or *Damini*, women are always portrayed as victims of abuse, who, need assistance from men to escape such conditions. Therefore, even such so-called 'women-centric' films are not free from gender stereotypes. There is no ambiguity as to the entertainment such films provide, but it is often at the cost of women's intelligence and dignity. In a deep contrast, movies like *Nayak, Deewar, Sholay, Krissh, Lakshya, Singham* that have strong male characters as protagonists, *celebrate* men in the roles of alpha males who triumph over social and political evils, and achieve their goals independently. This stark contrast delivers a message to the society which essentially declares that women can never be equal to men, either socially, or politically. In films, it is generally seen that some dialogues gain a somewhat landmark status. The larger point being made here is that even when a female movie character's role is more than decorative, the heavy emphasis on men's problems makes it appear as though it is the Indian man who is complex with real problems and the woman only serves as a support system. The dialogues of a movie reflect the popular culture of a society at that period of time. We have all heard the famous '*Mere pass maa haï*', however, other dialogues such as '*jaa choodiyan pehen ke beth jaa*' (go wear bangles and sit down, implying that a woman is incapable and useless) are frequently used in films and resonate the message that women are intellectually and socially inferior to men. Movies have found new cities, settings and even broader societal issues to tackle, yet, seem to be in a state of arrested development when it comes to the power dynamic in gender relationships. There are a few movies that have broken the mould and present women as strong independent characters. Bollywood is correct that it is free to express what it wants, and tell the stories it wants. They have rejected censorship as a tool to "elevate" the kind of content they generate. Some writers have argued that only blaming the producers of pop culture is dangerous, and that the audience needs to introspect as well — Shougat Dasgupta pleads with audiences to "question the invariably sexist, xenophobic, homophobic, plain stupid assumptions of the pop culture we consume". While, a 'Queen' or 'Kahaani' still manages to raise the bar and pave way for progressive approach to women-centric subjects, there are a dozen others which will still use the skimpy-clothes, trashy and offensive lyrics (most of Honey Singh's songs) to sell tickets and rake in the moolah. Is it fair to blame Bollywood, or even expect it to produce movies that adhere to a higher standard? Indians subconsciously or consciously believe that movies are a reflection of the Indian society. Therefore, it can be surmised that stereotyped portrayals of women in movies is contributing to rampant sexism prevailing in India. While the stories bring up different aspects of Indian society, and how women are victims to its ways, they are mainly served up as plot devices to show how the boys grow into men. The portrayal of women in Bollywood, and their larger effect on Indian society has been called into question following the brutal gang rape of a young girl in the capital, New Delhi. Many argue that Indian popular culture is full of misogyny, and Bollywood too needs to own up to its role in fuelling this culture. As Ritupurna Chatterjee writes, "it will be highly presumptuous to assume that Hindi cinema is the root cause of a spike in sexual assaults. But Bollywood and regional cinema in equal parts, because of their reach, scope and influence, have a larger role to play in assuming responsibility for the message it sends out to millions of audience, some highly impressionable. Bollywood is the biggest culprit as the reach and impact by Bollywood films is the most and it is shameful that such an industry still resorts to item songs and objectification of women without analysing the negating impact on society. If there has to be a certain sense of change in the way society treats women, even Bollywood needs to change its mentality and embrace subjects about womanhood and feminity without projecting women as a mere object of sexual gratification but as a person of her own with layers.

References

R.Burra, (ed.) 'Film India: Looking Back 1896-1960'. The Directorate of Film Festivals, New Delhi, 1981.

Indubala Singh, Gender Relations and Cultural Ideology in Indian Cinema: A Study of Select Adaptations of Literary Texts, Deep and Deep Publications, 2007.

Amitabha Bagchi,. Women in Indian Cinema, 1996, retrieved from http://www.cs.jhu.edu/~bagchi/women.html

S. Akbar Ahmed, 'Bombay Films: The Cinema as Metaphor for Indian Society and Politics'. Modern Asian Studies 26, 2 I992, pp. 289-320.

S. Basu, S. Feminist Film Review: „Fashion and other Bhandarkar Flicks. Retrieved March 3, 2012 from http://sanjukta.wordpress.com/2008/11/02/fashion-movie-review/

A. Joseph, and K. Sharma, Whose News? The Media and Women's Issues, New Delhi, Sage Publications, 1994

A. Roy, Images of domesticity and mother in Indian television commercials. Journal of popular culture, 32(3), 117-134, 1998

S. Datta, Globalization and Representations of Women in Indian Cinema. Social Scientist, Vol. 28, No. 3/4, (March. – Apr., 2000), pp 71-82 Retrieved March 5, 2012 from www.jstor.org/stable/3518191?origin=JSTOR-pdf

Chapter 26

Indian Cinema and Disabled Women: Beyond the Liberal Paradigm

*Suhasini Singh**

Disabled literally understand the disadvantaged group within the society, who is subjugated vie hegemonistic social structure. Similarly, having born with disability is to begin a life with social stigma and deprivation of opportunities for self development. This paper shall be based on the arguments that the disabled in Indian cinema has been largely framed by the liberal paradigm. The liberal paradigm undermines the issue of difference. There is no space for exercising particular roles in the society for them. This paper examines some of these challenges and demand politics of recognition in the context of disabled women.

Liberal Paradigm

Liberal paradigm based on two fundamental values: individualism and liberty. Firstly, it paradigm seats the individual at center of society and disputes that the social order is built around the individual. Secondly, the purpose of society consent to individuals to reach their full potential if they want to, and that the best way to do this is to give the individual as much liberty as possible.

Philosophically, liberal paradigm consists with the equality, rationality, liberty and individuality. Nevertheless, it paradigm combined these values in several and often opposed relationship, which reflect different social postulations. Usually,

**Research Scholar, Department of Sociology, Banaras Hindu University, Varanasi – 221 005*

liberals believed these values to be inscribed within the modern societies, reflecting via innovative technologies, and capital characteristic of the commercial and industrial age and its outcome.

Politically, liberal paradigm united against hierarchical societies, therefore, over whether it requires various political supports, such as the state regulation of markets. For now, liberal critics have either blamed it for all contemporary social ills as a transitory phase to be replaced by superior forms of social organization.

In social sciences, liberal paradigm has attributed in also divergent ways: as the 'natural' value system of modern societies, as moreover destructive or expressive of basic human goods.

Liberal feminists agree with these views, and persist on freedom for women. There is disagreement along with liberals about connotation of freedom, and thus liberal feminists take more than one form. This entry discusses on two manners of liberal feminism. Firstly, Classical-liberal or libertarian feminism conceives of freedom as freedom from coercive interference. Secondly, Liberal feminism conceives of freedom as personal autonomy and political autonomy. Therefore, liberal feminism is well-known in academics; much more classical-liberal or libertarian feminism.

Liberal feminists embrace that the personal autonomy depends on certain facilitating conditions that are insufficiently present in women's lives. Liberal feminists clutch autonomy deficits like these are due to the "gender system" (Okin, 1989). There is difference along with liberal feminists; nevertheless, about the role of personal autonomy in survives of life, the suitable role of the state, and how liberal feminism is to be vindicated.

Thus, the prevailing paradigm of liberalism undermines the issue of difference. It is based upon the idea of normality; based upon white, male, able people, European etc. Normality ignores the contextual condition of particular groups and led to exclusion. The structure of society constructs the whole system based on the idea of normality and similarity.

The methodology engaged in this paper based on an extensive review of the literature on the subject matter. This paper is qualitative and explanatory in nature and based on theoretical debate. This paper is written entirely on the basis of secondary sources that include review of books, journals, and other secondary materials.

Issue of Difference: Indian Cinema

Cinema, more than any other forms of art, has the power to manipulate people. Hence, cinema is considered to be a powerful medium that reflects what's going-on in a society. Although, it holds between the real and reel life, it still performs as a medium of entertaining people, educating them and bringing a behavior change in their practice and attitudes. So, cinema is believed to entertain, to take the watcher to a society that is basically different from the real one, a society which provides escape from the daily grind of life. There are people who believe in the power of cinema to change the society, there are others who say that its major purpose is to entertain people. It is very important to understand that how cinema is a popular medium of mass consumption which plays a key role in molding opinions, constructing images and reinforcing dominant cultural values.

The issues of cinema, beyond to normality and gender are being discussed all over today. Cinema related structures and systems have also undergone a deep change with privatization and globalization. Hence, several studies have recognized the implications of such a transformed cinema related environment on issue of difference access to media. This paper based on the arguments that the disabled women in Indian cinema have been largely framed by the liberalism paradigm. The liberalism paradigm undermines the issue of difference. In cinema that shows disabled women as a character and character shows to the viewers how individuals with that disability behave, feel, communicate and experience. Thus, it becomes important that disability is presented responsibility. This paper traces the portrayal of disabled women in Indian cinema from the 2005 - 2015 to the present using some select movies.

Indian cinema's approach can be traced back to the 2005 when a historic film "Black", the first by a major director to focus on a disabled girl got released. It's about a blind and deaf girl and his teacher who succumbs to Alzheimer. One of the most important films of last decade was "Taare Zameen Par" released in 2007 which turn around an eight-year-old boy suffering from mental disorder called Dyslexia. In 2008, "Ghajini" got released with the character of Aamir Khan suffers from Amnesia. The 2009 film "Lafangey Parinday" was central on a dancer played by Deepika Padukone who loses her sight before a major competition and as well, Indian cinema witnessed the great performance by Mr Amitabh Bachchan suffering from rarest disease called Progeria in movie "Paa". In 2010, "My name is Khan" released with starring Shah Rukh Khan who suffers from the disease Asperger's Syndrome. Anurag Basu's film Barfi released in 2012, starring Ranbir Kapoor and Priyanka Chopra in lead roles, is being touted as one that can change Indian cinem's perception about the abilities of the disabled.

Unlike the new millennium epoch and the emergence of communication revolution, cinemas were, though based on disease theme; entertainment touch was always the major focus. The recent trend has changed the notion of entertainment on various angels and explored an opportunity in making a serious film with a theme based on the disability related disease. Finally, the idea of portraying the disabled as independent and equally able but disabled specially women are widely misunderstood in Indian cinema. Recent studies have constantly found marginalization of disabled women and a lack of sensitization and awareness in Indian cinema. So, the traditional concept for disabled women continues to be a common belief in cinema related structures and systems. This paradigm shift (via beyond of normality) further strengthened the claim of Indian cinema as an instrument in creating the social awareness against various social evils and taboos.

Conclusion

Cinema is a powerful instrument for the reflection of different issues of society. Therefore, Cinema plays an important role in fostering equal chances for everyone and in combating stereotypes; strengths and interests regardless of traditional gender expectations. Consequently, this paper highlight that the disabled women in Indian cinema has been largely framed by the liberal paradigm. The liberal paradigm dented the issue of difference. So, approaching such concerns also tackle with various approaches and taking it through the different perspective.

References

Addlakha, R., *et. al.* (eds.), (2009). *Disability and Society*, New Delhi, Orient BlackSwan.

Bhargava, R. and Acharya, A., (2008). *Political Theory: An Introduction*, New Delhi, Pearson Langman.

Bryson, V., (1994). *Feminist Political Theory: An Introduction*, London, Macmillan.

Cumberland, G. and Negrine, R., (1992). *Images of Disability on Television*, New York, Rutledge.

Farrelly, C., (2004). *Contemporary Political Theory: A Reader*, London, Sage.

Mazumdar, R., (2001). *A Short Introduction to Feminist Theory*, Calcutta, Anustup.

Chapter 27

Psychology and Films

Gagan Prit Kaur and Richa Singh***

Psychology is the study of behavior and experience and films influence behavior and riches our experiences, so both the psychology and films are bound in a relationship that cannot be broken down. Indian cinema is successfully celebrating its century year. Indian cinema has influenced the life of Indians as well as people living outside India. It has influenced the behavior, life style as well as understanding about life. Psychology has played very important role in initiating and maintaining this influence.

Psychology and Cinemas

Psychology is the study of behavior, cognition and experiences of humans as well as animals. So it is everywhere in the world where humans and animals exist. Cognitive psychology is the study of how individuals perceive, learn, memorize and think about the information they receive from environment around them. It studies the entire phenomenon that takes place in the minds of human beings, *i.e.*, perception, attention, learning, memory, thinking, problem solving, reasoning etc.

Films or cinemas are made for human beings to pass their time, entertain them, some time teach and preach, and even demonstrate a particular point of view about some issues. Films are like imagination and fantasy, there isnothing real in them. They inviteus into different lives and worlds and sometimes don't letgo. Some show us things we've never seen before or perhaps only imagined; helping us

**Research Scholar, **Assistant Professor,
Department of Psychology,
Vasanta College for Women, Rajghat
Banaras Hindu University, Varanasi – 221 001*

safely (usually)venture into places and times we cannot enter in our normal lives and to imagine new possibilities.Some let us look into a world to which we may not have access andsometimes take us to future and sometimes to past. Good films stay with us, we talk about them with others and sometimes it becomes learning to us. The experience of films becomes part of our lives. Films often describe and explain the behavior of characters. These descriptions and explanations are all parts ofthe formal study of the field of psychology.

Psychology and cinemas were deeply related which resulted in first motion film in Paris (1895) was released in which with the help of movement illusion images were shown as moving. In early 1900s the questions were raised for the social and psychological impact of the filmsbefore it was assumed as cheap entertainment. Harvard psychologist Hugo was leading academicpsychologist of America at that time had tried to answer the question. He believed that films use such technologies that control thememories, perceptions and emotions of the humans.Munsterberg wrote a book, namely **The Photoplay** (1916), which showed the inner working of human mind.

Indian Cinema

The Indiancinema has completed its 100 years very successfully and with growth of day and night. Itconsists of films produced across India, Most famous amongst is Bollywood. As India consists of various cultures and states therefore various cinematiccultures of Bihar, Haryana, Andhra Pradesh, Telangana, Assam, Gujarat, Jammu and Kashmir, Jharkhand, Karnataka, Kerala, Maharashtra, Manipur, Odisha, Punjab, Rajasthan, Tamil Nadu and West Bengal are also involved in this industry and as many as 1,600 films in various languagesof India are produced annually.

In India cinema or films have gained immense popularity and influences on people.It is not only followed by Indians but also from people outside India.Dadasaheb Phalke is known as the *father of Indian cinema*. He was the producer, director as well as screenwriter offirst full-length Indian motion, but silent picture *Raja Harishchandra* (1913). To honor his contribution to cinema Government of India in 1969 named an award to Indian cinema by him as the DadasahebPhalkelifetime achievement Award. This is the most prestigious award in Indian cinema.As of 2013, in terms of annual film output, India ranks first, followed by Nollywood, Hollywood and China (Times of India, 2011). In 2015, India had a total box office of US$1.6 billion, the fourth largest in the world outside NorthAmerica.India's first talkingpicture was *Alam Ara*.Technological advancementupgraded cinema and its contents. Now movies based on visual effects, science fiction, and epic films like Enthiran,Baahubaliand Krrish are also being shown and becoming blockbusters and this led the path for Indian cinema to gain fame in other countries also. This led to the investments of foreign production houses, such as Sony Pictures, Walt DisneyPictures etc. in Indian cinema. Indian cinema's AVM Studios in Chennai is

India'soldest surviving film studio as well as Ramoji Film City located in Hyderabad, India holds Guinness World Record as theWorld's largest film studio for this. And Prasads IMAX Theatre located atHyderabad, is the world's largest 3-DIMAXscreen, and also the mostattended screen in theworld. Thus Indian cinema industry is very large and famous film industry.

Psychocinematics

Psychocinematics is a term coined by Shimamura (2012), whois Professor of Psychology at the University of California, Berkeleyand faculty member of the Helen Wills Neuroscience Institute. Hewas awarded with a fellowship to study links between art, mind, and brain. He is coeditorof **Aesthetic Science: Connecting Minds, Brains, and Experience**.

Psychocinematics is a new discipline that studies the relationship between human psychology and movies. It would be best to explain this relationship in terms of behavior as movies affect the behavior of the humans and psychology studies the behavior. Psychocinematics is a discipline to studyscientifically movie experiences that connect minds, brains, and experience at themovies. Filmmakers conceal themselves behind a screen and offer a mesmerizing experience that engages our sights, thoughts, andemotions. They have developed an assortment of magical "tricks" of acting, staging; sound, camera movement, and editing that create a sort of sleight ofmind (Shimamura, 2012). All these techniques have been developed gradually and now we are in the era of science fictions and amazing and heart throbbing action scenes. Films capture our attention and perceptual system thus we get attached with it, we portray ourselves with the characters of the films and we become happy, sad etc. according to them. Thus films capture our emotions also. If it does not involve it we will not be able to engage ourselves with the movie and get bored of it. For this engagement some factors are responsible such as script or story, acting done by the actors, scenes, songs and some suspense.

Psychological Effect of Cinema

Various types of researches have been done to study all these effects of movies. Some have developed models or theories and others have done empirical researches. According to Shimamura for a scientific understanding, one needs evaluate these rather subjective features by developing a theoretical framework for empirical research.

Shimamura (2012) have developed a model namely, ISKE model. The name is an acronym for intention (I) of the filmmaker and **s**ensation, knowledge, and emotion of the viewer.The ISKE model describes humans' aesthetic response to visual art. This model says that when we experience anything our experience is influenced by the factors of the things as well as our existing knowledge. We are never in the blank state because we always have knowledge about the world around us with our past experience. And this model says that we apply all those previous knowledge in experiencing new things. Ernst Gombrich called this influence "the beholder's share." The ISKE model explains that filmmakers with their intentions, that is expressed in the films, plays with this previous knowledge of the humans. The ISKE model describes this previous knowledge breaking them in three components, called sensory, conceptual (knowledge), and emotional features of film. When all these three components are at maximum intensities then the movie is called satisfying and people rate it good and this becomes blockbuster. Psychocinematics considers the impact of these ISKE components and how they interact with each other (Shimamura, 2012). With the advent of brain imaging techniques, particularly functional magnetic resonance imaging (fMRI), it is easy to measure the brain (neural) activity while watching and experiencing movies.

Psychology is everywhere in the films from the starting to the end and even after that. Cognitive psychology especially can be seen in movies as cognitive psychology includes all higher mental processes, *i.e.*, sensation, perception, thinking, memory and learning. Films play with all these fundamental aspects of life as they are essential parts of the films. To have initial experience sensations are used, to see objects being moved perceptual concepts are used, thought processes are used to understand the movie and memories are used to remember the character or story throughout the movie and even after so that impact of the films stay long with us. Noam Chomsky founded the field of cognitive science to study the acquisition and processing of knowledge. But Ulric Neisser is the father of cognitive psychology as he published the book cognitive psychology (1967) and documented this term first. Initially cognitive psychologists developed theories of mind that explains the physical aspects of how the brain works. **Performance and Cognition: Theatre Studies and the Cognitive Turn**(2006) was first survey book on cognitive psychology and films, which was edited by Bruce McConachie and F. Elizabeth Hart. In 2008 the first full-length monographs **Engaging Audiences: A Cognitive Approach to Spectating in the Theatre and Blair's The Actor, Image, and Action: Acting and Cognitive Neuroscience** were published by McConachie (Blair and Lutterbie, 2011). Cognitive theory for films study was proposed by David Bordwell in 1989 in cinema and cognitive psychology. This theory is concerned with the normal and successful actions of the humans unlike Freud's interests in incomplete tasks.

With the passage of time scientific knowledge and understanding of the people have been increased and this led to change in cinemas themes and stories. In early cinema, mentally ill were presented as a very deviant personalities who can be extremely dangerous to others and they could not be treated and become normal or live normal life. In Indian cinema they were not even shown in the movies as they were considered as ignorant. And if they were shown they were represented as very dangerous personalities, one such character is shown in movie Darr by Shahrukh Khan, who was having the Border Line Personality disorder. Other films such as "Baazigar", "Gupt","PyaarTune Kya Kiya" and more recently "Ranjhanaa" also have shown border line personality disorder. With the attempt to normalize the disorders and its successful treatment paved the way to accept these illnesses and treat them properly through pharmacological intervention, psychotherapy, or a combination of the two. Such films really now helping to overcome the stigma of mental illness and going to the therapist, counselors and psychiatrist as they go to the physician, or surgeons to treat their physical illnesses with dignity. Such as a film is Bhool Bhulaiyaa characters were played by Vidya Balan as dissociative personality disorder patient and Akshay kumar playing role of psychiatrist. In this film it was shown that the disease can be treated and patient become normal after treatment. Another films showed the same disorder namely "Aparichit", "Karthik Calling Karthik" etc. Many other films have now shown the mental disorders to make people learn about these disorders as the mental illnesses simply as physical illnesses. Such as "Taare zameen pe" has shown the learning disorder Dyslexia, "Burfi" has shown autistic personality, these films helped parents to understand the problems of their children. "Highway" has shown Stockholm syndrome, "Woh Lamhe", "Phir Teri Kahani Yaad Aye" and "Shabd" showed schizophrenia, "Ghajini" showed Anterograde amnesia etc. All these movies were blockbusters and had developed knowledge about the mental illnesses and their treatment.

Conclusion

Thus, we can say that psychology is also playing its role in story writing as the subject matter of the films. And this really has changed the viewpoints of the people towards mental disorders and their treatment. This shows that same mechanisms are used to know about or understand stories and real life. Films are making good contribution with the help of psychology to change the understanding and life style of the people as well as making people live life healthily and with full potential.

Chapter 28

Precarious Social and Political Issues in an Eternal Love Story- *Manjhi: The Mountain Man*

*Supriya Singh**

Though consumerism and capitalism have dominated the world to such an extent that one cannot see beyond, except what it shows. However skilled artists have enough space to find realism out of it and, now a days, they have made several attempts to carve out reality and to touch the real ground. Not only this but through logical surveys they try to achieve the truth, depleting all the artificial layers. *Manjhi: The Mountain Man* is the consequence of Ketan Mehta's struggle to locate the group of doubly marginalized society and accepting a dalit's achievement as something extraordinary.

This movie portrays a periodic map of certain age of our society and it comes to strike our mental faculty through several issues but it has attacked particularly those nook and corners which were undiscovered and untold till now. It has presented a dalit protagonist in a positive mode and most significantly based on real life story of a dalit man who should be proclaimed as a real hero. This is even rarer because it is among the one where a dalit character has created a space in the mind and heart of the audience.

**Assistant Professor,*
Department of English, Vasant Kanya Mahavidyalaya,
Kamachha, Varanasi – 221 010

Manjhi: The Mountain Man is a 2015 Indian biographical film based on the Dashrath Manjhi's eternal love for his wife. The film based on the theme of taking an oath or a solemn promise of carving way out of mountain because taking her injured wife to the hospital across the mountain to Wajirjang was a lengthy and time taking affair and in the process he lost his wife. This attempt of Manjhi made him an extraordinary man. Though in the beginning "people called him a lunatic but that only ironed his resolve further and after twenty two years of back breaking labour, he carved a path 360 feet long, 25 feet deep in places and 30 feet wide, without a single penny help by Government and it is only after four years of his death that government made a metalled road to Gehlaur in 2011".

It is an inspiring and touching tale of a common man Ketan Mehta has ensured that the film is true to its hero. Manjhi, widely known as the 'Mountain Man' was a poor labourer in Gehlaur village, near Gaya in Bihar, India, carved a path using only hammer and chisel. This biopic film is directed by Ketan Mehta and "jointly produced byViacom 18 Motion pictures and NFDC India'[1] and was released on 21 August, 2015. The role of Dashrath Manjhi is enacted by Nawazuddin Siddiqui while Radhika Apte played Manjhi's wife, Phalguniya. The plot of the movie goes to the period of 1960s in the village of Gehlaur, beside the Rocky Mountains where people either had to climb over or travel round the mountain to have access to medical care at the nearest town Wazirjung. One day Manjhi's wife fell while crossing the mountain and she died in the way to the hospital and here starts the effort of Manjhi to break the huge Rocky Mountains. Nawazuddin breathed and lived the character with accurate exactness and gave an effortless performance to every part-be it revolting against the Zamindar, celebrating when the regulation was passed regarding social equality of all the castes, or toiling for decades in the memory of his wife. He brings out all the emotions to the fore with his brilliant facial as well as eye expressions. Siddiqui acted out so naturally that one can feel the pain that he feels. For instance, when he is bitten by a snake, he staggers, cries out in pain and soon cuts out the thumb that was bitten. The most striking and heart breaking scene is the one where Dashrath is arrested and told that he might have to stay in jail for rest of his life. Then he says to himself, "*Hum haar gaye Phalguniya, lagta hai bina rasta banaye hi mar jayenge*".

The movie has also attempted to focus over serious social and political evils prevalent in the years of 60s like notorious and rigid system of caste or experiences of dalit for instance in a scene where dalits were celebrating the regulation declaring the social equality of all castes or untouchability, created a sense of dissatisfaction among upper middle class as this law would inhibit their uncontrolled use of those under-privileged section who were moving about with a sense of fear and inferiority complex. For instance Dashrath was harshly beaten when the chief of village gets touched by him and nails were strucked in a dalit's foot as he dared to put on shoes. Thus the director has made the audience familiar with the expected obstacles of that section of society and particularly Manjhi.

Ketan Mehta has also brilliantly portrayed the political milieu of the contemporary time. He has thrown light over the political side of class and caste with remarked expertise. In an ironical manner it appears to us in a scene where Prime Minister Indira Gandhi is delivering her speech raising the slogan 'Gareebi Hatao', but when the stage crumbles, people from the crowd were asked to support the stage. There, we see Gandhi as leader, talking about poor and to bring about change in their life, is seeking support of the shoulders of the common man, particularly those marginalized men who were there to look at her with hope for certain positive change in their life. The scene leaves a question in our mind 'who is supporting whom?' The scene further followed by a period when emergency was declared, and Manjhi was told by the cops and the upper class men that he has chosen the wrong time to revolt against the corrupt bureaucrates and that he could be put into jail.

Apart from class and caste, Ketan Mehta has also raised the gender issue as to how upper castes men used to exploit dalit women sexually and kill their family members if they come for the rescue of their women. Rape and then killing dalit women was a very common practice these days. Life of dalits was worthless to them, even less than a commodity, as in a scene a dalit worker named 'Bhura' fell in the brick kiln and when his co-workers were making attempts to extinguish fire, chief's son stopped them for the bricks would get ruin. Thus, Ketan Mehta has addressed all possible social evils in interesting manner to captivate the audience as well as to guess the difficulty that Manjhi had gone through. Manjhi didn't deviate even when there was drought and scarcity of food and water and when other villager's were migrating to some other place. His determination to complete his task while living in this village is made reasonable through flashbacks that focus how he is tied with the memories of his wife.

The story is an epitome of eternal love and one could consider it more inspiring and worthy as compared to Shah Jahan's expression of love for his begum Mumtaj Mahal. As Taj Mahal is an historical building to visit at and admire its beauty. It is to be noted that during her last breath, Mumtaz Mahal asks Shah Jahan to construct her tomb in a beautiful mausoleum to express their love, for each other, to all who visit it and as a consequence we see TheTaj Mahal, the seventh wonder of the world but the expression of love by Mountain Man is something done by a common man or better to say a man who is doubly marginalized by his class as well as caste and has no approach to any authoritative party and even no financial help has been given to him. Thus, facing all sorts of economical, social and political obstructions he was able to achieve something that is not merely a piece of art to appreciate but the task is accomplished with the sense of welfare for the whole society or the whole village.

Dashrath was born a '*Musahar*' (a caste of bonded farm laborers once known for killing and eating rats). And therefore can be considered as a man belonging to the doubly marginalized groups in India and have suffered all sorts of discrimination at the hands of the upper caste. Married in childhood, Dashrath and Phalguniya hardly spent four to five years together before she dies and the compatibility and love that developed during these years can be clearly seen as the reason behind the twenty two year-long struggle Dashrath undertakes to ensure that no one else dies the way his wife did. The Director of the movie has truly depicted their romance and that retains its intensity even after Phalgunia's death and after so many obstacles that Dashrath finds in his target to achieve. It is everytime when Dashrath is about to lose his patience, he regains strength as Phalguniya's spirit appears again and again to remind him why he needs to do it, charging him up all over again. Phalguniya appears again in the end dancing and celebrating with the villagers at the ultimate victory of her lover and husband.

The chief motives that pervade the plot of the movie are love, passion and strength of a man's will power. From fighting corrupt bureaucrats to villagers and non supportive family members, Dashrath fights everyone and odd to ensure the completion of task that he took upon himself, a task that will serve mankind and not just an expression of his selfish emotion.

The make-up, performance, acting, language, dialect and even the accent are in accordance with the setting, the culture and the class of the people in contemporary time. Though delicately woven within the limitations of the class and caste, the portrayal of the romance is extraordinary. Thus the overall performance comes out to present a powerful love story and has created a paradigm on the earth. Varadraj Swami and Shaiwal has presented their expertise in dialogue writing and the paper comes to its conclusion with a meaningful dialogue- "Bhagwan ke bharose mat baitho, ka pata u hamre bharose baitha ho".

References

"Manjhi The Mountain Man Movie Review". The Times of India. 21 August 2015.

Mehta, K. Manjhi: The Mountin Man. 21 August, 2015. DVD.

Index

A

Aadmi 3
Achhut Kanya 30, 78, 83, 84, 85
Agantuk 52, 56, 58
Aged 49
Alam Ara 6, 51, 74, 78, 124, 165, 172, 190
Aligarh 45, 46, 48
All India Women's Conference (AIWC) 94
Anand 40, 134, 175
Animals 62
Annadurai 6, 7, 9, 10, 11, 12, 13, 14
Annapurna Mandir 94
Anti-stereotype 96
Apur Sansar 113
Audio-Visual Mass Medium 29, 31, 33, 35, 37
AVM studio 11
Avtaar 53
Avvayar 11

B

Baghban 53
Bandit Queen 84, 87, 89, 90, 136, 142, 143, 146, 182
Bawandar 84, 87, 88, 89
Bharati Dasan 9
Bimal Roy 75, 85, 122, 173, 174, 178
Bombay 2

C

Caste dynamics 83, 85, 87, 89
Charulata 113, 114
Cheluvi 59
Child marriage 2
Chitrangada 45, 48, 153
Cinema and power 3
Cinematic journalism 63, 65, 67, 69
Classic collections 153
Commodified women 77, 79, 81
Computerized box-office ticketing 23
Confluence 5, 7, 9, 11, 13, 15

Corporatisation 166
Corruption 2
Criminalization of politics 2

D

Dadasaheb Phalke 74, 77, 172, 190
Dahej 2
Darmiyan 42
De-colonizing 71, 73, 75
Delhi Safari 59
Desya Muropokku Dravida Kazhayagam 14
Devdas 33, 113, 130, 131, 151, 154, 177, 178
Dharma Production 19
Dialectics 39, 41, 43, 45, 47
Digitalization 17, 20, 23, 27
Digital technology 21-24, 26, 27
Dilwale Dulhania Le Jayenge 132
Dirty Picture 99, 145, 146, 183
Disabled women 185, 187
Distributions platforms 24
Dostana 40, 43, 48
Dowry 2
Dowry system 30, 36
Dunia na Maane 3

E

Ecological concern 59, 61
Education 2, 105
English Vinglish 3, 163
Ethics 65, 68, 76

F

Family planning 30, 37
Father of Indian cinema 77
Film distribution 21
Film ecosystem 19, 20
Film industry value chain 19
Film production 20, 168
First information report (FIR) 87
Folk theatre 7
Fox Star Studios 20

G

Garm Hawa 52
Gay 39
Gemini pictures 11
Girlfriend 46, 48
Golden era 174
Gurudev Rabindranath Tagore 1

H

Haider 76, 119, 120-122, 152
Hijra 39, 42
Hindocha eunuchs 41
Historical element 157
Homosexuals 41, 43, 44
Human development 36
Human settlements 61, 62

I

Indian Cinema 1-3, 39, 83-104, 119, 121-163, 171-190
Indian film industry 18, 19, 152, 171
Indian penal code (IPC) 40
Intercaste marriages 7, 30, 37
International film festival awards (IIFA) 129
International year of the aged 49
Iron man of India 123-127

J

Journalism films 64-70
Justice party 6

K

Kabhi Khushi Kabhi Gham 32, 130, 132

Kalandar 43, 48
Kalidas 6, 159, 173
Keecchaka Vadam 5

L

Lagaan 30, 130, 131, 177
Lesbian 39
Literature 147

M

Mahabharat 7
Mahanagar 113, 116
Manimekalai 8
Manusmriti 93
Masaan 3
Masala and art movie era 174
Mata Bahuchara 41
Media ethics 68
Mekhala pictures 12
Memories in March 44, 48
Mother India 11, 35, 51, 52, 78, 95, 96, 128, 143, 146, 161, 174, 181
Murder 2 42, 48
Murosoli 6, 7
My Brother Nikhil 44, 48, 177

N

Namak Haraam 40
National integration 30, 37, 105, 155, 177
National year for older persons 51
Natsamrat 53
Newspapers 33, 63, 64, 66, 68, 91, 117, 126, 148
No One Killed Jessica 99, 142
Nostalgia 66, 70

P

Padosi 3
Parineeta 78
Pather Panchali 56, 113, 174
Pinjar 149, 153
Political tool 9
Psychocinematics 191
Psychology 189
Puranas 7, 8
Purdah system 30, 36

Q

Queen 3, 20, 80, 84, 87, 89, 90, 94, 101, 136, 142, 143, 146, 163, 182, 183
Queer 39

R

Rafoo Chakkar 43
Raja Harishchandra 18, 29, 51, 74, 124, 153, 172, 190
Rajkamal pictures 12
Rajshree production 19
Ramayana 8, 9
Rang De Basanti 32
Regional cinema 6
Regional films 10
Reliance entertainment 20
Religious stories 2
Roja 2
Rupkonwar Jyoti Prasad Agarwala 103-109, 111

S

Saaransh 52
Sanskrit literature 7
Sardar Vallabhbhai Patel 123-128
Satellite channels 24
Sati Charitra 94
Sati Parvati 2
Satyajit Ray 30, 52, 55-58, 75, 113, 115-118, 124, 134, 135, 151-156, 174, 175

Screens 22
Sexual gratification 80, 182, 184
Shanti Theatres 12
Shivaji Kanda Indu Rajyam 12
Sholay 30, 40, 98, 143, 175, 183
Silent era 171, 172
Sillapadikaram 8
Social identity 92
Social questions 83
South Indian Liberation Federation 6

T

Talking era 172
Tamil Filmland 5, 7, 9, 11, 13, 15
Tamil literary revival 6, 8
Tanu weds Manu 3
The Dowry Prohibition Act 1961 2
The Mirror 1
The Namesake 149
The National Council of Indian Women (NCIW) 94
Thinkalaazhcha Nalla Divasam 52
Tirukural 8
Tolkapyam 8
Transsexuals 39, 41

U

Untouchability 30, 36, 51, 85, 94, 95, 178
UTV production 19

V

Values and culture 2
Viacom18 Motion Pictures 20

W

Women characters 161
Women in Indian Cinema 81, 91, 93, 95, 97-101, 155, 156, 184
Women's India Association (WIA) 94

Y

Yash Raj Films 19, 146

Z

Zubeidaa 77, 144, 146